More P
The Spirit of Early

"Robert Wilken offers here a rich ...
Christian faith as seen through the eyes of its most formative
exponents — the theologians, bishops, poets, and hymn writers of
the early church. Written with clarity and conviction, this book is a
window onto the landscape of the Christian soul."
— Timothy George, Dean of Beeson Divinity School of Samford
University and executive editor of *Christianity Today*

"By turns scholarly, contemplative, and argumentative, this is an
exposition in which the early Christian writers
speak for themselves — and to us."
— Jaroslav Pelikan, author of *The Christian Tradition*

"A stunning achievement aimed at the general reader. . . .Rich in
learning and insight, [it] is one of the best and most meaningful
Christian books this reviewer has ever read."
— W. L. Prehn, *The Living Church*

"An elegant and learned introduction to the giants of Christian
antiquity, this book shows brilliantly how the Church can live by
continually pondering the Word of God."
— Avery Cardinal Dulles, S.J., Fordham University

"An eminent scholar of early Christianity . . . has again put
scholarship on early Christianity in his debt. . . . Should be in the
library of every university, seminary, and church."
— James R. Payton, Jr.,
St. Vladimir's Theological Quarterly

The Spirit of Early

Christian Thought

SEEKING THE FACE OF GOD

Robert Louis Wilken

YALE UNIVERSITY PRESS   NEW HAVEN & LONDON

Designed by Rebecca Gibb. Set in Fournier type by Keystone Typesetting, Inc.
Printed in the United States of America by R. R. Donnelley & Sons,
Harrisonburg, Virginia.

The Library of Congress has cataloged the hardcover edition as follows:
Wilken, Robert Louis, 1936–
The spirit of early Christian thought : seeking the face of God /
Robert Louis Wilken.
p. cm.
Includes bibliographical references (p.   ) and index.
ISBN 0-300-09708-5
1. Church history—Primitive and early church, ca. 30–600.
2. Theology—History—Early church, ca. 30–600. I. Title.
BR165 .W65 2003
230'.11—dc21
2002011130

A catalogue record for this book is available from the British Library.

The paper in this book meets the guidelines for permanence and durability of the
Committee on Production Guidelines for Book Longevity of the Council on
Library Resources.

ISBN 978-0-300-10598-8 (pbk. : alk. paper)

12   14   16   18   20   19   17   15   13   11

TO RICHARD

amico in Christo dilectissimo et fidelissimo

Take every thought captive to obey Christ.

2 CORINTHIANS 10:5

What is more magnificent than the beauty of God?

SAINT BASIL OF CAESAREA, *DETAILED RULES*

poi dietro ai sensi
vedi che la ragione ha corte l'ali.
[reason, even when
supported by the senses, has short wings.]

DANTE, *PARADISO* 2.56−57

the heart
must bear the longest part.

GEORGE HERBERT, ''ANTIPHON''

Contents

Acknowledgments

I AM GRATEFUL to Stanley Hauerwas, Richard John Neuhaus, Robin Darling Young, Lewis Ayres, and Rowan Greer, who read the manuscript and made helpful suggestions. The writing of this book has stretched over several years, and many people have made a difference at key points in its composition. Among them are Gary Anderson, David Burrell, Robert Dodaro, Jeremy Driscoll, Allan Fitzgerald, Harry Gamble, David Hart, David Hunter, Robert Jenson, David Kovacs, Judith Kovacs, George Lawless, Bruce Marshall, Bernard McGinn, Thomas F. X. Noble, Abram Ring, Nathan Scott, Basil Studer, Daniel Westberg, David Yeago, and John Yiannias. I also wish to thank Charles

Grench, my former editor at Yale University Press, for his support of my work, my present editor, Larisa Heimert, Lawrence Kenney for his careful copyediting of the manuscript, and Keith Condon for help with the illustrations and book jacket.

Introduction

THE CHRISTIAN RELIGION is inescapably ritualistic (one is received into the church by a solemn washing with water), uncompromisingly moral ("be ye perfect as your Father in heaven is perfect," said Jesus), and unapologetically intellectual (be ready to give a "reason for the hope that is in you," in the words of 1 Peter). Like all the major religions of the world, Christianity is more than a set of devotional practices and a moral code: it is also a way of thinking about God, about human beings, about the world and history. For Christians, thinking is part of believing. Augustine wrote, "No one believes anything unless one first thought it believable. . . . Everything that is believed is believed after being preceded by thought. . . . Not everyone who thinks believes, since many think in order not to believe; but everyone who believes thinks, thinks in believing and believes in thinking."[1] From the beginning the church has nurtured a lively intellectual life.

It is the purpose of this book to depict the pattern of Christian thinking as it took shape in the formative centuries of the church's history. I have tried to see things whole, to present persons and ideas as part of a common tradition rooted in a specific historical period yet not bound to time. Though long dead, the church fathers maintain their ground. This is not a history of early Christian thought. There are chapters on the doctrine of the Trinity and on Christ, but I have also included a chapter on Christian poetry and one on the moral life. My aim is less to describe how certain teachings emerged and developed than to show how a Christian intellectual tradition came into being, how Christians thought about the things they believed.

Although I deal with ideas and arguments, I am convinced that the study of early Christian thought has been too preoccupied with ideas. The intellectual effort of the early church was at the service of a much loftier goal than giving conceptual form to Christian belief. Its mission was to win the hearts and minds of men and women and to change their lives. Christian thinkers appealed to a much deeper level of human experience than had the religious institutions of society or the doctrines of the philosophers. In this endeavor the Bible was a central factor. It narrated a history that reached back into antiquity even to the beginning of the world, it was filled with stories of unforgettable men and women (not all admirable) who were actual historical persons rather than mythical figures, and it poured forth a thesaurus of words that created a new religious vocabulary and a cornucopia of scenes and images that stirred literary and artistic imagination as well as theological thought. God, the self, human community, the beginning and ending of things became interwoven with biblical history, biblical language, and biblical imagery.

The church gave men and women a new love, Jesus Christ, a person who inspired their actions and held their affections. This was a love unlike others. For it was not only that Jesus was a wise teacher, or a compassionate human being who reached out to the sick and needy or even that he patiently suffered abuse and calumny and died a cruel death, but that after his death God had raised him from the dead to a new life. He who once was dead now lives. The Resurrection of Jesus is the central fact of Christian devotion and the ground of all Christian thinking. The Resurrection was not a solitary occurrence, a prodigious miracle, but an event within the framework of Jewish history, and it brought into being a new community, the church. Christianity enters history not only as a message but also as a communal life, a society or city, whose inner discipline and practices, rituals and creeds, and institutions and traditions were the setting for Christian thinking.

From the time Christianity first came to public attention, Greek and Roman writers took note of the new religion and wrote learned and informed works of criticism. In an earlier book, *The Christians as the Romans Saw Them*, I presented the thought of these ancient critics of Christianity, philosophers like Celsus and Porphyry and the zealous Roman emperor Julian. That book was a self-conscious attempt to understand the critics of Christianity on their own terms within the context of ancient thought. Although they were often hostile and condescending, there is much to learn from them, not least about Christianity itself. But the reason for the study was eventually to take up the Christians' response to their critics. It has taken me much longer to return to this task than I anticipated, and my thinking has changed as I have read more widely and deeply in ancient texts and in early Christian literature. Though the present book is a fulfillment of that project, its plan is quite different from the one I envisioned some years ago.

I had intended to write a history of Christian apologetics, that is, how Christian thinkers answered the arguments of their critics as they defended and explained Christian belief to a world that knew little of Christ. But as compelling as that task remains, I have found that Christian thinking is much too independent to be treated chiefly in relation to Greco-Roman thought. It is instructive to hear the voices of the critics of Christianity, and that is where this book begins, but the energy, the vitality, the imaginative power of Christian thought stems from within, from the person of Christ, the Bible, Christian worship, the life of the church. Some of the most valuable sources, for example, are sermons. The agenda of this book is set by the things Christians cared most about.

The notion that the development of early Christian thought represented a hellenization of Christianity has outlived its usefulness. The time has come to bid a fond farewell to the ideas of Adolf von Harnack, the nineteenth-century historian of dogma whose thinking has influenced the interpretation of early Christian thought for more than a century. It will become clear in the course of this book that a more apt expression would be the Christianization of Hellenism, though that phrase does not capture the originality of Christian thought nor the debt owed to Jewish ways of thinking and to the Jewish Bible. Neither does it acknowledge the good and right qualities of Hellenic thinking that Christians recognized as valuable, for example, moral life understood in terms of the virtues. At the same time, one observes again and again that Christian thinking, while working within patterns of thought and conceptions rooted in Greco-Roman culture, transformed them so profoundly that in the end something quite new came into being.

There are many ways to account for this transformation—for example, the person of Christ and the events associated with him, the sacramental character of Christian worship, the communal life of the church—and each has its place in the story I tell. But what has impressed me most is the omnipresence of the Bible in early Christian writings. Early Christian thought is biblical, and one of the lasting accomplishments of the patristic period was to forge a way of thinking, scriptural in language and inspiration, that gave to the church and to Western civilization a unified and coherent interpretation of the Bible as a whole. Needless to say, this means that any effort to mount an interpretation of the Bible that ignores its first readers is doomed to end up with a bouquet of fragments that are neither the book of the church nor the imaginative wellspring of Western literature, art, and music. Uprooted from the soil that feeds them, they are like cut flowers whose vivid colors have faded.

The distinctive marks of early Christian thinking can be set down in a few sentences. Christians reasoned from the history of Israel and of Jesus Christ, from the experience of Christian worship, and from the Holy Scriptures (and earlier interpretations of the Scriptures), that is to say, from history, from ritual, and from text. Christian thinking is anchored in the church's life, sustained by such devotional practices as the daily recitation of the psalms, and nurtured by the liturgy, in particular, the regular celebration of the Eucharist. Theory was not an end in itself, and concepts and abstractions were always put at the service of a deeper immersion in the *res*, the thing itself, the mystery of Christ and of the practice of the Christian life. The goal was not only understanding but love, and at various points in the book, in discussing the knowledge of God, the Trinity, the virtues, and especially in the final chapter on the passions, I have tried to show the indispensability of love to Christian thinking.

In an essay on the church fathers, Hans Urs von Balthasar once wrote, "Greatness, depth, boldness, flexibility, certainty and a flaming love—the virtues of youth, are marks of patristic theology. Perhaps the Church will never again see the likes of such an array of larger-than-life figures that mark the period from Irenaeus to Athanasius, Basil, Cyril, Chrysostom, Ambrose and Augustine—not to mention the army of the lesser fathers. Life and doctrine are immediately one. Of them all it is true what Kierkegaard said of Chrysostom: 'He gesticulated with his whole existence.' "[2]

Early Christian thought, as these words suggest, is the work of an unparalleled company of gifted thinkers whose lives are interwoven with their thought. No discussion is worth much if it does not keep close to the concrete, and I have presented the thinking of the early church by reference to distinct persons and issues. I have not sought to be comprehensive. There is only passing reference to the Pelagian controversy over grace, for example, and I discuss only one aspect of the debate over the person of Christ. As far as possible, each chapter focuses on one or two persons whose thinking illustrates one of the themes of the book, and I have said little that cannot be related to specific texts. To fill out the pattern of early Christian thinking, however, I draw freely from works of writers spread out across seven centuries and beyond.

I have tried to write for the general reader, avoiding modern scholarly debates about the interpretation of early Christian history and thought. These are best carried on in learned journals and monographs. With few exceptions the notes are to the ancient sources. The suggestions for further reading list some books and articles that have formed my thinking or elaborate on topics treated in a chapter.

Although I cite many writers, including Justin Martyr, Irenaeus, Clement of Alexandria, Lactantius, Athanasius, Basil of Caesarea, John Chrysostom, Ambrose of Milan, Cyril of Alexandria, and others, I found that I turned consistently to four: Origen in the third century, Gregory of Nyssa in the fourth, Augustine in the fifth, and Maximus the Confessor in the seventh. In the early church these four stand out as the most rewarding, the most profound, and the most enduring. They can be read as living interpreters, not just as historical sources. Yet few will quarrel with the conventional wisdom that Augustine stands at the summit. He is the most discerning, his thought flows at a deeper level, his range of interests is greater, he wrote with more elegance, and he has been the most influential, at least in the West. But he was not alone, and he has much in common with others, especially with Gregory of Nysssa and Maximus the Confessor and in places with Origen. Like all great Christian thinkers he consciously moved within a tradition he had himself not created. He was most comfortable with a page of the Bible open before him in a basilica in the midst of the community of faith to which he was accountable. The church fathers wrote "as those who are taught" (Isa. 50:4).

A few words on the organization of the book. The first three chapters deal with foundations: how God is known, Christian worship and sacraments, the Scriptures. From the beginning Christian thinkers recognized the centrality of biblical history in Christian thinking. God was made known in the history of Israel and in the events of Christ's life, and Christian thinking begins with these events and is sustained by them. Chapter 2, on Christian worship, shows that early Christian thinkers were men of prayer who knew the person of Christ not only as a historical memory, but as a fact of experience in the liturgy, in which the events recorded in the gospels, particularly the death and Resurrection of Christ, were "made present." In the third chapter I have tried to give a sense of how fresh, even astonishing, the Bible appeared to thinkers schooled in ancient literature. The Scriptures disclosed a world unlike anything they had known before, and reading and expounding the Bible left a lasting imprint on their vocabulary and altered their patterns of thought.

Next come three chapters on Christian teachings: the Trinity, the work of Christ, and the creation of the world and of human beings. Chapter 4 recapitulates points made in the first three chapters to illustrate how history (the Resurrection of Christ), the Trinitarian formulas of Christian worship, and the Scriptures all worked together to forge a Christian doctrine of the Trinity. Chapter 5 discusses the work of Christ in relation to one event in the gospels, the "agony" of Christ, when Jesus said, "Not my will but thine be done." The key person here is Maximus the Confessor. By thrusting his mind into this event, Maximus was able to find language and concepts to express the mystery of Christ's humanity with a clarity and depth that had eluded earlier thinkers. Christian thinking is nourished by constant immersion in the evangelical history. Chapter 6 has as its focus the account of creation in the first chapter of the book of Genesis, the opening words, "In the beginning God created," and the phrase "made in the image and likeness of God" (1:26). Here I draw chiefly on the interpretation of these texts in the writings of Basil of Caesarea and Gregory of Nyssa. Their goal was to forge a view of creation and of human beings that was biblical, yet intelligible and coherent to all reasonable persons.

Then come two chapters dealing with the believer, chapter 7 on faith as a way of knowing, and chapter 8 on the fellowship of believers, the church in relation to society. In these chapters I depend on Augustine. The chapter on faith expands on a theme introduced in the first chapter, that the knowledge of God is participatory; hence it is reasonable to say that God can be known only in faith and love. At points in the book I call attention to the importance of the church as the context for Christian thinking, and in chapter 8 I discuss the role of the church in Augustine's understanding of a just society.

Chapters 9 and 10 deal with things, the stuff of Christian culture, the former on things that are words, that is, Christian poetry, the latter on things that are wood and paint, that is, icons. Just as some Christians tried to understand the central mysteries of the faith, for example, the Holy Trinity and the person of Christ, in words and concepts, others sought to give expression to Christian truth in literature and art. The Christian poet Prudentius, the subject of chapter 9, celebrated the "glorious deeds of Christ" in verse and invited readers through poetry to make place for the Trinity in their hearts. Icons are, of course, objects of veneration and are best discussed in relation to Christian worship and devotion. But the defense of icons, the subject of chapter 10, provides an occasion to examine the intimate relation between material things and spiritual realities in Christian thinking and to underscore observations made in the first chapter about the primacy of the Incarnation in Christian thinking.

Augustine wrote that the only purpose in doing philosophy is to attain happiness.[3] The prodigious intellectual effort of the early church had as its aim to lead men and women to holiness of life. Hence the final two chapters of the book deal with the Christian life, chapter 11 with the moral life and chapter 12 with the spiritual life. Although Christian thinkers worked within a Greek and Roman tradition of moral philosophy that preceded them, they transformed what they received. The goal of life came to be understood as likeness to Christ, the cardinal virtues were reinterpreted as forms of love, and the list of virtues was expanded to include distinctively biblical virtues, for example, patience (or long-suffering) and humility. Finally, I turn to the passions (or affections) and hence to love. In the thinking of the church fathers, desire, the energy that moves one to do the good, gives way to love, the blessed passion that binds one to God. The knowledge of God, in the words of Beatrice in Dante's *Paradiso*, "is buried from the eyes of everyone whose intellect has not matured within the flame of love."[4]

The subtitle *Seeking the Face of God* is based on Psalm 105:4 in the Latin version, "Seek his face always" (Quaerite faciem eius semper). This verse is cited four times by Saint Augustine in his work *The Trinity*. More than any other passage in the Bible it captures the spirit of early Christian thinking.

The Spirit of Early Christian Thought

Chapter 1

Founded on the Cross of Christ

> "Precious in the sight of the Lord is the death of his saints"
> (Ps. 116:15). No degree of cruel inhumanity can destroy the religion
> founded on the mystery of the cross of Christ.
>
> LEO THE GREAT

FROM THE BEGINNING Christians were conscious of the other. The first Christians had to explain to their fellow Jews why they venerated a man who had been executed by the Romans. Within a few decades of Jesus' death, as some Christians ceased observing the Jewish Law, Christian leaders had to answer charges they had abandoned the ancient traditions of the Jewish people. Later, in Greece, as Paul began to move beyond the Jewish world to address the Gentiles, the citizens of Athens brought him to the famous hill west of the Acropolis, the Areopagus, and asked him to justify his new teaching. "It sounds rather strange to our ears," they said, "so we would like to know what it means" (Acts 17.21).

Of course all efforts to explain or to justify what one believes are undertaken as much for oneself as for others. If the questions are genuine, if they go to the heart of the matter and are not simply rhetorical flourishes to score points in a debate, over time they will be asked even in the absence of the other. Dialogue inevitably leads to a more solitary and sustained inquiry. Nevertheless, even if there is no philosophical necessity for dialogue, it is no idle matter to have the questions posed by someone else, especially if the inquirer belongs to a neighboring community that lives by different answers.

Although Christianity began as a movement among Jews in Palestine, it spread swiftly to other parts of the Roman Empire, to Syria and to Egypt, to Asia Minor and to Greece, to Rome and from there across the Mediterranean to Roman Africa. Initially many of the converts were Jews, but within a few decades others began to join the new movement. For these people, many of whom had little contact with Judaism, to become a Christian meant abandoning a way of life that had been practiced for generations, even centuries, and rending the social fabric that bound family and neighborhood and city. Christianity was a novel, alien way of life, seemingly disdainful of custom and tradition and making extravagant claims about a man who had lived only recently. Christians, it was thought, jettisoned the wisdom of the past.

An early and astute critic reproached Christians for abandoning the "ancient doctrine" that had been taught by "the wisest peoples and cities and sages."[1] In different dress this charge was brought against Christianity by all Greek and Roman observers during the first few centuries. Their accusation cut deep because Christian thinkers, like their critics, had been educated in the literature and philosophy of the ancient world. What is more, they cherished that past—it was their inheritance as well as that of their critics. Christians could not escape the claims of the other, whether as a social fact or as an intellectual challenge, and in its formative period Christian thought was in continuous conversation with the classical intellectual tradition.

Early Christian thinking, however, was as much an attempt to penetrate more deeply into the mystery of Christ, to know and understand what was believed and handed on in the churches, as it was to answer the charges of critics or explain the faith to outsiders. Christian thinkers were not in the business of establishing something; their task was to understand and explain something. The desire to understand is as much part of believing as is the drive to act on what one believes. In the course of this book there will be many occasions to observe how Christian thought arose in response to the facts of revelation, how its idiom was set by the language and imagery of the Bible, and how the life and worship of the Christian community gave Christian thinking a social dimension that was absent from ancient philosophy. But the place to begin is with questions posed by outsiders. For the critics of Christianity had an uncanny sense of what made the new religion unique, and in their response the earliest Christian thinkers saw with unparalleled acuity what gave Christianity its distinctive character.

A Fire in the Soul

The earliest Christian writings were composed by Christians for Christians. These include the gospels, epistles written by Saint Paul to Christian congregations scattered about the Mediterranean world, letters of bishops like Ignatius of Antioch and Clem-

ent of Rome at the turn of the first century, an occasional sermon, a manual to aid in regulating the life of an early Christian
community, an account of the martyrdom of an aged bishop.
Some writings, the *Acts of the Apostles,* for example, may have
envisioned a wider audience, but it was not until the middle of
the second century that Christians began to compose literary
works consciously addressed to outsiders.

The authors of these books are called apologists, and in this
context the term *apology* means a defense and explanation of
one's way of life and beliefs. The early apologists were faced
with the daunting task of presenting Christianity for the first
time to a society that knew nothing of the Christian religion.
Christianity had begun in the fourth decade of the first century
in Jerusalem, on the eastern periphery of the Roman Empire,
and a hundred years later few people across the empire had any
firsthand knowledge of the new movement. What they knew
was based on hearsay. The first mention of Christianity by a
non-Christian writer does not occur until the second decade of
the second century. Pliny, a Roman governor in Asia Minor
(modern-day Turkey), dismissed the new movement as a "de-
praved foreign cult carried to extravagant lengths."[2] Given
views like Pliny's, the new religion needed defenders.

Among the earliest apologists the most sophisticated was Justin Martyr, who was born in Palestine at the beginning of the
second century. He calls himself a Samaritan, probably because
he was born at Neapolis (modern Nablus) in Roman Palestine,
but his family was Greek, and he seems not to have heard of
Moses and the prophets until as an adult he met a Christian. He
practiced philosophy before becoming a Christian and after his
conversion remained a philosopher and continued to wear the

philosopher's garb. Justin settled in Rome, the home of a vibrant Christian community, and there taught the "the word of God," as an ancient historian put it, and used his pen to defend his new faith to other philosophers in the city.[3]

Justin wrote several works to the Romans in defense of Christianity, but he also addressed a long work to the Jews. Christian thinkers had to address two sets of critics simultaneously, one representing the cultural traditions of Greece and Rome, the other the people from whom Christianity had sprung and whose Bible (what Christians called the Old Testament) they made their own. In his work dealing with Judaism, the *Dialogue with Trypho*, Justin offers a detailed exposition of select passages from the Septuagint (the Greek translation of the Old Testament), his purpose being to show that these books must be given a Christian interpretation. But he prefaces his work with an artful account of how he came to embrace Christianity. Because the chronicle of his conversion is consciously literary and modeled on conventional depictions of conversion to philosophy, some have suggested that his account is not wholly biographical. No doubt there is truth in this view, yet, whatever the literary background of the work, it is not insignificant that Justin chose to present his embrace of Christianity as a conversion to philosophy. For the term for philosophy in his day was *life*, and Justin wanted his readers to know that in turning to Christianity he had embraced a new way of life.

According to the *Dialogue with Trypho* Justin first went to study with a Stoic philosopher. But after listening to him, he learned, as he puts it, nothing about God. Indeed, his mentor seemed bored with the subject. Next Justin turned to a Peripatetic, that is, a follower of Aristotle, but this philosopher seemed interested only in talking about fees. After that he approached a Pythagorean, who cared chiefly about mathematical theorems. Finally he turned to a Platonist and for the first time sensed he was making genuine progress. His mind had been given wings, and he hoped in time to "see God."[4]

One day, however, while walking on a beach he fell into conversation with an old man about Plato. As they talked, the sage gradually began to modulate into another key. Unlike Plato, who taught that the soul is immortal and has life in itself, the old man said that the soul's life is a wondrous gift of God, the source of all life. When Justin sensed that this man uttered things he had not heard before he asked, If one is to follow this way of life, does one need a teacher? His aged companion responded that long ago, even before the Greek philosophers, there lived teachers called prophets, who wrote about "the beginning and end of things." In contrast to the philosophers, who rely chiefly on demonstration, the prophets spoke about what they had seen and heard and were "witnesses to the truth."[5] The Word of God makes its way not by argument but as men and women bear witness to what has happened.

As Justin finished his conversation, the old man, to Justin's surprise, did not try to convince him of the teachings he had presented but ended the colloquy with a prayer that the "gates of light" would be opened and Justin would be receptive to what he heard. After his prayer the old man left, but his words had fallen like hot coals on dry kindling. "A flame was kindled in my soul," writes Justin, "and I was seized by love of the prophets and of the friends of Christ. While I was pondering his words in my mind, I came to see that this way of life alone is sure and fulfilling."[6]

Whatever the historical kernel behind Justin's account of his spiritual odyssey, what he wished to convey to his readers is set forth with admirable grace and clarity. God, as he learned from this sage, is known primarily through events that take place in history. When speaking of how God is known, the Bible seldom speaks of insight or illumination or demonstration; rather, it says that God appeared, did something, showed himself, or spoke to someone, as in the beginning of the book of Hosea: "The word of God came to Hosea" (Hos. 1:1). Accordingly, the way to God begins not with arguments or proofs but with discernment and faith, the ability to see what is disclosed in events and the readiness to trust the words of those who testify to them.

By presenting his embrace of Christianity as a conversion to a way of life that is "sure and fulfilling," Justin let his readers know that the truth of Christ penetrates the soul by means of our moral as well as our intellectual being. The knowledge of God has to do with how one lives, with acting on convictions that are not mere premises but realities learned from other persons and tested by experience.

Justin's account also makes place for the affections. Jesus had taught that the first and greatest commandment was, "You shall love the Lord your God with all your heart and with all your soul and with all your might." The language of love pervades the New Testament. Nevertheless it is noteworthy, especially at the very beginning of the Christian intellectual tradition, that in describing his response to the words of the old man Justin said that he was set ablaze by the fire that breaks from God and was "seized by love." Only when wounded by love can one know the God of the Bible. As Augustine would write several centuries later, it is love that "sets us on fire" and "lifts us" to God.[7] To love God is already to be on the way of understanding.

Seeing God

In A.D. 165, Justin, who had been living in Rome, was condemned to death for refusing to venerate the gods of Rome. With a group of his companions he was beheaded. Hence he received the name Justin Martyr, Justin the Witness, for by his death he bore witness to the truth of Christ. During his lifetime some Greek thinkers had begun to take note of the new movement and to read Christian writings. The physician-philosopher Galen, a younger contemporary of Justin, was acquainted with the account of creation in the book of Genesis. He thought it irrational that God would create the world by an act of will without regard to the laws governing nature, and he ridiculed the biblical notion that with God all things are possible. A few years after Justin's death another Greek philosopher by the name of Celsus wrote a book on Christianity entitled *True Doctrine*. Celsus had made it his business to become well informed about Christian teaching and practice and had read several books of the New Testament as well as writings of Christian thinkers of his own day, including one of Justin's apologies in defense of Christianity. From Celsus we have an informed portrait of what thoughtful outsiders knew about the new religion and what in their view set off the spiritual vision of Christianity from the religious beliefs and practices of the Roman world.

Among ancient philosophers it was axiomatic that all knowledge of God came through the activity of the mind purged of impressions received by the senses. Only when freed from the perception of tangible objects can the mind lift itself to God. In this view the knowledge of God was achieved by very few, and even the seer divined but little of God. One of the texts cited most often by philosophers during this period was a passage from Plato's treatise on cosmology, the *Timaeus*: "Now to find the Maker and Father of this universe is difficult, and after finding him it is impossible to declare him to all men." Celsus was familiar with this text, and in his book *True Doctrine* he cites the authority of Plato to deride Christians for their claim that God had been revealed in a historical person. God, he said, can be known only through the mind's eye: "If you shut your eyes to the world of sense and look up with the mind, if you turn away from the flesh and raise the eyes of the soul, only then will you see God."[8]

Another philosopher, Alcinous, a contemporary of Celsus, stated the conventional opinion in this way: The "first God" is unlike objects in this world. He is "eternal, ineffable, self-sufficient, without need . . . and perfect in every respect." To acquire knowledge of God one must train the mind to turn away from sensible things and rise to higher spiritual realities: "First one contemplates the beauty found in bodies, after this one passes on to the beauty of the soul, then to the beauty in customs and laws, then to the vast ocean of beauty; after this one conceives of the Good itself . . . which appears as light and shines on the soul as it makes its ascent. Then one comes to the idea of God because of his preeminence in honor."[9]

In his *True Doctrine* Celsus appeals to this philosophical commonplace to drive home his argument against the Christians. Christians, he says, are so taken up with sensible things, with a person of flesh and blood, that they are unable to breathe the pure intellectual air where true knowledge of God is found. The idea that God should appear to humans, that the knowledge of God should be a matter of revelation in a historical person, was contrary to God's nature. In Celsus's mocking and mordant taunt, "What is the purpose of such a descent on the part of God. Was it in order to learn what was going on among men? Doesn't God know everything?" By challenging Christians at this point Celsus hoped to lay the axe to the root of the new movement.

The distinctive feature of Christianity, as Celsus realized from reading the New Testament, was that "God or a son of God had come down to earth" in the person of Jesus of Nazareth and was seen by human beings. If God entered space and time, argued Celsus, the fundamental order and structure of the world would be irrevocably disrupted. In the memorable lines of W. H. Auden, "How could the eternal do a temporal act? / The infinite become a finite fact?" The laws that govern the cosmos are fixed and immutable, and a spiritual entity cannot be subject to the constraints that govern terrestrial life. "If you changed any one quite insignificant thing on earth," writes Celsus, "you would upset and destroy everything."[10]

A Proof Proper to the Gospel

Celsus wrote his book against Christianity about A.D. 170, and for several generations it received no response. But in the middle of the next century Origen of Alexandria, one of the boldest and most original minds in the church's history, wrote a detailed refutation of Celsus's *True Doctrine*. Entitled *Against Celsus*, Origen's treatise adroitly fields Celsus's criticisms, patiently explains where he misunderstands things, and on the points that count meets him argument for argument. It is a learned, subtle book, and among early Christian writings written in defense of the faith only Augustine's *City of God* rivals it in profundity. More remarkable, Origen took great care to present the views of his opponent to his readers. (Perhaps this is why Thomas Jefferson had two copies of *Against Celsus* in his library, the Greek text and a French translation.) In it the case against Christianity was stated with uncommon intelligence. Origen's citations of Celsus's *True Doctrine* are so extensive that one can reconstruct not only the arguments but many of the actual words of Celsus's treatise.

Origen was born in Alexandria, the large cosmopolitan city on Egypt's Mediterranean coast, about A.D. 185. His parents were Christian, and he received a Christian formation as a boy, which accounts for his familiarity with the Bible. But as a young man he also gave himself to the study of philosophy. Origen was as comfortable in the cultured intellectual world of the early Roman empire as he was at home in the church. One of his critics, the philosopher Porphyry, thought Origen was more Greek than Christian in his thinking, an opinion that is shared by some to this day. Origen was a man of the church first, however, and most of his writings are expositions of the Bible. Even those dealing with philosophical matters are studded with citations from the Scriptures and appeal to biblical history. In responding to Celsus, Origen relies not only on philosophical arguments, but also on the biblical account of the Jewish people recorded in the Old Testament. Origen spent his mature years in Caesarea in Palestine, the home of a large Jewish community, and *Against Celsus* was written there in A.D. 248, when he was in his early sixties. Two years later he was imprisoned by the Roman authorities during the persecution of the emperor Decius, and he died a martyr in 250 after being subjected to prolonged torture.

Celsus had urged that the way to God was through the ascent of the mind. One must turn away from what can be perceived with the senses and by a series of mental steps rise to God. As another critic of Christianity put it, "Intellectual matters are known intellectually, and sensible things are known through the senses." In response Origen makes the extraordinary statement that the knowledge of God begins not with the ascent of the mind, but with God's descent to human beings in a historical person: "I admit that Plato's statement quoted by Celsus is noble and impressive. But consider whether the Holy Scripture shows more compassion for humankind when it presents the divine Word (*logos*), who was in the beginning with God . . . as becoming flesh in order to reach everyone."[11]

Origen acknowledges that the seers of old had a glimpse of God, but their knowledge was partial and defective. The most telling evidence against them is that the philosophers who claimed to know God continued to live as though they did not know God, revering many gods instead of worshiping the one God. "If God really had been found by Plato or one of the Greeks," Origen writes, "they would not have venerated something else and called it God and worshiped it, abandoning the true God or associating things with him that are incompatible with God's majesty."[12] Origen was convinced that the knowledge of God acquired solely by the activity of the mind was imperfect—it brought no change of worship—and it is at this point that he joins the debate with Celsus.

The early apologists, like apologists in every age, shared many ideas with thinkers of their day and highlighted aspects of Christian teaching that could be readily understood within the cultural milieu in which they lived. In his first Apology Justin presents Jesus as a teacher of the moral life and illustrates his teaching by sayings from the gospels that have parallels in the moral essays of contemporary Greek philosophers. Christian thinkers also drew on the cardinal virtues, prudence, justice, courage, and temperance, a staple of classical moral philosophy, to present the distinctive features of Christian ethics. Others noted points of correspondence between biblical terms designating God's transcendence and Greek philosophical terms for God, such as *eternal, invisible* and *unchanging*. At one point in *Against Celsus* Origen said even that "the doctrines of our faith are in complete accord with common notions" shared by philosophers and other thoughtful people.[13]

Yet when one looks more closely at the writings of the early apologists, it is apparent that Christian thinkers had seen something in Christ and the Scriptures that would not yield easily to conventional philosophical reasoning. Celsus had chided Christians that the source of their teaching was "originally barbarian," by which he meant Christianity was not Greek and had begun among the Jews. Origen cheerfully granted Celsus's point and even complimented him for not dismissing Christianity simply because the gospel arose among non-Greeks. Celsus, however, adds that if Christianity is to be taken seriously by thinkers like himself, Christians must subject their teaching to a "Greek proof," that is, measure it by current philosophical standards as to what is reasonable. "The Greeks," he writes, "are better able to judge the value of what the barbarians have discovered and to confirm their teachings and adapt them to the life of virtue." How presumptuous, says Origen. Is the gospel to be judged by a criterion external to itself? The "gospel," he responds, "has a proof that is proper to itself and is more divine than the dialectical arguments of the Greeks." This more divine proof, he adds, is called "proof of the Spirit and of power" (1 Cor. 2:4) by Saint Paul.[14]

By insisting the gospel has a "proof proper to itself," Origen wished to say that Christianity had its origin in "God's revelation, not in human wisdom." From this truth, however, he did not draw the conclusion that Christian thinkers should ignore the arguments of the philosophers or dismiss questions that arose from logic, history, or experience. "It is far better," wrote Origen, "to accept teachings with reason and wisdom than with mere faith." As Clement his predecessor in Alexandria knew, one cannot respond to one's critics without understanding what they say. First one must "closely examine" what they teach, and only after setting down the opinions of the philosophers side by side with those of the Christians can one claim to have arrived at the truth.[15] Some critics, notably Galen, had tried to brand the Christians as fideists because their teachings seemed to be based solely on faith. But these cultured despisers soon learned that Christian thinkers were as conversant with the philosophical tradition as they were and respected arguments from reason. In their works in defense of Christianity the apologists met Greek and Roman thinkers argument for argument, a dialogue that was carried on without interruption for three centuries and resumed in the high Middle Ages. Even the Bible was a book to be argued from, not simply an authority to brandish when arguments failed. Origen's assertion that the gospel had a "proof proper to itself" was not a confession of faith, but the beginning of an argument.

In the debate between Christian thinkers and their critics the central issue was where in the search for God reason is to begin. Christians argued that Christ had brought something new; the life he lived, though fully human, was unlike that of anyone who had lived earlier. In the "face of Christ," Saint Paul had written, the "knowledge of the glory of God" (2 Cor. 4:6) had shone forth. Once a person had seen such splendor "what once had splendor has come to have no splendor at all" (2 Cor. 3:10). Early in the second century Ignatius of Antioch had written, "The Gospel has something remarkable: the coming of the Savior, our Lord Jesus Christ, his suffering and resurrection." And centuries later at the end of the formative period of Christian history in the seventh century, Maximus the Confessor said that Christ's life was "strange and wondrous," for it was "imprinted with the new power of a person who lived life in a new way." After the coming of Christ, human reason had to attend to what was new in history, the person of Jesus Christ. For the Greeks, God was the conclusion of an argument, the end of a search for an ultimate explanation, an inference from the structure of the universe to a first cause. For Christian thinkers, God was the starting point, and Christ the icon that displays the face of God. "Reason became man and was called Jesus Christ," wrote Justin. Now one reasoned from Christ to other things, not from other things to Christ. In him was to be found the reason, the *logos,* the logic, if you will, that inheres in all things.[16]

The Christian gospel was not an idea but a certain kind of story, a narrative about a person and things that had actually happened in space and time. It was, says Origen, an "event recorded in history." In its proper sense the term *gospel,* as he explained in his commentary on the *Gospel according to John,* refers to those books that include a "narrative of the deeds, sufferings and words of Jesus." But this narrative was not a bare report of what had taken place. The gospel, he writes, is "an account of things that . . . make the hearer glad when he accepts what is reported." It is centered on a specific human being, Jesus of Nazareth, but as Celsus realized, God is the protagonist.[17]

As much as the apologists were convinced that God's fullest self-disclosure was in Christ they also recognized that God was known through creation. Athenagoras, a contemporary of Justin, wrote that "heaven and earth are filled with God's beauty" and from what is made people can know that God "must be one."[18] But early Christian thinkers offer no philosophical argument for the existence of God drawn from the world of nature. When speaking of the revelation of God in creation they cite the Scriptures, usually Romans, "God's invisible nature . . . is clearly perceived in the things that have been made" (Rom. 1:20), sometimes the psalm, "the heavens declare the glory of God" (Ps. 19:1). They did not argue that there is a God because there is order; rather, they saw design in the universe because they knew the one God. God was not a principle of explanation. In seeking God they sought to understand the God they already knew.

The Elect People of God

When Origen is defending Christianity to the Greeks and Romans, the Jews play a prominent part in his argument. He knew he could not present what is distinctive about Christ without first speaking about God's relation to the Jewish people. God's "descent" into history in the person of Christ was not a solitary, isolated event: it stood in a long train of earlier appearances of God to the people of Israel. Without this history the significance of Christ's coming was hidden. The same God, says Origen, who "first established Judaism, afterward established Christianity."[19] The God who appeared in Christ was the God who appeared to Abraham, Isaac, and Jacob, to Sarah, and Rebecca and Rachel, to kings and prophets and sages of old. The Christian gospel does not appear in a vacuum, it is of a piece with the revelation of God to Israel.

Origen's appeal to Moses is neither casual nor perfunctory. Celsus was critical of the Jews because they had held fast to their own law "as though they had some deeper wisdom." In their ignorance (thinking their doctrine was unique) they had turned away from the society of the nations. Origen does not dispute Celsus's point; indeed, he accentuates it. The Jews are different from other people. They *do* consider themselves "an elect portion of the supreme God preferred before any other nation." *Elect* is Origen's word, not Celsus's, and it is of course taken from the Bible. What set the Jews apart was that they ordered their life on the basis of God's revelation of the Law to Moses. If one studies their "society in their early days when the Law was given one would find that they were a people who manifested a shadow of the heavenly life on earth." They served the one God and "would not allow makers of images to be citizens. There were no painters of idols or image-makers in their society, because the Law banished from it any people of this sort. In this way they made sure that there would be no occasion for the making of images that could take hold of simple people and drag the eyes of their soul from God down to earth."[20]

This exchange between Origen and Celsus is part of the central debate between Christians and their critics: should the one God alone be worshiped? or should God be worshiped as one (the highest to be sure) of a company of deities? Celsus, like other philosophers of his day, believed in an inclusive monotheism, the view that there was one high god who presided over a

hierarchy of lesser gods ranked in descending order. The worship of God became more perfect by venerating all the gods.
Origen would have none of this; in his view such inclusive piety
was an offense to God. What is instructive, however, is that to
answer Celsus Origen does not bring forth a philosophical argument about the uniqueness of the one high god. Instead he takes
an apparently roundabout route that traverses the history of the
Jews, that people who had worshiped and served the one God
for centuries. His is an argument from history and communal
experience. By the example of a life devoted to the one God, the
Jewish people introduced others to the worship of God.

The Jews, however, are a single people, and there came a
time, says Origen, when the Jewish way of life "needed to be
altered so that it was suitable for people everywhere." This
change took place at the time of Jesus, whose "noble religion"
was given to those who believe "in all places," not only in one
land and among one people: "He overthrew the teaching about
the daemons on earth, who delight in frankincense and blood
and the odors rising from burnt sacrifices, and drag men down
from the true conception of God."[21] Through Jesus the worship
of the one God found a home among all the peoples of the world.

The Grace of Revelation

In the passage from *Against Celsus* that began this discussion,
Origen says that when God became flesh in the person of Christ
human nature was able to "find God." But then he adds, "We
affirm that human nature is not sufficient in any way to seek God
and find him with purity unless it is helped by the one who is the
object of the search." When Saint Paul testified that the Greeks
"knew God," he also said, "They did not achieve this without

God's help." For "God manifested it to them" (Rom. 1:19). Unlike other forms of knowledge, the knowledge of God begins with God's movement toward human beings, what in the language of Christian theology is called grace. Early on this biblical teaching sank deep into the Christian mind. Irenaeus, bishop of Lyons in France at the end of the second century, wrote, "The Lord taught us that no one is able to know God unless taught by God. God cannot be known without the help of God."[22]

To see how Christian thinkers came to this conviction one must begin, as they did, with the Scriptures. In a homily on the Gospel according to Saint Luke, Origen explains how it is that human beings can "see God." The text he was expounding was Luke 1:11: "Then there *appeared* to him [Zechariah] an angel of the Lord, standing at the right side of the altar of incense." Origen distinguishes two types of seeing, the normal way human beings perceive physical objects and spiritual seeing, that is, knowing God. "For corporeal things to be seen," he writes, "it is not necessary that they do anything." One needs only "an eye that focuses on the objects." When someone directs his gaze at the object he sees it whether the object wills to be seen or not. With "divine matters," however, something else is required: "For when something is present it will not be seen if it does not will to be seen." When God appeared to Abraham or to any of the saints, two things were needed: Abraham had to have a pure soul capable of seeing God, and God had to "present himself" to Abraham: "It was by an act of grace that God appeared to Abraham and the other prophets. The eye of Abraham's heart was not the only cause of his seeing God; it was God's grace freely offered to a just man that allowed him to see."[23] The knowledge of God begins with God.

As this passage suggests, when speaking of how God is known early Christian thinkers favored the metaphor of seeing, not hearing. In his response to Celsus Origen cites a series of biblical texts that have to do with seeing: "Blessed are the pure in spirit for they shall see God" (Matt. 5:8); "He who has seen me has seen the Father" (Jo. 14:9); and "Christ is the image of the invisible God" (Col. 1:15). From these he draws the conclusion that people come to know the "Father and maker of this universe by looking at the image of the invisible God."[24]

Beauty is the corollary of seeing. In the Scriptures many of the key terms used of God's self-disclosure, words such as *glory, splendor, light, image,* and *face,* have to do with the delight of the eye. When we speak of the pleasure the eye takes in what it sees the term that comes to mind is *beauty.* The psalmist wrote, "One thing have I asked of the Lord . . . that I will behold the beauty of the Lord" (Ps. 27:4). As early as the second century the apologist Athenagoras of Athens included the term *beauty* in a list of words depicting God. The God we set before you, he says, is "encompassed by light, beauty, spirit, and indescribable power." In his commentary on the Song of Songs Origen wrote that the "soul is moved by heavenly love and longing when it beholds the beauty and the comeliness of the Word of God." God's revelation can be seen from the perspective of its ineffable beauty as well as of its truth and goodness.[25]

Just how important seeing is in early Christian thought can be seen in another homily of Origen on Saint Luke. In the account of the giving of the Law on Mount Sinai, Origen observed that the Scriptures say that the people "saw the voice of the Lord" (Exod. 20:18 in the Septuagint). Obviously a voice cannot be seen with the eyes. Yet that is what the Scripture says. The biblical expression, says Origen, means that the voice of the Lord is "seen by those to whom it is given to see," that is, it is heard by those who have the capacity to grasp what is disclosed. Hence the term *eyewitnesses* in the prologue to the Gospel of Luke does not simply signify seeing Christ with the eyes. When Luke says that the disciples were "eyewitnesses of the *word*," he means "not only that they saw Jesus in his bodily form, but also that they were eyewitnesses of the *Word of God*," that is, they knew Christ the divine Son of God. If seeing Jesus in his bodily form is the meaning of *eyewitness*, then Pilate or Judas or those who cried out, "Crucify him, crucify him" would also be eyewitnesses, and that, says Origen, is surely false. The expression "seeing God" is to be understood in the sense of the words from the Gospel of John: "Who has seen me has seen the Father."[26]

Origen overstates the matter. If the Logos truly became flesh, there is a sense in which whoever sees Jesus sees the Logos, whether pure of heart or hard of heart, whether in unbelief or in faith. Yet what Origen is driving at is clear. In the Scriptures, seeing is never simply beholding something that passes like a parade before the eyes; it is a form of discernment and identification with what is known. What one sees reflects back on the one who sees and transforms the beholder. As Gregory the Great will put it centuries later, "We are changed into the one we see." There can be no knowledge of God without a relation between the knower and God. To see light is to share in light and to be enlightened. In the words of Irenaeus, "Just as those who see the light are illuminated by the light and share in its brilliance, so those who see God are in God and share his splendor." In the Scriptures, says Origen, the term *know* means to "participate in something" or to be "joined to something." This is why in

Galatians Paul says that believers "have come to know God," but then immediately adds, "or rather to be known by God" (Gal. 4:9). The Lord knows those who know him because "he has been made one with them and given them a share in his divine life." At a key place in the *Contra Celsum,* in response to Celsus's mocking question as to why God descended to human beings, Origen says that it was "to implant in us the happiness which comes from knowing him."[27]

When Origen's defense of Christianity to the Greeks is read in conjunction with his homilies on the Bible, the pillars on which Christian thinkers erected a kind of theological epistemology, a way of knowing God, become apparent. Although there was a well-developed tradition in the Greco-Roman world of thinking about how God is known, Christian thinkers set out on a different path. They began with the history of Israel and the revelation in Christ as presented in the Scriptures. In the Bible God is the actor and revelation is a drama in which God acts and man responds. Origen called the knowledge of God "reciprocal," by which he meant that without love, there can be no knowledge of God. Yet he insisted, and he does not consider it paradoxical, that even the response to God is itself God's work: "Our will does not suffice to give us a wholly pure heart. We need God to create such a heart. That is why the one who prays with understanding said: '*Create* in me a clean heart O God.' "[28] To know and love God is a gift bestowed by God.

In the early church no text was more beloved than John 1:18: "No one has ever seen God. It is God the only Son, who is close to the Father's heart who has made him known." So certain was this truth that it changed everything. In his Gifford lectures of 1931–32 Etienne Gilson observed, "Now it is a fact that between

ourselves and the Greeks the Christian revelation has inter-
vened, and has profoundly modified the conditions under which
reason has to work." What one thinks is now to be measured by
reference to a series of contingent events that happened in Palestine in the first century. Reason can no longer be exercised
independently of what had happened in Christ and, it must be
added, came to be because of Christ. In the final paragraphs of
the *Contra Celsum* Origen points the reader to the church, whose
"sacred words" and "acts of worship" instruct others in the
worship of the one God.[29]

It has been said that Christianity brought a loss of nerve and a
distrust of reason. But one might argue that Christian revelation
put an end to skepticism and gave men and women new confidence in reason. Whether one reads Saint Augustine, who wrote
that "anyone who supposes that the senses are never to be
trusted is woefully mistaken," or Saint John of Damascus, who
said that the "mind which is determined to ignore corporeal
things will find itself weakened and frustrated," under the tutelage of historical revelation, reason became more certain of its
starting point, more confident, less abstract, and more purposeful. Though respectful of its limitations, reason's scope was also
expanded and enlarged. That God was known in history, in the
life of a human being, validated experience; it allowed Christian
thinkers to appeal to the lives of holy men and women, especially
the martyrs and saints, and to the experience of the church, as
testimony to the truth of God.[30]

When Saint Paul appeared before the Athenians and spoke to
them the "good news of Jesus and the Resurrection," they said,
"It sounds rather strange to us, so we would like to know what it
means." In their writings to outsiders as well as in homilies

preached before Christian congregations the earliest generation of Christian thinkers set about the task of explaining "what it means." What had been handed on in the church's worship and practice, in prayers and catechetical instruction, in the words and images and stories of the Bible was set on a firm intellectual foundation. Yet, and this is the central point, the biblical narrative was not reduced to a set of ideas or a body of principles; no conceptual scheme was allowed to displace the evangelical history. Christianity, wrote Leo the Great, bishop of Rome in the fifth century, is a "religion founded on the mystery of the cross of Christ."[31] Christian thinking did not spring from an original idea, and it was not nourished by a seminal spiritual insight. It had its beginnings in the history of Israel and the life of a human being named Jesus of Nazareth, who was born of Mary, lived in Judea, suffered and died in Jerusalem, and was raised by God to new life. That this history was the history of God's self-disclosure does not make it any less historical, but it does mean that what is seen with the eyes is not the fullness of what there is to see. In a different way, as we shall see in the next chapter, what was seen when the church gathered to pray was not all there was to see.

Chapter 2

An Awesome and Unbloody Sacrifice

Making remembrance of his life-giving sufferings, his saving cross
and death, his burial and resurrection on the third day from the dead,
and his session at the right hand of You his God and Father, and his
second glorious and fearful coming when he will judge the living and
the dead. . . . we offer to You O Lord, this awesome and unbloody
sacrifice, beseeching You to deal with us not according to our sins . . .
but according to Your great mercy and love.

ANAPHORA OF THE LITURGY OF SAINT JAMES

ALL THE FIGURES portrayed in this book prayed regularly,
and their thinking was never far removed from the church's
worship. Whether the task at hand was the defense of Christian
belief to an outsider, the refutation of the views of a heretic, or
the exposition of a passage from the Bible, their intellectual work
was always in service of praise and adoration of the one God.
"This is the Catholic faith," begins an ancient creed, "that we
worship one God in Trinity and Trinity in Unity." Often their
treatises ended with a doxology to God, as in Augustine's *On the
Spirit and the Letter:* "to whom be glory forever. Amen."[1] They
wished not only to understand and express the dazzling truth
they had seen in Christ, by thinking and writing they sought to

know God more intimately and love him more ardently. The intellectual task was a spiritual undertaking. In the oft-cited words of the desert monk Evagrius, "A theologian is one who prays, and one who prays is a theologian."

The point may seem obvious, yet it is often forgotten. More often than not the church fathers have been interpreted as solitary intellectuals, each working out his own system, beholden chiefly to the world of ideas and arguments, as though they were clandestine members of an ancient philosophical guild. To be sure, many of the best minds in the early church were philosophically astute and moved comfortably within the intellectual traditions of the ancient world. They knew the argot of philosophy, and their books and ideas were taken seriously by Greek and Roman intellectuals. But if one picks up a treatise of Origen or Basil of Caesarea and compares it with the writings of the philosopher Alcinous or the neo-Platonist Plotinus, it is apparent at once that something else is at work.

For one thing, as we shall see in the next chapter and throughout the course of this book, they turn always to the Bible as the source of their ideas. No matter how rigorous or abstruse their thinking—for example, in dealing with a complex and subtle topic like the distinctive identity of each person of the Trinity— Christian thinkers always began with specific biblical texts. I have found that it is not possible to read the church fathers without the Bible open before me. The words of the Scriptures crowd the pages of their books and essays, and their arguments often turn on specific terms or phrases from the Bible.

But one can detect something else in their writings, at once closer to experience yet more elusive. On page after page the reader senses that what they believe is anchored in regular, indeed habitual, participation in the church's worship, and what they teach is confirmed by how they pray. At one point in his work against the Gnostics, Irenaeus observed that they say the "bread over which thanks have been given is the body of the Lord and the cup is his blood," yet they do not worship Christ as the Son of God. Either they should alter their view of Christ or give up the practice of celebrating the Eucharist. To which he adds, "Our teaching is consonant with what we do in the Eucharist, and the celebration of the Eucharist establishes what we teach."[2]

One reason Christian thinking is so resolutely trinitarian is that from the beginning the language of Christian worship was unequivocally tripartite. In an age in which thinkers of all kinds, even poets, are creatures of the academy, it is well to remember that most of the writers considered in this book were bishops who presided regularly at the celebration of the Eucharist, the church's communal offering to God, and at the annual reception of catechumens in the church through baptism at Easter. The bishop also preached several times a week and could be seen of a Wednesday or Friday or Saturday as well as on Sunday seated before the Christian community expounding the Sacred Scriptures. Some of the most precious sources for early Christian thought are sermons taken down in shorthand as they were being preached in the ancient basilicas. In them the bishop speaks as successor of the apostles to a community that looks to him as teacher and guide. For intellectuals of this sort, even when they were writing learned tomes in the solitude of their studies, there was always a living community before their eyes. Faithfulness, not originality, was the mark of a good teacher. Some early Christian thinkers were monks who spent many hours each day in prayer, particularly in the daily recitation of the psalms and in the devotional reading of the Bible. Even laymen like Clement of Alexandria moved effortlessly between the study and the sanctuary.

If we are to enter into the spirit of early Christian thinking, then, we must consider not only what early Christian thinkers thought but also what they did when they lifted up their minds and hearts to worship God, the Father, Son, and Holy Spirit. A good place to begin is a memorable and singular passage in the first Apology of Justin Martyr.

Offering up Prayers and Thanksgiving

Origen once observed that in conversations with non-Christians he first tried to establish points of commonality before introducing the name of Christ. Athenagoras of Athens, another apologist, does not even mention the name of Jesus in his work. When he cites sayings of Jesus from the gospels he identifies them simply as "the teachings on which we were brought up."[3] Justin Martyr, however, names Jesus Christ at the very beginning of his apology and identifies him as "our teacher." What is more surprising, toward the end of the work he provides his readers a detailed description of Christian worship, first of baptism and then of the Eucharist. Here is what he says about the celebration of the Eucharist in his time, the middle of the second century:

> On the day called Sunday all who live in the cities or in
> the country gather at one place and the memoirs of the
> apostles or the writings of the prophets are read as long as
> time permits. When the reader has finished, the one who
> is presiding instructs us in a brief discourse and exhorts us
> to imitate these noble things. Then we all stand up to-

gether and offer prayers. . . . When we have finished the prayer, bread is brought forth, and wine and water, and the presiding minister offers up prayers and thanksgiving to the best of his ability, and the people assent, saying the Amen; after this the consecrated elements are distributed and received by each one. Then a deacon brings a portion to those who are absent. Those who prosper, and who so wish, contribute what each thinks fit. What is collected is deposited with the presiding minister who takes care of the orphans and widows, and those who are in need because of sickness or some other reason, and those who are imprisoned, and the strangers and sojourners among us.[4]

The simple ritual that Justin describes was practiced throughout the Christian world, and from other sources we know its basic shape differed little from place to place. The exact wording of the prayers varied, but the central features were the same wherever Christians could be found. With little alteration this early form of Christian worship remained intact until the Reformation and to this day can be found in most Christian churches.

As is evident from the passage in Justin the Eucharist consisted of two chief parts. The first was centered on the Bible and comprised a series of biblical readings interspersed with prayers and psalms. It had close parallels to the synagogue, though in Jewish worship the central reading was from the Torah, that is, the five books of Moses, whereas in the churches it was a selection from the gospels, what Justin calls the "memoirs of the apostles." The scriptural readings were followed by an exposition of the text, a sermon or homily, that applied what had been read to the lives of the members of the assembly. In Justin's words, the presiding minister exhorted those gathered "to imitate these noble things." After the sermon the leader led the assembly in common prayers "for ourselves . . . and for all others everywhere," and all joined in the prayers by saying, "Amen."[5]

On finishing these prayers the faithful greeted each other with a kiss. At this point the action turned from a reading desk to a table, that is, an altar, which had been prepared for the offering. Bread and wine and water are brought forward and placed on the altar, and the presiding minister "offers up praise and glory to the Father of the universe through the name of the Son and of the Holy Spirit and offers thanksgiving[6] at some length." At the end of the prayer the congregation says, "Amen," and the "consecrated" bread and wine, that is, bread and wine over which the prayer of thanksgiving has been spoken, are distributed to the faithful.

Justin not only gives an account of the chief components of Christian worship, but also explains to his readers (the apology is addressed to the Roman emperor) the meaning of what takes place: "This food we call Eucharist, of which no one is allowed to partake except one who believes that the things we teach are true, and has received the washing for forgiveness of sins for rebirth, and who lives as Christ taught us. For we do not receive these things as common bread or common drink, but *as Jesus Christ* our Savior who became incarnate by God's word and took flesh and blood for our salvation. So also we have been taught that the food consecrated by the word of prayer which comes from him, from which our flesh and blood are nourished by being renewed, *is* the flesh and blood of that incarnate Jesus."

Remarkably, Justin does not try to reinterpret the language of Christian worship in terms that might be more congenial to outsiders. This is all the more noteworthy when one recalls that the people to whom he addressed his apology thought that Jesus had died an ignominious death in Palestine more than a hundred years earlier. Nonetheless, Justin says that in the Eucharist the members of the assembly receive a living person, Jesus Christ, and that the food they eat *is* the body and blood of Christ. His explanation of what happens in the Eucharist is not idiosyncratic, though its appearance in a work written to outsiders is uncommon. What he says is confirmed earlier in the century by Ignatius of Antioch in Syria, who said that "the Eucharist is the flesh of our savior Jesus Christ who suffered for us." And Irenaeus, writing from southern Gaul at the end of the century, said, "The bread over which thanks have been given is the body of the Lord and the cup is his blood." What Justin and others believed in the second century is documented in the texts of actual prayers in liturgical documents from a somewhat later time. In the "thanksgiving" of the church of Jerusalem, for example, the bishop prayed that the Holy Spirit come upon "these holy gifts" to "sanctify and make this bread the holy Body of Christ" and "this cup the precious blood of Christ."[7]

The first point, then, is that Christian liturgy was a celebration of the presence of the living Christ. It is not a memorial meal commemorating something that happened in the past. As Augustine said in a sermon on Psalm 22, the great psalm of Christ's passion, the liturgy "makes present what took place in time past, and in this way it moves us as if we were actually watching our Lord hanging on the cross." The second point is that the liturgy is explicitly trinitarian. Before there was a "doctrine" of the Trinity, Christian prayers invoked the Holy Trinity. Justin says that the presiding minister offers up prayers of "praise and glory to the Father of the universe through the name of the Son and of the Holy Spirit." What Justin reports is echoed in the prayer over the gifts of bread and wine in the early liturgies. In the *Apostolic Tradition* of Hippolytus, a little book with prayers for the Eucharist, baptism, ordination, and other rites reflecting practice in Rome at the end of the second century, the prayer began with an address to God the Father followed immediately by a mention of Christ,

> through whom you made all things and in whom you are well pleased, whom you sent from heaven into the womb of the Virgin, and who was conceived within her and made flesh, who was manifested as your son, born of the Holy Spirit and the Virgin. . . . Who gave himself up willingly to suffering; that he might destroy death . . . and manifest his resurrection, taking bread and giving thanks to you said: "Take eat: this is my body, which is broken for you." And likewise also the cup, saying: "This is my blood, which is shed for you. As often as you do this, do it to remember me."

The prayer concludes with an invocation of the Holy Spirit: "We pray that you would send your Holy Spirit upon the offerings of your holy church."[8]

Besides its trinitarian shape, the prayer of thanksgiving, or the *anaphora* (offering), as it was called, has two other notable features. Although it is a prayer of adoration, thanksgiving, and supplication, it has a distinct narrative structure. In this way it follows biblical precedent. Psalm 150, for example, the last psalm in the psalter, begins, "Praise the Lord! Praise God in his sanctuary; praise him in his mighty firmament!" But then the psalmist adds, "Praise him for his mighty deeds." In some psalms these deeds are enumerated, for example, in Psalm 136: "[Give thanks to] him who by understanding made the heavens . . . to him who brought Israel out from Egypt . . . to him who led his people through the wilderness . . . who gave a heritage to Israel his servant." The psalmists do not simply praise the majesty and goodness and power of God, they identify God by his actions, "his mighty deeds." To praise God is to narrate what he has done.

In the same way the prayer of thanksgiving in the liturgy begins with praise and adoration of God but then retells, in capsule form, the biblical story from creation through the giving of the Law to the people of Israel to the coming of Christ, his death and Resurrection, and the expectation of his coming again: "You are holy, ruler of all things . . . who made man from the earth in your own image, who did not forsake him when he transgressed your command . . . who called him by the law and instructed him by the prophets, and in the last times you sent your only begotten Son our Lord Jesus Christ into the world that by his coming he might renew and restore your image. . . . In the night in which he was betrayed . . . he took bread . . . saying, 'Take eat this is my Body which is given for you.' "[9] The liturgy kept intact the biblical narrative, and by recounting the story of Israel and Christ in ritual form it confirmed Christian belief that God's fullest revelation came through historical events.

Yet it is apparent from the wording of the prayers that something more is at work here than recalling ancient history. After reciting the history of salvation leading up to the "night on which he was betrayed," the prayer continues as follows: "And we sinners *make remembrance* of his life-giving sufferings, his death, and resurrection on the third day from the dead and ascension to the right hand of You, his God and Father, and his second glorious and fearful coming." The key term here is the Greek word *anamnesis,* usually translated "remembrance," which in this context means "recall by making present."

There are parallels between this sense of *remembrance* and the way the Exodus out of Egypt is remembered in the Jewish Passover. In the *Mishnah,* the collection of Jewish law from the early third century, it is reported that Rabbi Gamaliel used to say, "Whosoever has not said these three things at Passover has not fulfilled his obligation. And they are these: Passover, unleavened bread, and bitter herbs. 'Passover' because God passed over the houses of our fathers in Egypt, 'unleavened bread' because our fathers were redeemed from Egypt, 'bitter herbs' because the Egyptians embittered the lives of our father sin Egypt." Then Gamaliel says, "In every generation a man must so regard himself as if he came forth himself out of Egypt, for it is written, 'And you shall tell your son on that day saying, "It is because of that which the Lord did for me when I came forth out of Egypt." ' " Those who celebrate Pesach are not spectators, they are participants. "It is I who came forth out of Egypt," says Rabbi Gamaliel. Remembrance is more than mental recall, and in the Eucharist the life-giving events of Christ's death and Resurrection escape the restrictions of time and become what the early church called mysteries, ritual actions by which Christ's saving work is re-presented under the veil of the consecrated bread and wine. Speaking of the Christian paschal celebration Origen wrote, "The passover still takes place today" and "Those who sacrifice Christ come out of Egypt, cross the Red Sea, and see Pharaoh engulfed." What was once accomplished in Palestine is now made present in the action of the liturgy, as the prayers indicate: "We offer to You O Lord, this awesome and unbloody sacrifice, beseeching You to deal with us not according to our sins."[10] Liturgy is always in the present tense. The past becomes a present presence that opens a new future.

In the New Testament Christ's death and Resurrection were presented not simply as past events but as a living sacrifice offered up to God in the present: "For Christ has entered, not into a sanctuary made with hands . . . but into heaven itself, *now* to appear in the presence of God on our behalf" (Heb. 9:24). This relation between past event and present reality was as mysterious to the ancients as it is to moderns. In Constantinople in the early fifth century some wanted to know how the one sacrifice could be re-presented again and again in different places. In a sermon on this passage from Hebrews John Chrysostom, the most popular preacher in the early church, explained the matter this way:

> Do we not offer the sacrifice daily? Indeed we do offer it daily, re-presenting his death. How then is it one sacrifice and not many? . . . We offer the same person, not one sheep one day and tomorrow a different one, but always the same offering. . . . There is one sacrifice and one high priest who offered the sacrifice that cleanses us. Today we offer that which was once offered, a sacrifice that is inexhaustible. This is done as a remembrance [*anamnesis*] of that which was done then, for he said, "Do this in remembrance of me." We do not offer another sacrifice as the priest offered of old, but we always offer the same sacrifice. Or rather we re-present the sacrifice.[11]

The repeated celebration of the liturgy worked powerfully on the imagination of early Christian thinkers. It brought them into intimate relation with the mystery of the Christ, not as a historical memory, but as an indisputable and incontrovertible fact of experience. Leo the Great, bishop of Rome in the fifth century, put it this way: "Everything that the Son of God did and taught for the reconciliation of the world, we know not only as an historical account of things now past, but we also experience them in the power of the works that are present."[12] Before there were treatises on the Trinity, before there were learned commentaries on the Bible, before there were disputes about the teaching on grace, or essays on the moral life, there was awe and adoration before the exalted Son of God alive and present in the church's offering of the Eucharist. This truth preceded every effort to understand and nourished every attempt to express in words and concepts what Christians believed.

Christ Never Without Water

The Eucharist was the central act of Christian worship, and its communal celebration each Sunday set the rhythm of Christian life. In the early church there was no Christianity without an altar. But there was also no Christianity without a bath, without passing through the waters of baptism. In his Apology to the emperor Justin Martyr briefly mentions the rite by which people were received into the church, the "way in which we dedicated ourselves to God when we were made new through Christ." Those who are persuaded that "the things we teach and say are true," he says, "and undertake to live in accord with them, are instructed to pray and ask God with fasting for the remission of their past sins, while we pray and fast with them. Then they are brought by us where there is water and are born again in the same manner of rebirth by which we ourselves were born again, for they then receive washing in water in the name of God the Father and master of all, and of our Savior, Jesus Christ, and of the Holy Spirit."[13]

The earliest Christian baptisms took place at natural sources of water, a river or spring or even the ocean. Tertullian of Carthage in North Africa, the first Christian to write theological works in Latin, at the end of the second century, said it made no difference whether one was baptized "in the sea or pond, in a river or at a spring, in a lake or in a pool." From the book of Acts it appears that in the first generations baptism took place immediately on acceptance of Christ. But by the end of the second century baptism was preceded by a period of elaborate and intense preparation. Baptism was a ritual for adults, not infants, and the months, even years, leading up to it were a time of formation in the Christian life, through example and practice, and of instruction in the creed. Baptism was a moral as well as a spiritual experience.[14]

When a person had completed the initial period of formation and was ready to apply for baptism he indicated his desire by an act of enrollment. This included a formal interrogation, followed by the making of the sign of the cross on the forehead, an initial exorcism of evil spirits, the imposition of hands by the bishop, and the eating of a tiny bit of salt. Egeria, a visitor to Jerusalem in the fourth century, described the scene as follows:

> Names must be given in before the first day of Lent, which lasts eight weeks here. . . . When the priest has taken down all the names the bishop's chair is placed in the middle of the Great Church. The priests sit in chairs on either side of him and the other clergy stand nearby. One by one

the candidates for baptism are led forward, men coming with their godfathers and women with their godmothers. As they come in one by one, the bishop asks their neighbors questions about them: "Is this person leading a good life? Does he respect his parents? Is he a drunkard or a boaster?" . . . If the candidate proves to be without fault in these matters the bishop writes down his name; but if someone is accused of anything, he is asked to leave and told: "Amend your life and when that is done approach the baptismal font."[15]

Toward the end of the weeks leading up to Easter (what became Lent), during which the candidate for baptism fasted, abstained from public entertainments and sexual intercourse (assuming one was married), and faithfully attended the word service of the Eucharist, the bishop preached a sermon in which he recited each article of the creed and explained its meaning. The *competentes*, those seeking baptism, were asked to repeat the phrases after the bishop. Later the sponsor helped the candidate memorize the creed. Eight days later the community gathered in the evening for a vigil of prayers, psalms, and homily. On this occasion there was a fuller rite of exorcism in which the priest laid his hand on the *competentes*, invoked the Holy Trinity, and rebuked the devil.

Finally the day of baptism arrived. In the early church the great liturgy of Easter took place on Saturday evening at the depth of the night—as it does to this day in the Eastern Church —and continued till the morning. After listening to the reading of the Scripture the catechumens would "hand back the creed," that is, recite the words they had learned from the bishop weeks earlier. Toward dawn, psalm 42, "As the deer yearns for flowing streams, so yearns my heart for You, O God," was sung, and the catechumens proceeded to the font, a small pool usually six to ten feet long, about three to six feet wide, and approximately three feet deep. At either end there were steps to walk down into the pool, and curtains enclosed the area. The catechumens went down naked into the pool and were immersed in the water as the bishop spoke each person's name and recited the baptismal formula: "I baptize you in the name of the Father and of the Son and of the Holy Spirit." When they came out of the water they were anointed with oil and clothed in a garment of white linen. After the baptism the catechumens returned to the main basilica for the Easter Eucharist. At their first Eucharist they received a cup of milk and honey, and during Easter week they attended services in their white garments.

As can be seen from this brief description, in the early church baptism was not a private affair but a communal celebration of the entire community. Everyone had a role, the bishop and other clergy, neighbors, friends, and family. Its recurrence each year in late winter and spring, the gravity of the interrogation, the rigor of fasting, the sonorous phrases of the creed, the drama of the exorcisms, the immersion in water—all heightened the experience. Baptism was the great Christian spectacle, and the excitement of seeing neighbors and friends step forward one by one to go down under the waters riveted the attention of the Christian community. At Rome when the famous philosopher Marius Victorinus mounted the steps in the basilica to confess his faith before being baptized, a murmur of astonishment went through the congregation as people realized who he was and whispered his name one to another, "Victorinus, Victorinus!"[16]

Baptism was a washing in water, a ritual washing to be sure, but a washing nonetheless. Early Christians did not sprinkle or pour, they immersed. Christianity is an affair of things, of bread and wine, of water, and of oil, and its beliefs are anchored in things and the actions that accompany their use. What took place in the liturgy often became the occasion for thinkers to reflect more deeply on the words of the creed and the stories in the Scripture. In a beautiful treatise on baptism written about the year 200, Tertullian observed that water was created at the very beginning of time, and in the book of Genesis it is written that the Spirit "was carried on the waters." Water, he says, was the first element "to produce things that would live." It is not surprising that water, ordinary water, used in baptism "already knows how to give life." Through the presence of the Holy Spirit water that was precious in itself "took on the ability to make holy."[17]

In Tertullian's discussion of water in baptism, the central Christian conviction, that God is known in a human being who could be seen and touched, is now extended to other tangible things, water and oil, bread and wine, milk and honey, and salt, and, as we shall see in a later chapter, the bones of the saints, the holy places touched by Christ's body, the wood and paint of icons. When God is invoked, writes Tertullian, "water acquires the mysterious power of conveying sanctity." So much is water part of God's way of relating to human beings, he writes, that

Christ was never without water. He himself was baptized with water; when invited to a marriage he inaugurates the exercise of his power with water; when talking he invites the thirsty to partake of his own everlasting water; when teaching about charity he approves among the works of love the offering of a cup of water to a neighbor; he refreshes his strength at a well-side; he walks on water; he crosses it at will; he uses water to do an act of service to his disciples. This witness to baptism continues right up to the passion. When he is handed over to the cross, water plays a part (witness Pilate's hands); and when he is pierced, water gushes out from his side (witness the soldier's spear).[18]

As in the Eucharist, the liturgical texts read and sung during the rite of baptism were trinitarian, beginning of course with the formula of baptism itself. But it was not simply the formula that was trinitarian: the biblical event celebrated at baptism also had a trinitarian shape. In the early church the model for Christian baptism was the baptism of Jesus in the Jordan river. At the beginning of the second century Ignatius of Antioch wrote, "Christ submitted to baptism so that by his passion he might sanctify the water." Gregory of Nyssa said that from the Jordan "the grace of baptism was spread throughout the whole world." Along with the Incarnation, death, and Resurrection, the baptism of Jesus was one of the mysteries presented to the catechumens in the period of instruction prior to baptism. Jesus's baptism was a singular moment of divine revelation, for in it the Holy Trinity was first made known. In the biblical accounts of the baptism of Jesus the Father speaks to Jesus, "You are my beloved Son, with you I am well pleased," and the Holy Spirit descends on him in the form of a dove. The Syriac writer Jacob of Sarug put it this way: "At the time of the Epiphany [that is, the baptism] of Christ, the Trinity appeared at the Jordan."[19]

At the solemn ritual of baptism the bishop presided, and

during the period of preparation he instructed those who were to be baptized. His role was spiritual, moral, and catechetical, and the ancient "catechetical lectures," talks given to the catechumens, display early Christian thinkers in a role that is not always evident in their dogmatic and polemical writings. Yet in many ways it was the most congenial, expounding the teachings of the church as confessed in the creed, introducing the catechumens to the distinctive idiom of the Bible, outfitting tyros in the faith for the arduous demands of a new life, and encouraging them to combat the forces of evil. Here Christian teachers learned as well as taught. In a revealing aside in a sermon preached on the anniversary of his ordination Augustine said, "I nourish you with what nourishes me; I offer to you what I live on myself."[20] By apprenticing themselves to the church's inner life, the bishops acquired skill in using the church's language, discovered anew the implications of biblical images by trafficking in a world of things that could be seen and touched, not just opined, and in all, learned that what they taught had to do not only with words and ideas but palpable realities.

The Present Grace

Saint Augustine's biographer, Possidius, who shared his table for many years, said, "Right down to his final illness he preached the word of God in the Church without interruption, zealously and courageously, and with soundness of mind and judgment."[21] As I have already observed, most, if not all, of the figures treated in this book preached regularly in the churches. In the Eucharist after the reader has finished reading the "memoirs of the apostles" or the "writings of the prophets," said Justin, the presiding minister "urges us in a discourse to the imitation of these noble things."

In the early church preaching was biblical. It customarily took the form of an exposition of a passage from the Bible. Over time the portions of the Scripture to be read in the Sunday liturgy were compiled in a lectionary, an organized selection of readings from the Scriptures. On Sunday it was customary to read a passage from the Old Testament and a selection from one of the four gospels, the chief reading for the day. As a Christian calendar developed, readings were assigned to the principal festivals of the year, Christmas, Easter, Pentecost. The calendar, like the liturgy itself, accentuated the narrative character of Christian revelation.

The words of the Scripture made a temple deep within the hearing of early Christian preachers. Not only in sermons but also in theological works, in letters, and in spiritual writings the church fathers display an enviable verbal command of large sections of the Bible. In contrast to modern theological writings in which the Bible is cited in support of theological ideas, and hence usually relegated to the footnotes, in the early church the words of the Bible were the linguistic skeleton for the exposition of ideas. Even in the writings of the most philosophical of early Christian thinkers their thoughts are expressed in the language of the Bible, seldom above it. The liturgy provided a kind of grammar of Christian speech, a key to how the words of the Bible are to be used.

But preaching in the liturgy was not just about words. The Eucharist was a celebration of the living Christ present in the offering of bread and wine. In the sermon the preacher sought not only to explain the words but also invited the congregation to enter into the reality itself, the mystery of Christ, by the use of words. As Christian thinking was grounded in the events recorded in the Bible, the *res gestae,* the things that had taken place, so it was nourished in worship by the *res liturgicae,* the things enacted in the liturgy. This is vividly displayed in sermons on the great festivals, Christmas, Easter, and Pentecost, and no preacher in the early church grasped this more fully than Leo. In a sermon on the nativity of Christ he said, "Today's festival renews for us the holy childhood of Jesus born of the Virgin Mary, and in adoring the birth of our Savior, we find that we are celebrating the commencement of our own life. For the birth of Christ is the source of life for the Christian people, and the birthday of the head is the birthday of the body."[22]

Leo was not unique. Similar language can be found in John Chrysostom and Augustine and Ambrose and Gregory the Great and others. In a sermon preached at the great Vigil of Easter Gregory of Nyssa again and again uses the phrase "the present grace." The term refers not simply to the grace that flows from Christ's Resurrection, but to the actual liturgical celebration of the Resurrection. The night of Easter was resplendent, he proclaims, for on every other day of the year the light of the sun gives way in the evening to darkness. But at Easter the torches were lit at dusk and the brilliance of the Easter procession met the last rays of the setting sun. Night was canceled by the light of the torches, which seemed to prolong the day. Even though "according to the clock it is night," said Gregory, "according to the light it is day." And in the morning the rays of the torches called out in welcome to the beams of the rising sun. Easter inaugurated a day unbroken by the intervention of night.

What is read in the Scriptures is fulfilled in the Eucharist, in the "present brightness" of the Easter liturgy. With Christ's Resurrection there is "another birth, another life, another form of life, a transformation of our nature."[23]

Nothing in the mind can ever have the solidity and mystery of what is seen and touched. By constant immersion in the *res liturgicae* early Christian thinkers came face to face with the living Christ and could say with Thomas the apostle, "My Lord and God." Here was a truth so tangible, so enduring, so compelling that it trumped every religious idea. Understanding was achieved not by stepping back and viewing things from a distance but by entering into the revealed object itself. As we shall see in a later chapter, only as Christian theologians penetrated more deeply into a specific event in Christ's life, that moment in the Garden of Gethsemane when he said, "Father, if thou art willing, remove this cup from me" (Luke 22:42), were they able to to express the belief that Christ was "truly man." This converse with the *res,* the thing itself, was the gift of the liturgy.

With Angels and Archangels

All the ancient liturgies included prayers commemorating the "faithful departed." The church, as Augustine put it in one of his sermons, "does not include merely ourselves"; it is a great "city whose head is Christ" and counts among its members those who lived before, those who are yet to be born, and the angels, "our fellow citizens." In some liturgies these prayers for the faithful departed took the form of a brief remembrance of "those who have fallen asleep before us." But often the prayers were more elaborate, as in the following example from the Apostolic Constitutions, a collection of liturgical sources from the fourth century: "We present the offering to you for all the saints who have been pleasing to you from the beginning, patriarchs, prophets, the just men, apostles, martyrs, confessors, bishops, priests, deacons, subdeacons, readers, singers, virgins, widows, lay people, and for all those whose name you know."[24] Sometimes the actual names were mentioned, martyrs and saints, a former bishop of the city, a holy woman venerated in the local church.

Christianity began with the testimony of those who had known the risen Christ. Their witness, as Saint Paul puts it in 1 Corinthians, was "handed over" to others, and in time this handing over came to be called tradition. Although tradition has to do with handing on practices, teachings, and institutional forms, human beings do the handing on. From the beginning Christians honored those who had given witness to what they had received, most notably the martyrs and holy men and women. Christian faith is inescapably bound up with the lives and words of actual persons, for the truth of what was handed on rested finally on the faithfulness of the *traditores*, those who did the handing on.

Early in the church's history Christians gathered at the tombs of martyrs to pray and celebrate the Eucharist. The faithful of one generation were united to the faithful of former times, not by a set of ideas or teachings (though this was assumed), but by the community that remembered their names. This bridge to earlier generations and through them to the apostles gave Christian thinkers the confidence to speak boldly and act courageously. They trailed their thoughts after the lives of others. Just as there was no Christianity without an altar and no faith without the bath of baptism, so there was no Christian thinking without the church. The communion of saints was a living presence in every celebration of the Eucharist.

The faithful departed were not simply remembered, they were welcomed as participants in the liturgy. Here, too, John Chrysostom, ever mindful of the limitations of his hearers, found it necessary to explain to his congregation why the liturgy included such prayers: "In the divine mysteries," he says, "we do not make mention of the departed in vain, but we approach God on their behalf, beseeching the Lamb of God who is before us [note his language], he who takes away the sins of the world . . . that they receive some comfort." When the "awesome mysteries are celebrated," he writes, the priest says that the sacrifice is offered "for all those who have fallen asleep in Christ as well as for all who make commemorations on their behalf." For good measure he adds that we would not do these things unless we thought they had some effect: "Our worship is not a stage show."[25]

In the liturgy all the members of the church, past, present, and future, were fused into a single community that included the patriarchs and prophets, the Virgin Mary and apostles, martyrs and saints, and those whose names are known only to God. In the words of the Te Deum, "The glorious company of the apostles, the noble fellowship of prophets, the white-robed army of martyrs praise you." The company that celebrated the liturgy was not confined to this world. The hymn of the seraphim was given to us, says Cyril of Jerusalem, "that we might be participants with the heavenly hosts in their hymn of praise." When the people of God lifted their voices to worship the Triune God they joined the hymn that was being sung by the heavenly host. This is made explicit in the prayer leading up to the singing of the "Holy, holy, holy," immediately prior to the great prayer of thanksgiving over the gifts of bread and wine: "You are attended by thousands upon thousands, and myriads upon myriads of angels and archangels, of thrones and dominions, of principalities and powers. Beside you stand the two august Seraphim with six wings; two to cover their face, two to cover their feet, two with which to fly. They sing your holiness. With their praise, accept also our acclamations of your holiness: Holy, holy, holy is the Lord Sabaoth! Heaven and earth are filled with your glory. The heaven is filled, the earth is filled with your wonderful glory!"[26]

In the ancient versions of Psalm 138 the first verse read, "In the presence of the angels I will sing a psalm to you." In an interjection in one of his writings Gregory the Great asked, "Can any of the faithful doubt that at the hour of the Eucharistic sacrifice of Jesus Christ the choirs of angels are present, the heights joined to the depths, earth linked with heaven, the visible united with the invisible." Gregory was not a solitary voice. Centuries earlier Origen had said, "I do not doubt that angels are even present in our assembly." There is "a double church present, one of men, the other of angels."[27]

By actions and words the liturgy engraved the communion of the saints on the minds and hearts of Christian thinkers. They praised God in the presence of others, and when they returned to their studies this company remained present. There is no intellectual elitism among the church fathers. Their thinking was not only nourished by the communal experience of the church, but also beholden to a community that reaches back in time and will exist in the future as a city whose purpose is to "worship the Lamb" (Rev. 22:3). What they wrote in their books and essays they preached to their congregations, often in the same words. The liturgy drew bishops and faithful into a shared public life whose central activity was the worship of the Triune God, and Christian thought developed in intimate connection with the church's life, her sacraments and practices, Scripture and creeds, martyrs and saints, and in the company of the whole host of heaven.

Chapter 3

The Face of God for Now

For now treat the Scripture of God as the face of God.
Melt in its presence.

SAINT AUGUSTINE

WHAT WOULD IT have been like to have lived before there was a Bible? In the cupboards where educated Romans kept their books one would have found, among Greek speakers, the *Iliad* and the *Odyssey,* whose tales were learned by schoolchildren, Hesiod's *Theogony* with its myths of the genealogy of the gods, tragedies of Sophocles and Euripides, and comedies of Menander. In the homes of educated Romans whose language was Latin there would have been the *Aeneid,* Virgil's epic poem of the wanderings of Aeneas toward Italy to found a city, Ovid's *Metamorphoses,* a collection of stories of cosmic and historical transformations beginning with the emergence of order out of chaos, and Livy's history of Rome, especially the first book on the city's founding. There would have been sayings of the venerable sages Thales and Pythagoras, dialogues of Plato, especially the *Timaeus*, Aristotle's *Nicomachean Ethics*, writings of Zeno the Stoic, the histories of Thucydides and Herodotus. Romans would have had copies of Cicero's speeches and his *De Republica* and perhaps the moral essays of Seneca.

In these and other books one could read of Apollo, who had killed the great dragon Python that guarded Delphi, of the adventures of Odysseus returning from Troy, of the labors of Heracles, of Dido's grief at Aeneas's departure from Carthage, of the myths of the cave and of Er in Plato's *Republic*. One could ponder Aristotle on friendship, Cicero's telling of Scipio's dream of the future life, Seneca on the happy life, Cleanthes' Hymn to Zeus, the funeral oration of Pericles, the story of Lucretia's purity and Antigone's loyalty, and much more. These myths, histories, tales, sayings, speeches, and stories comprised the wisdom of ancient Greece and Rome. There was little, it seemed, wanting.

Yet for those who followed Christ this world seemed distant and unreal. For its wisdom did not include the Bible with its account of the creation of the world out of nothing in the book of Genesis, the story of the temptation and fall of Adam and Eve, Abraham's sacrifice of his only son, Isaac, the deliverance of the Israelites from Egypt, Moses receiving the Law on Mount Sinai, David's desire for Bathsheba, Job's suffering, the oracles of the prophets when the Jewish people were captives in Babylon, the servant songs of Isaiah, the tales of Judith and Susanna, the story of the birth of Christ from a virgin, Christ's temptation in the wilderness, the parables of the good Samaritan and the prodigal son, the story of the rich man and Lazarus, the betrayal of Christ by Judas, his death on a cross and Resurrection three days later, the account of the church's early history in the book of Acts and the conversion of Saint Paul.

Neither would ancient Greeks and Romans have been familiar with the biblical images of the heavenly Jerusalem or City of God, the second Adam or the body of Christ, the poetry of the Song of Songs or the canticle of Mary in the Gospel of Luke, the vivid theological locutions of Saint Paul, "image of the invisible God," "first born of all creation," the hymn on Christ's "emptying" in Philippians, the prologue to the Gospel of John and Saint John's meditation on love in his first epistle. Their prayer books would have been innocent of the intensely personal language used by the psalmists to address God: "Against you, you alone, have I sinned," (Ps. 51) and "O Lord, you have searched me and known me. You know when I sit down and when I rise up; you discern my thoughts from far away. . . . Where can I flee from your presence?" (Ps. 139). Though ancient writers would have used many of the words found in the Scriptures, the overtones of such terms as *grace, faith, obedience, love, truth, patience, hope, image of God, adoption, servant, creation, will of God, election, law, God the Father, Word of God, Holy Spirit* would have escaped them. They would not have looked upon the history of the Jewish people as their own history. The Bible formed Christians into a people and gave them a language.

As intellectuals formed by the classical tradition, the first Christian thinkers belonged to a learned and contented club, secure in the confidence they knew whatever was useful to know. In school they had memorized long passages from Homer or Virgil, and by imitating the elegant sentences of Isocrates or Cicero they had learned to write graceful prose and speak with polished diction. Before reading Genesis they had read Plato, before reading the prophets they had read Euripides, before reading the books of Samuel and Kings they had read Herodotus and Thucydides, and before reading the gospels they had read Plutarch's *Lives.* Intensely proud of their ancient culture, they took pleasure in the beauty of its language, the refinement of its literature, and the subtlety of its sages.

Yet when they took the Bible in hand they were overwhelmed. It came upon them like a torrent leaping down the side of a mountain. Once they got beyond its plain style they sensed they had entered a new and mysterious world more alluring than anything they had known before. As a Syriac Christian said of Genesis,

I read the opening of this book
And was filled with joy,
For its verses and lines spread out their arms to
    welcome me;
The first rushed out and kissed me,
And led me on to its companion;
And when I reached that verse
Wherein is written
The story of Paradise,
It lifted me up and transported me
From the bosom of the book
To the very bosom of Paradise.[1]

Our Wisdom

The impact of the Scriptures on Christian thinking is apparent in all the earliest Christian writers, Justin Martyr, Melito of Sardis, Irenaeus of Lyon, Tertullian of Carthage, and, of course, Origen of Alexandria. But how the fresh water of the Bible seeped drop by drop into the mind of the early church can be observed best in the writings of Clement of Alexandria, improbable as this may seem. Among early Christian writers Clement is the most Greek, the most literary, a savant so immersed in the high culture of the Hellenic world that he effortlessly cited hundreds of passages from poets, philosophers, playwrights, and historians in his writings. To this day he is an unparalleled source of citations from lost works, including many precious passages from the writings of pre-Socratic philosophers. He is the first Christian writer to use literature as an instrument of peaceful labor within the church itself, not simply as a tool to combat heretics. He was also a layman, not a bishop, and bore no responsibility to oversee the life of the church or to preach. For this reason it is all the more illuminating to see how the Bible formed his intellectual outlook.

The place of Clement's birth is not known, but it is likely he was born in Athens in the middle of the second century about A.D. 160. There he received his early education and as a young man traveled to various parts of the Mediterranean world to study with philosophers. At some point he embraced Christianity and began to seek out Christian teachers, one in Greece, another in Syria, another in Palestine until at last in Egypt he found the one he was seeking. This teacher, says Clement, was "the true Sicilian bee who gathered honey from the flowers of the prophetic and apostolic meadow." His name was Pantaenus, and he may have been head of a Christian school in Alexandria, but all we know of him is that Clement studied with him and considered him "first in power."[2]

Clement's first work, a kind of apology for Christianity entitled "Exhortation to the Greeks" begins, "Amphion of Thebes and Arion of Methymna were both singers, both famed in legend, and to this day they are celebrated in a chorus sung by the Greeks, one for having charmed a dolphin, the other for having fortified Thebes with walls. Another, a Thracian skilled in his art (and also celebrated in Hellenic legend) tamed wild beasts solely with song and even transplanted oak trees with music. I might also tell you the myth of another, a brother to these and also a singer, Eunomos the Locrian and the Pythic grasshopper."[3]

Clement is strutting before his readers, brandishing his command of Greek literature to play to the gallery. But it does not take him long to come to the point. The time has come for the Greeks to hear a new song. "Let us," he writes, "bring down from the heavens truth with wisdom in all its splendor and the sacred choir of the prophets to the holy mount of God." Let men "abandon Helicon and Cithaeron [two mountains in Greece, sites of ancient cults to the gods] and take up a dwelling place in Zion, 'For out of Zion shall go forth the law, and the word of the Lord from Jerusalem.' "[4]

For Clement the word that came forth from Jerusalem, the "heavenly word," was the divine Logos who had become flesh in the person of Christ and lived on this earth. Through his song men and women had been brought back to life, the eyes of the blind had been opened, the ears of the deaf unstopped, the lame had learned to walk, the rebellious been reconciled to God, and through him, says Clement, we are able to "see God." Generation after generation this Word of God, the Divine Logos, had spoken to God's people in the words of Moses, in the oracles of the prophets, in the exhortations of the proverbs, and finally in the writings of the apostles, particularly the gospels. These writings Clement calls the "holy scriptures" or "divine scriptures," and he sees them as a guide to a holy life and a source of truth: "Free of pretensions of style and elegant diction, of useless and beguiling words, they raise up those who have been drawn down by vice and offer a firm path amidst the treacheries of life."[5]

In Clement's writings the Bible emerges for the first time as the foundation of a Christian culture. His writings are suffused with its language, its forms of expressions, its images and metaphors, its stories. Its heroes become his heroes, and its history his history. This is all the more remarkable when one realizes that for him the Bible was an alien book, written in a plain and unadorned style, a product of Jewish culture, quite unlike the artful and polished works of Greek literature. He came to the Bible as an adult after being educated in Greek literature. In places Clement will quietly rewrite biblical passages to make them sound more like the prose his readers were accustomed to. As he embraced the Bible, Clement remained very much the Greek, and the unschooled reader of his works will be puzzled by the juxtaposition of citations from Homer and Plato and passages from the prophets or the writings of Saint Paul.

Yet Clement's intellectual work is inconceivable without the Bible. Consider a few statistics. A rough calculation indicates that on average there are seven or eight biblical citations on every page of his writings. There are more than fifteen hundred references to the Old Testament alone and close to three thousand to the New Testament. The Gospel of Matthew is cited more than five hundred times, John more than two hundred, the Psalms more than three hundred, the books of Isaiah and Proverbs more than two hundred times.

Of course one might object that the simple piling up of biblical citations is no evidence that a writer understands the Bible or that the Bible has shaped his thinking. In Clement there are *more* references to Greek literature, to Homer, Plato, Aristotle, Euripides, Chrysippus, Plutarch, and other Greek authors than to the Bible. Yet there is a difference. Clement cites Greek literature to illustrate a point, to give flourish to an argument, to delight and amuse his readers. When he cites the Scriptures there is a sense of discovery, that something extraordinary is to be learned in its pages, that it is not one book among many. For Clement the Bible was a source of revelation and instruction, "our wisdom," as he called it in one place. In one case, when Clement is drawing directly on a legacy from Hellenic culture, he presents it as wisdom drawn from the Bible. He knew, for example, that the cardinal virtues were to be found in the Greek moralists, yet when he presents them to his readers he cites a passage from a biblical book, the Wisdom of Solomon, as the source of his teaching: "She [Wisdom] teaches self-control and prudence, justice and courage; nothing in life is more profitable for mortals than these."[6]

A Book about Christ

How the Bible came to figure in Clement's thinking can be seen by considering one passage in detail. Clement's major work, *Stromateis,* is a series of rambling and often elusive discourses on theological and philosophical topics bearing on the Christian life. At one point he begins a discussion by citing a passage from Plato's *Laws.* "According to ancient tradition," writes Plato, "God is the beginning, the end and the center of all things that exist. . . . With God is to be found justice . . . and every person who would be happy cleaves to justice."

In Plato's *Laws* this axiom, which Plato himself had inherited from earlier tradition, had to do with the role of law in the life of the city, its divine authority and the duty of human beings to God and to one another. In the centuries after Plato's death, however, the passage was disengaged from this setting and circulated, probably through handbooks of citations, as a moral axiom. Alcinous the second-century philosopher took the passage to be speaking about the end, that is, the goal, of human life, which he defined, following Plato, as "likeness to God": "We can attain likeness to God if we are endowed with a suitable nature, if our habits, education and way of life are in accord with the law, and most important, if we use reason, and study the teachings in the philosophical tradition."[7]

Clement was familiar with Alcinous's interpretation of Plato, but before introducing the passage from Plato, he quotes a passage, as he puts it, from one of "our writers." The text is the well-known passage in Genesis 1 on the creation of human beings: "Let us make man in our image, according to our likeness," which includes the term *likeness* used by Alcinous and Plato. At the very outset of his discussion Clement gives an unexpected turn to the argument by reminding his readers that consideration of man's likeness to God must begin not with man as he is presently known, but with man as created by God and made "in the image" of God. He suggests that Plato's "likeness" is to be interpreted in light of the biblical notion of image. "Image," in his reading of Genesis, refers to what human beings received when created by God, "likeness" refers to the goal, the end toward which our lives aspire. Human destiny is linked to its origin in God, and likeness with God is possible because we were made in the image of God.

By introducing the theme of likeness Clement shows himself to be thoroughly Greek and, what is more, dependent on a contemporary philosophical interpretation of the premier Greek philosopher, Plato. Yet by citing the passage from Genesis, Clement orients the discussion to the God of the Bible. Next Clement cites several other biblical texts to explain the meaning of "likeness to God." Likeness to God, he writes, means "restoration to perfect adoption by the Son . . . the great high priest who has considered us worthy to be called brothers and fellow-heirs" (Heb. 4:14, 2:11). To which he adds, "And the apostle succinctly depicting the *end* writes in the epistle to the Romans: 'But now that you have been freed from sin and enslaved to God, the advantage you get is holiness. The *end* is eternal life' " (Rom. 6:22).

The term *end*, *telos*, is the same term that is used in the passage from the Laws. Clement, like Alcinous, takes *end* to mean the goal of human life, holiness, or life with God, what Paul calls "eternal life." But Clement says that the first step on the way to this end is not the cultivation of good habits or wholesome practices or a good education, but deliverance from sin. Likeness to God requires a transformation that begins with God, not with human striving. Again citing the Bible, Clement says the goal humans seek is "laid up for us" (Heb. 4:9), that is, it is a gift to be received in faith: "In Christ Jesus neither circumcision nor uncircumcision counts for anything; the only thing that counts is faith working through love."

Finally, Clement gives the entire discussion a distinctively biblical sheen by interpreting "likeness to God" in terms of discipleship, specifically, following Christ. He cites Saint Paul: "Be followers [or imitators] of me as I am of Christ" (1 Cor.

11:1). To be "like God" is be made over in the image of Christ. The end that God has promised to human beings, the "aim of faith," is to be conformed to Christ.

It will be said, and has been said, that a passage such as this is evidence of how deeply early Christian thought was permeated by the spirit of Hellenism. What makes the whole passage work, it seems, is the notion of "likeness to God," an idea that was at the center of the Hellenistic moral tradition. Yet that is where Clement begins, not where he ends. In his hands this Hellenistic notion is set within a new, and for the Greeks alien, context drawn from the Bible and Christian tradition. "Likeness to God" means becoming Christ-like.

Clement is not about the business of proof texting, that is, citing passages from the Bible that have only verbal resemblance to the topic at hand. He surrounds the citation from Genesis and the passage from Plato's Laws with a vocabulary and a conceptual framework drawn from the Bible. Note how many new terms accompany the notion of likeness to God: made in God's image, sin (citing Ezekiel 18:4–9, "the soul that sins shall die"), grace, faith, hope, love, imitation of Christ, restoration, eternal life. And though Clement does not mention it here, he probably also had in mind the words from 1 John 3:2, "We will be *like* him [God] for we will see him as he is," a text that is often cited in this connection.

Ideas do not exist disembodied from language. When Plato's "likeness" is paired with the biblical expression "image of God" and interpreted as "imitation of Christ" it acquires a meaning that cannot be found in Plato. Likeness to God has become concrete, visual, human, accessible. No longer is it simply a philosophical ideal; it was embodied in the life of an actual person who lived on this earth, Jesus Christ. The goal toward which humans strive has already been reached by someone who shared human life and suffering, and by looking at Christ it is possible to know what likeness to God means for human beings.

For Clement the Bible was a book about Christ. It was not simply a collection of ancient and venerable oracles or an account of what happened centuries earlier, but a book about a living person, Jesus Christ, who is the divine son of God. "If you truly desire to see God," he writes, "betake yourself to Christ." In its pages one came to know a person whose life could be told in words and deeds from the past, but who lives still. "It is no longer I who live, but Christ who lives in me," writes Saint Paul (Gal. 2:20). Christ is the goal, the end of all striving, the one who alone can satisfy human longing. As an early medieval commentator on the psalms, Cassiodorus, put it, "When we have reached the 'end' we shall seek nothing further; we shall be content in this end of happiness and enjoy the fullest sweetness."[8]

A Single Story

By the time Clement was writing, the Christian Bible had taken the form we know today. It consisted of two parts, the Greek translation of the Jewish Bible (which was written in Hebrew and Aramaic), and the apostolic writings. According to Jewish tradition the Bible was translated in Alexandria in the second century B.C. by seventy-two translators, hence it is usually called the Septuagint. In truth, the translation was done by different scholars working in different places over a longer period of time. This Greek Bible, however, is not just a translation of the Hebrew Bible; it also included other books that are today known as the Apocrypha. Some were written in Greek, for example, the books of the Maccabees and the Wisdom of Solomon, while others were translations from Hebrew, for example, the book of Sirach. It was this Greek Bible that was used by the first Christians, who were, of course, Jews, and it is this version that is usually cited in the New Testament and other early Christian writings. By the end of the second century the Greek Bible came to be known as the Old Testament of the Christian Church. To this were added the apostolic writings, that is, the epistles of Saint Paul, the Gospels, the Acts of the Apostles, 1 Peter, and other books, what came to be called the New Testament. Together these two collections of books comprised the Christian Bible and presented itself to Christian readers as a single book. As Cyril of Alexandria wrote in the fifth century, "The entire Scripture is one book and was spoken by one Holy Spirit."[9]

In the second century, however, it was not so obvious that the Christian Bible should include the Jewish Scriptures, and one of the first great struggles in the church's history erupted over the unity of the Bible. Some Christians, notably Marcion and the Gnostics, believed that the Old Testament was a book about a lesser God who had created the world of matter, a jealous and vengeful deity, the votary of a single people, the Israelites. The demiurge, as this God was called by them, had nothing in common with the universal and loving God who had sent his son into the world. In response to this challenge, in the first extended theological essay in the church's history, Irenaeus, bishop of Lyon in southern Gaul, argued, by detailed exposition of passages from the Bible, that there was one God, "maker of heaven and earth, who formed man . . . called Abraham, led the people from the land of Egypt, spoke with Moses, gave the law, sent the prophets," and is also the "father of our Lord Jesus Christ."[10]

For Irenaeus the Bible was a single narrative whose chief actor was God. Of course much in the Bible is not narrative, but, except for the Wisdom books (for example, Proverbs and Ecclesiastes), even those books that are not historical (for example, the Psalms), take the form of an interpretation of events that had happened (or will happen) in space and time. Without a knowledge of the history of Israel, the writings of the prophets are only beautiful sentiments, and apart from the life, death, and Resurrection of Jesus of Nazareth, the epistles of Paul are pious fantasies. Two histories converge in the biblical account, the history of Israel and the life of Christ, but because they are also the history of God's actions in and for the world, they are part of a larger narrative that begins at creation and ends in a vision of a new, more splendid city in which the "Lord God will be their light." The Bible begins, as it were, with the beginning and ends with an end that is no end, life with God, in Irenaeus's charming expression, a life in which one is "always conversing with God in new ways."[11] Nothing falls outside of its scope.

In the ancient world few books had as much reach as the Bible. One of the most ambitious was Ovid's *Metamorphoses*, but even a surface reading will show how different it is from the Bible. Ovid's great poem begins with the creation of the world and brings the story down to his own day, the reign of Julius Caesar, whose apotheosis symbolized the final transformation to which all human beings aspire. Yet the stories that make up the poem are mythical—tales of Apollo and Daphne, Perseus and Andromeda, of the daughters of Minyas, the Minotaur, of Daedalus and Icarus, of Hercules and Orpheus and Midas—and related to one another by ideas and themes, not by a historical narrative. The *Metamorphoses* is a book of episodes, not a continuous story, and the stories Ovid tells are universal in that they are typical. As events they lead nowhere. They depict transformations of the soul in the course of life. The poem has no real ending and no future expectation. It comes to an end in the present with only a vague allusion to a "far off dawn." The final lines of the poem express Ovid's fervent and vain hope that his poem will outlast the passage of time: "My name will never die," he writes. "Wherever through the lands beneath her sway / The might of Rome extends, my words shall be upon the lips of men."[12]

The Bible is a book of events with consequences, not only for those who lived through them or were influenced by them, but for all men and women. Its meaning turns on the history it records, whether it be God's creation of all things at the beginning of time, the sin of Adam, the giving of the Law to Moses, Christ's birth from a virgin, or his Resurrection on the third day. A key text for Irenaeus's interpretation was Romans 5, in which Saint Paul had drawn parallels between Adam and Christ. Irenaeus paraphrases the passage from Romans as follows: "Just as through the disobedience of one man, the first made from the virgin earth, many were made sinners and lost life, so it was necessary that through the obedience of one man, the first born of a Virgin, many should be made righteous and receive salvation." In the prologue to the Gospel of John the evangelist had cast the coming of Christ in universal terms by identifying him with Logos, Reason, but Irenaeus sensed that Paul proposed another path to universality. In the epistle to the Romans Christ is universal because he is particular and singular. He is the second first man, the second Adam, who by his obedience undid the work of the first Adam. Christ did something without precedent, and Irenaeus, ever sensitive to the historical shape of Christian revelation, highlights the novelty of Christ's coming. Christ, he says, brought "something wholly new by bringing himself," and it was this "new thing that brought about the renewal and revivifying of mankind."[13]

The key to understanding the Bible, then, was what had happened in Christ, in Augustine's words, the "dispensation of divine providence *in time,*" that is, "what God has done for the salvation of the human race to renew it and restore it." Hilary of Poitiers, whom we will meet in the next chapter, says that the "spiritual order" of the Scriptures is "preserved in the events." But which events? The Bible is large and diffuse, and it is bewildering if read simply as a book, as any reader discovers who tries to read it in its entirety by beginning with the first chapter of Genesis. Yet its central plot can be told rather simply. It is a story, in the language of medieval theology, of a going out from God, an *exitus,* and a return to God, a *reditus.* Irenaeus puts it this way:

> This, then, is the ordering of our faith. . . . God, the Father, uncreated, incomprehensible, invisible, one God, creator of all. This is the first article. The second is the Word of God, God the Son, Jesus Christ our Lord, who was revealed to the prophets. . . . At *the end of times,* to sum up all things, he became man among men, visible and palpable, in order to destroy death and bring to light life, and bring about communion with God. And the third is the Holy Spirit, by whom the prophets prophesied and the patriarchs were taught about God and the just were led into the path of justice, and who *in the end of times* was

poured forth in a new manner upon men all over the earth renewing man to God.[14]

Irenaeus's summary resembles what later was to become the Apostles' Creed. In his day there were no creeds as such, but at baptism catechumens answered a set of questions that took the form of a simple statement of belief, or "rule of faith." "Do you believe in God the Father Almighty?" "Do you believe in Jesus Christ his only Son our Lord?" "Do you believe in the Holy Spirit?" The rule of faith had a trinitarian structure whose narrative identified God by the things recorded in the Scriptures, the creation of the world, the inspiration of the prophets, the coming of Christ in the flesh, and the outpouring of the Holy Spirit. The rule of faith, which, of course, was drawn from the Bible, reverberated back on the Bible as a key to its interpretation. Yet in practice it stood apart from the Scriptures as a confession of faith received from tradition and recited at baptism during the liturgy of Easter. An arc of understanding stretched from what the church practiced to what it read in the Scriptures.

Although the central event that held together the biblical narrative was the coming of Christ, his death, and Resurrection, Irenaeus always sets Christ's coming against the backdrop of creation. He favors terms like *renew* and *restore*, and, drawing on the language of Saint Paul in Ephesians, he says that Christ "summed up" or "united" all things in himself (Eph. 1:10): "When he was made flesh and became man, he united in himself the long history of mankind and gained salvation for all so that what we had lost in Adam, the image and likeness of God, we might receive in Jesus Christ." Though Irenaeus says that what was lost in Adam was regained in Christ, suggesting that redemption was a return to an original state, he is careful to explain that the perfection brought by Christ was never granted to Adam. Adam was but a child who needed to grow into a mature human being to reach full perfection. In Irenaeus's view the fall was a necessary stage in the growth to maturity, and the whole of human history is a long process leading from infancy to maturity. Christ does not simply reverse what had been lost in the fall: he brings to completion what had been partial and imperfect.[15]

The Bible is thus oriented toward a future still unfolding. Christ, says Irenaeus, not only gathers into himself all previous generations, but also bears within himself "the future dispensation of the human race." The Christian Bible, to reiterate the point, begins at the beginning and ends with an end that is no end. Its final chapters in the book of Revelation depict the heavenly city, and Irenaeus ends his work against the Gnostics with a vision of the ultimate restoration of all things. He looks back over the whole biblical history and, citing Saint Paul, says there will come a time when creation "shall be free from the bondage of corruption," and the "same God and father who fashioned human beings, and gave promise of the inheritance of the earth to the fathers, who brought creatures forth from bondage at the resurrection of the just, and fulfils the promise for the kingdom of his Son, this God will be revealed in all his majesty and splendor. On that day all things will be brought to perfection and God will be 'all in all'" (1 Cor. 15:28).[16]

The Scriptures are the "ground and pillar of our faith," says Irenaeus. If the Bible is dismembered to serve an exotic theological program and biblical texts are deployed willy-nilly (as the Gnostics did), the Scriptures will remain a closed book and it will not be possible "to find the truth in them." Without a grasp of the plot that holds everything together, the Bible is as vacuous as a mosaic in which the tiles have been arbitrarily rearranged without reference to the original design or as a poem constructed by stringing together random verses from the *Iliad* and *Odyssey* and imagining it was Homer. In Clement of Alexandria the Bible's plan is implicit, suggested by a word here, a phrase there; in Irenaeus the outline is set out in bold. So successful was Irenaeus's approach to the interpretation of the Bible that it informed all later interpretation. Whether one reads Athanasius against Arius, Augustine against Pelagius, or Cyril of Alexandria against Nestorius, all assume that individual passages are to be read in light of the story that gives meaning to the whole.[17]

In sermons and in theological writings, in devotional books and in prayers, and in commentaries on specific books of the Bible, the core narrative, the "ordering of our faith," as Irenaeus puts it, suffuses Christian thinking about God, Christ, the world, human beings, the church, the moral and spiritual life. Centuries later it was stated with exemplary clarity and brevity by Hugo of Saint Victor, a monk living in medieval Paris:

> The subject matter of all the Divine Scriptures is the works of restoring humankind. For there are two works in which all that has been done are contained. The first is the work of foundation; the second is the work of restoration. The work of foundation is that by which those things that were not came into being. The work of restoration is that by which those things that had been damaged were made better. Therefore, the work of foundation is the creation of the world with all its elements. The work of restoration

is the Incarnation of the Word with all its sacraments, those which have existed from the beginning of time, and those which came about later until the end of the world.[18]

The Inevitability of Allegory

The Roman Empire was a rhetorical culture, a society that loved words, especially spoken words. Even letters to personal friends were an occasion to display rhetorical virtuosity. The recipient would read a letter aloud for friends to savor (and perhaps judge) its sonority, vocabulary, choice of metaphors. Cities staged rhetorical contests in which skilled orators vied with each other to win the applause of the audience. Most of the church fathers were practiced in rhetoric and skilled in public speaking, and they too loved words. And though they found the style of the Scriptures plain and inelegant, the words of the Bible were radiant with light, incandescent, and bursting with a power so palpable, said Augustine, that they "pummeled" his heart.[19]

In early Christian writings and sermons it is the words of the Bible that are the bearers of ideas. A writer will begin with a particular text, and a word in the text will suggest other passages, sometimes predictable, sometimes surprising, whose words in turn form the writer's thought. The technique was learned from Saint Paul. In Romans 10, for example, Paul cites Isaiah 53:1: "Lord, who has believed what he has heard from us?" The word *heard* indicates that something was spoken, and Paul says that what is heard comes from the "words of Christ." This in turn reminds him of the term "words" in Psalm 19: "Their voice goes out through all the earth, and their *words* to the end of the world." Though the psalm celebrates the heavens that tell the glory of God, even though there is no "speech, nor are there words," Paul takes it to refer to the apostles, who go out into the world to proclaim the words of the Gospel. His interpretation is different from the plain meaning of the psalm, yet it took hold in Christian prayer. To this day Psalm 19 is read in the church's daily prayer on days commemorating an apostle.

In modern times there has been something of a consensus among biblical scholars that words have only one meaning and that the task of biblical interpretation is to discover the original meaning of the words of the Bible. The church fathers, however, took it as self-evident that the words of the Bible often had multiple meanings and the plain sense did not exhaust their meaning. "No Christian," said Augustine in the first paragraph of his *Literal Commentary on Genesis,* "would dare say that the [words of the Scripture] are not to be taken figuratively." As authority he cites Saint Paul in 1 Corinthians, where he said that the things that happened of old to the Israelites were said "as figures" (1 Cor. 10:11), and in Ephesians, where the phrase "and the two shall become one flesh" is called a mystery that refers "to Christ and the Church" (Eph. 5:31–32). Even John Chrysostom, whose exegesis is always firmly rooted in the familiar, praised Abraham because he "preferred the less obvious to the more obvious."[20] Figurative speech is the natural clothing of religious thought.

Allegory, as this way of interpreting the Old Testament was called, was adopted early in the church's history. I have already cited one example, Paul's interpretation of Psalm 19 in Romans 10, but the most striking instance is found in Galatians 4, where Saint Paul calls his interpretation of Abraham's wives, Hagar and Sarah, an allegory. Over time allegory achieved almost universal acceptance as a way to give the Old Testament a Christian interpretation. Though Christians had adopted the Jewish Bible, the Septuagint, as their sacred book, large sections—for example, laws in the book of Leviticus, the book of Joshua, even passages in the prophets—seemed impenetrable to Christian readers. When Augustine was preparing for baptism he asked Ambrose what he should read "to receive so great a grace." Ambrose told him to read the prophet Isaiah, but when Augustine took up the book its meaning eluded him: "I did not understand the first passage of the book and thought the whole would be equally obscure." So he put it aside, he says, until "I had more practice in the Lord's style of language."[21]

Origen was the first Christian scholar to deal directly with the question of how Christians were to interpret the Old Testament. In a homily on the book of Exodus he observed that Saint Paul had shown Christians "how the church gathered from the Gentiles ought to interpret the books of the Law." The text he took as exemplary was 1 Corinthians 10, where Paul had written, "I want you to know, brethren, that our fathers were all under the cloud, and all passed through the sea, and all were baptized into Moses in the cloud and in the sea, and all ate the same supernatural food and all drank the same supernatural drink. For they drank from the supernatural Rock which followed them, and the Rock was Christ" (1 Cor. 10:5). Paul's interpretation of the Exodus and the wanderings of the Israelites in the desert, says Origen, differs from the "plain sense" of the text. What the Jews understood to be "crossing of a sea," he writes, "Paul calls baptism," and what they thought "was a cloud Paul says is the Holy Spirit." Paul dealt with only a few passages and the Old Testament was a very big book. So Origen proposes that the several examples proffered by Paul should be taken as models to guide Christians in their interpretation of the Old Testament. Let interpreters take what they have learned from Paul and apply it to other passages, he says. Augustine makes exactly the same point, also citing 1 Corinthians 10: "By explaining one passage, [Paul] shows us how to understand others."[22]

Now the topic of allegory (or the spiritual interpretation of the Bible) is much too large to discuss even in cursory fashion in these pages. But its practice in the early church helps one understand how the Septuagint came to figure so large in Christian thinking. With the help of allegory Christians learned to read the Bible as a single book about Christ. Speaking of patristic exegesis of the Old Testament, Henri de Lubac wrote, "Jesus Christ brings about the unity of Scripture, because he is the endpoint and fulness of Scripture. Everything in it is related to him. In the end he is its sole object. Consequently, he is, so to speak, its whole exegesis." Put another way, Christ is the subject of biblical interpretation. The words of the Scriptures are the signs given to the church to understand the mystery of God present in human flesh in the person of Jesus Christ. It is only if one knows the *res*, the subject matter of the Scriptures, that one can understand its words. "If I am given a sign [that is, a word]," wrote Augustine, "and do not know the thing [*res*] of which it is the sign, it can teach me nothing."[23]

A few examples must suffice. The word *cleave*, *adhaerere* in Latin, appears again and again in Augustine's writings. It is taken from Psalm 73:28, "For me to *cleave* to God is good." "Does not this one word 'cleave'," writes Augustine, "express all that the apostle says about love?" No other biblical word seemed to Augustine to embody the entire mystery of the faith so fully. Augustine's interpretation of "cleave" cannot, however, be drawn directly from the text of Psalm 73. Augustine explains the verse in light of the promise in the book of Leviticus: "I will walk among you, and will be your God, and you shall be my people" (Lev. 26:12). Already in the New Testament Saint Paul had made a connection between the words of Leviticus and fellowship with God (2 Cor. 6:14–7:1). Augustine, following Paul, writes, "This passage ["I will be their God" in Leviticus] is the reward of which the psalmist speaks in his prayer, 'For me to cleave to God is good.'. . . . There can be no better good, no happier happiness than this: life for God, life from God, who is the well of life, in whose light we shall see light. Of that life the Lord himself says, 'This is life eternal, that they may know you the one true God, and Jesus Christ whom you have sent' (John 17:3). . . . This is his own promise to his lovers: 'He that loves me keeps my commandments; and he that loves me is loved of my Father and I will love him and will show myself to him' (John 14:21)."[24]

For Augustine, Psalm 73:28 recalls God's word in Leviticus to the Israelites and anticipates Jesus' words in the Gospel of John. The verse invites a Trinitarian exposition; indeed, it requires it, because it is only through the outpouring of the Holy Spirit that humans are able to love God and cleave to God. To support his interpretation Augustine cites Romans 5:5: "God's love has been poured into our hearts through the Holy Spirit which has been given to us." Augustine takes love here to refer to our love for God, for it is only through love given by the Holy Spirit that we are able to have fellowship with God. Besides receiving the commandments that instruct us in how one is to live, a person also "receives the Holy Spirit, whereby there arises in his soul the delight in and the love of God, the supreme and changeless

Good . . . and he may be fired in heart to 'cleave' to his Creator, kindled in mind to come within the shining of the true light; and thus receive from the source of his being the only real well-being."[25]

For Augustine and other early Christian interpreters the meaning of Psalm 73 was not to be found by analyzing the word *cleave* in biblical Hebrew (or biblical Greek) or by constructing the historical context in which the psalm was written. If Psalm 73 was written "for our instruction" it must be interpreted in light of what is known of God through the revelation in Christ and the sending of the Holy Spirit. Through exegesis, Christian interpreters discovered in the words and images of the Scriptures the signs given by God, what they celebrated in the church's Liturgy, heard in its preaching, learned in its catechesis, confessed in its creeds.

Interpretation has to do with context. As moderns we are so accustomed to think of context as literary or historical that we forget that the words of the Scripture come to us in many ways. Think how differently a verse from the Scriptures touches us when it is sung or spoken in the Liturgy. In the little entrance of the Liturgy of Saint Mark, for example, immediately before the reading of the first lesson, Psalm 43:3, "Send out your light and your truth," is read. In the psalm the phrase is part of a prayer for deliverance, but in the Liturgy it serves to introduce the reading of the Scriptures. The liturgy "generates a new 'us,'" observes Paul Ricoeur; it creates a framework of meaning that is other than the literary or historical setting of the text. When the text is reused in its new setting, an exchange takes place between the words of the text and the liturgical action. As Ricoeur says, "The rite opens the space of 'sacramental mystery' to the poem [he is speaking about the Song of Songs], the poem gives the rite the rightness of an appropriate word." The *res*, the theological truths and spiritual realities, known and lived within the church invest the words of the Bible with meanings that are other (that is, allegorical) than the original sense, yet over time become what the text means. Whatever meaning Psalm 19 may have had originally (which of course remains one interpretation), it is now indisputably and irrevocably a psalm about the apostles, as Psalm 22 ("My God, my God, why have you forsaken me?") is a psalm about Christ's passion.[26]

A different kind of example can be found in Gregory of Nyssa's exposition of Song of Songs 4:12–15.[27] The text from the Song of Songs reads, "A garden locked is my sister, my bride, a garden locked, a fountain sealed. Your shoots are an orchard of pomegranates with all choicest fruits, henna with nard, nard and saffron, calamus and cinnamon, with all trees of frankincense, myrrh and aloes, with all chief spices—a garden fountain, a well of living water, and flowing streams from Lebanon."

The phrase that caught Gregory's attention in this passage was "living water." This image, familiar to readers of the Bible, is capable of differing interpretations, and in its original setting within the Song it is crowded in with a number of other images. In the literary context of the fourth chapter of the Song of Songs it appears relatively innocuous. In his homilies on the Song of Songs, however, Gregory of Nyssa takes "living water" to be an image of the divine life which is "lifegiving" and interprets it in light of Jesus' words in John about the living water that Christ gives. Gregory writes, "We are familiar with these descriptions of the divine essence as a source of life from the Holy Scriptures. Thus the prophet, speaking in the person of God, says: 'They have forsaken me, the fountain of living water' (Jer. 2:13). And again, the Lord says to the Samaritan woman: 'If you knew the gift of God, and who it is that is saying to you, "Give me a drink," you would have asked him, and he would have given you living water' (John 4:10). And again he says: 'If any one thirst, let him come to me and drink. He who believes in me, as the scripture has said, "Out of his heart shall flow rivers of living water"' (John 7:38–39). Now this he said about the Spirit, which those who believed in him were to receive." After the coming of Christ, "living water" could not be interpreted without reference to Christ and his words in the Gospel of John. The Old Testament as read by Christians was a different book from the Hebrew and Aramaic writings that have come down to us from the ancient near East. Having the New Testament in hand, Christians saw terms take on different hues, certain images spring to life, persons and events privileged, and everything woven together in a tapestry imprinted with the face of Christ. In one of his sermons Augustine calls the Scriptures "God's face for Now."[28]

The Christian Bible (the Greek Old Testament and the apostolic writings) created a distinctive universe of meaning. As its words took up residence in the minds and hearts of Christian thinkers, it gave them a vocabulary that subtly shaped their patterns of thought. What the Bible spoke of could not be expressed apart from its unique language and its singular history. Gregory of Nyssa was aware that images other than living water were used to express the nature of God. Plotinus, for example, had used such expressions as "inexhaustible infinity" and "boiling over with life" for the divine.[29] One can speak of God as the source of life without using the language of the Bible. The point is not that "living water" expresses things better than "inexhaustible infinite" or "boiling over with life." What is significant is that "living water" is found in Bible and would always be found in the Bible. Metaphors and images and symbols drawn from elsewhere, no matter how apt, do not stir the Christian imagination in the same way as those drawn from the Scriptures. Like rhetorical ornaments that momentarily delight the hearer, they are as insubstantial as breath blown on glass.

Because the words and images of the Bible endure, they provided scaffolding on which to construct the edifice of Christian thought. The Bible was, however, more than a platform on which to build something else, and biblical interpretation was not a stage on the way to the real work of thinking. Thinking took place through exegesis, and the language of the Bible became the language of Christian thought. Christians thinkers returned again and again as to a bountiful spring from which, says Ambrose, flow "rivers of understanding, rivers of meditation and spiritual rivers."[30]

Seeing Oneself in What Is Written

For early Christian thinkers the Bible, finally, was a book about how to live. God's Word is not something to be looked at, but acted on. Saint Bernard, the medieval mystic, said it well: the interpreter must see himself in that which is said. In the early church Gregory the Great stated this spiritual truth more eloquently than anyone else. In Gregory's life of Saint Benedict he was asked by Peter his interlocutor what it means for Benedict to "live with himself." Gregory took the phrase to be an interpretation of the words of the prodigal son, who had journeyed to a far county only to squander his inheritance. When the country was ravaged by a great famine he became so hungry that he would gladly have eaten the slop fed to swine. At that point in the parable he realizes how grievously he has sinned against his father and the evangelist says, "He came to himself" (Luke 15:17).[31]

How is it, asks Gregory, that a person who is always with himself can be said to have "come to himself"? The phrase, says Gregory, means "search one's soul continuously" and see oneself always in the presence God and attend to one's life and actions. Job came to himself when he heard the words of God, "Where were you when I laid the foundation of the earth?" (Job 38:4). In the same way, explains Gregory, "it is right for us to be brought back to our own hearts by the things that were said to holy Job. For we understand the words of God more truly when we 'search out [ourselves] in them.' "[32]

Gregory's most charming statement of the mysterious relation between reader and text occurs in his homily on the famous allegory of the living creatures and the wheels in the first chapter of the prophet Ezekiel. The text reads, "Now as I looked at the living creatures, I saw a wheel upon the earth beside the living creatures. . . . And when the living creatures went, the wheels went with them; and when the living creatures rose from the earth, the wheels rose" (Ezek. 1:15–19). Gregory took the wheels to be the Scriptures and the living creatures to be readers of the Scriptures. When Ezekiel says, "And when the living creatures went, the wheels went together with them, and when the living creatures were lifted up from the earth the wheels also were lifted up with them," he means that the Scriptures grow with the reader. The more profoundly one understands the Scriptures the more deeply one penetrates into them. The wheels would not be lifted up if the living creatures had not been lifted up. . . . But if the living creature moves and seeks the path that leads to a virtuous life, and through the footsteps of the heart learns to do good works, the wheels keep pace with him. You will progress in understanding the Holy Scripture only to the degree that you yourself have made progress through contact with them.[33]

Chapter 4

Seek His Face Always

Let us set out on the street of love together making for Him of whom
it is said, "Seek his face always" (Ps. 105:4).

SAINT AUGUSTINE

IN AUGUST 1941 in the desert south of Cairo, Egypt, while
clearing out rubbish in several caves to make room for ammuni-
tion, a group of British soldiers uncovered a bundle of ancient
papyrus rolls buried under the dry sand. When the rolls were
examined by an archaeologist it was discovered that they contained writings of several early Christian thinkers, including
Origen of Alexandria and the fourth-century author Didymus
the Blind, also from Alexandria. Though less heralded than the
discovery of a library of Gnostic writings at Nag Hammadi in
Egypt a few years later or the Dead Sea Scrolls, this collection
included a work of Origen that was previously unknown. What
is more, it is an unusual writing, not a theological essay or a

commentary on the Bible, but the record of a colloquy between Origen and a bishop from Arabia named Heraclides on the doctrine of the Trinity and other subjects.

Dialogue with Heraclides, as this work is now entitled, is a transcript of a meeting that had taken place in A.D. 245, a few years before Origen's death. From hints in the text it appears that the discussion between Origen and Heraclides was attended by neighboring bishops as well as lay members of Heraclides' church. Apparently some of the bishops had doubts about Heraclides' orthodoxy and had invited Origen, the most famous theologian of his day, to clarify the issues. This was not a judicial proceeding, but a genuine theological interchange carried on with mutual respect and affection. At one point Origen says, "It is not right that there should be any difference in teaching between one church and another. You are not the false church."[1]

Origen's first question probed Heraclides' understanding of the relation of Christ to God the Father. He asks, "Do you believe that Christ Jesus was God before he came into the body?" Heraclides answers, "Yes." Origen asks, "Was he God distinct from the God in whose form he existed?" Heraclides again answers, "Yes." Then Origen poses a more provocative, even disturbing, question: "Is it the case then . . . that we are not afraid to say that in one sense there are two Gods and in another sense there is one God?" At this point Heraclides hedges a bit and Origen says, "You do not appear to have answered my question." So he puts it to him again in different words: "Is the Son distinct from the Father?" Heraclides answers, "Certainly! How can he be Son if he is also Father?" Then, after several more questions, Origen asks, "Do we confess two Gods?" To which Heraclides responds, "Yes. The power is one."[2]

The logic of Origen's questioning had led to a rather embarrassing admission (which of course he invited), so he halts his colloquy with the bishop to offer his own views on the matter at hand. Some, he explains, "take offense at the statement that there are two Gods," and for that reason "we must express the doctrine carefully to show in what sense they are two and in what sense the two are one God."[3]

Few Christian thinkers were as bold as Origen to use language such as "two Gods." Yet he knew what he was about, and, true to his character, he is supremely confident that the expression "two Gods" can be understood properly. This brief exchange between a learned theologian and an unknown bishop somewhere in the Arabian peninsula offers a precious glimpse of the linguistic and conceptual difficulties faced by Christian teachers as they sought to interpret what they read in the Scriptures and said in their prayers. There could be no believing without thinking about what was believed.

Christianity, like Judaism, confessed belief in one God, and being received into the church meant abandoning the worship of many gods. "We have one God the Father from whom are all things" (1 Cor. 8:6), wrote Saint Paul. According to the Shepherd of Hermas, a very early Christian writing, the first commandment is "Believe that God is one, who created and completed all things and made all that is from that which is not." At the same time, early in the second decade of the second century an outside observer, Pliny, the Roman governor of Bithynia, reported that Christians were in the habit of meeting on a fixed day before it was light to "recite a hymn to Christ as to a *god.*" Christians were baptized "in the name of the Father and of the Son and of the Holy Spirit," the early rules of faith, or creeds, were tripartite, and trinitarian formulas are sprinkled throughout the New Testament. As the English theologian Leonard Hodgson observed several generations ago, "Christianity began as a trinitarian religion with a unitarian theology. The question at issue in the age of the Fathers was whether the religion should transform the theology or the theology stifle the religion."[4]

How the trinitarian religion of the Bible, the liturgy, and the early creeds was to be expressed in light of the biblical teaching that God is one provoked a fervent and prolonged debate that occupied the church's most gifted thinkers for two centuries. The controversy pitted bishops against their own clergy, bishops against bishops; it rent the social fabric of cities and towns and even divided families. John Chrysostom urged members of his church to keep their distance from those who did not confess the full divinity of Christ, "even if they are your parents."[5] As Christian emperors were drawn into the disputes profound changes took place in the relation of the church to imperial authorities. The first general council (as distinct from regional and local councils) in the church's history was convened by the emperor Constantine in A.D. 325 at Nicaea (present-day Iznik in Turkey), a city in the province of Bithynia in northwestern Asia Minor. Constantine, who had only recently become a Christian, envisioned the church as a unifying, not a divisive, force in the empire and hoped that by calling the bishops together he could bring a swift end to the controversy. His hopes would be disappointed, at least in the short run.

At Nicaea the bishops adopted a creed and condemned the teachings of Arius, a priest in Alexandria, but like other councils in the church's history, most recently Vatican II in the 1960s, the Council of Nicaea did not halt debate but set terms for a new, more vigorous stage in the dispute. Only after the convening of many regional councils, intense political maneuvering, intervention by other emperors (not always on the same side of the debate), the exile of leading bishops, Athanasius and Hilary, for example, and heated theological argument carried on in doctrinal treatises and letters did another emperor, Theodosius, convoke a second general council in Constantinople in 381. Although the discussion continued after the bishops left Constantinople—Augustine's treatise on the Trinity was written three decades later—this council did bring peace to most of the church and adopted a creed that would become as authoritative and enduring as the earlier Apostles' Creed. Based on the creed of Nicaea but without its condemnations of Arius's teachings, the creed of the council of Constantinople also included an expanded section on the Holy Spirit, for example, "Lord and Lifegiver . . . who with the Father and the Son is together worshiped and glorified." The proper name for this creed is the Nicaeno-Constantinopolitan Creed, but it is understandably known as the Nicene Creed, and in this form it is confessed by most Christians in the Eucharist on Sundays to this day.

The history of the formulation of the Christian doctrine of the Trinity and the issues that dominated the thinking of the leading bishops of the church in the fourth century is well known and has been the subject of many books. It is not the purpose of this chapter to recount this history anew. I wish rather to examine certain aspects of early Christian thinking about God as triune to illuminate features of the emerging Christian intellectual tradition. My aim is to illustrate, by reference to specific writers, how Christian thinkers, when faced with questions arising out of Christian belief and practice—for example, baptizing in the name of the Father and of the Son and of the Holy Spirit—went about the task of giving conceptual form to their faith, that is, reasoned about what was believed.

As the exchange between Origen and Heraclides suggests, the facts of Christian revelation posed an acute problem for reflective Christians. Veneration of Christ, a man born of a woman, seemed to put in doubt the truth that God is one. How then did thinkers who believed in the one God, the God of Israel, come to formulate the doctrine that God is triune and defend this teaching as the definitive mark of orthodox Christianity?

The Resurrection of Christ and Plurality within God

The place to begin the discussion of the doctrine of the Trinity is the Resurrection of Christ. This may seem surprising. In the standard accounts of the history of Christian thought the Resurrection is usually discussed as a topic in itself, for example, as part of eschatology, the last things and future hope, and in relation to the understanding of salvation. Of course one might say that the Resurrection of Christ is implicit in everything Christians do and believe. The Eucharist is an empty ritual if Christ is not risen, and prayer to Christ is otiose if Christ is not alive. The New Testament affirms that belief in Christ as God is directly related to his Resurrection. At the beginning of his epistle to the Romans, Saint Paul says that Christ was "designated Son of God in power according to the Spirit of holiness by his *resurrection* from the dead" (Rom. 1:4).

Yet it is always satisfying to discover that what is taken for granted was actually stated explicitly. In the heat of the disputes in the fourth century, a bishop in the west, Hilary of Poitiers, writing in Latin, discerned with uncommon perspicacity the inner logic of Christian thinking about God. If we wish to understand how Christians learned to think differently about God and broke with established patterns of Greek and Jewish thought, Hilary offers a unique vantage point.

Hilary of Poitiers, sometimes called the Athanasius of the West because of his defense of the decrees of the Council of Nicaea in A.D. 325, was born in Poitiers in Gaul in 315 to a well-to-do family. Like others from his class he received a thorough education in the Latin classics, and as he grew to maturity he faced the prospect of a life imposed on him by family and society, the gentlemanly amusements of a man of wealth and leisure. Hilary, however, grew restless under these expectations and found himself turning to more spiritual pursuits. In his words he wished to pursue a life that was "worthy of the understanding that had been given us by God." Like Justin he began to read the Bible, and one passage that touched his soul was Exodus 3:14, where God the creator, "testifying about himself," said, "I am who I am." For Hilary this brief utterance penetrated more deeply into the "mystery of the divine nature" than anything he had heard or read from the philosophers. Shortly thereafter he was baptized and received into the church.[6]

When Hilary was in his midthirties the bishop of Poitiers died, and Hilary was elected bishop of the city by acclamation, a practice that is well documented in the early church. (Augustine avoided going to any place where he knew the chair of the bishop was vacant.)[7] Almost at once Hilary was drawn into the great debate over the Trinity that was dividing the church. When Hilary became a player in the dispute, the defenders of the Council of Nicaea were in disfavor with imperial authorities. The emperor Constantine had died in 337, and his son and successor Constantius was cool to the bishops who supported Nicaea. Hilary was sent into exile and was not able to return to his diocese in Gaul for four years. During his banishment, however, he had contact with eastern writers and found time to write a large, diffuse work, *The Trinity,* a treatise that displays not only mastery of the arguments of earlier writers but the imagination to rework them in light of the debates of a new generation. Written in Latin, it displayed the growing sophistication of western Christian thinking on the Trinity.

The Trinity also breathes a spirit of devotion, and Hilary reminds the reader again and again that the subject of the discussion is the living God. Although the book is a technical theological treatise it begins with an account of his conversion, and in the first book he lays down some guidelines for the discussion that follows. He cites the words from Exodus 3:14, "I am who I am," several times in the book, most notably at the very beginning in connection with his conversion and again in the final chapter. He clearly wants the reader to take note of this verse. The reason is that in answer to the question What is your name? God uses the word "is," "I am," a form of the word "to be." What the Scriptures teach, says Hilary, is that in seeking to know and understand God, we discover that God is always "prior to our thinking." For it is the "nature of the one who *is*" to *be,* that is, to exist. If something *is,* neither thoughts nor words can claim that it does not exist. Therefore, even if we try to reach back into eternity we discover that God is already there. As the psalmist wrote, "If I ascend to heaven thou art there! If I make my bed in Sheol thou art there!" (Ps. 139:8). Thinking about God begins when one "stands before the certain reality" that is God.[8]

The only way to stand before God, however, is in humble

adoration. If we are to discuss the "things of God," writes Hilary, we must learn obedience and serve God with devotion and reverence. Only by yielding to God and giving ourselves to the object of our search can we know the God we seek. The careful reader of a book, says Hilary, realizes that he will not understand what is written in it if he does not expect more from the book than he brings to it. If he approaches the book only as a critic he will never allow his thoughts to be shaped by what is found there. Applied to theology, that is, thinking about God, this axiom means that we must allow the reality of God to stretch our thoughts so that they become worthy of the God we seek, befitting God, rather than limit God by imposing on him arbitrary standards of our own making. This is why, says Hilary, "God can only be known in devotion." The form of knowledge that is appropriate to God, he writes, is "thinking with understanding formed by piety," approaching God with a devout mind. Theology requires the "warmth of faith."[9]

Like Origen and Irenaeus, Hilary believed that God can be known only as God "has made himself known to us."[10] The knowledge of God begins in receptivity, in openness to what is revealed and the willingness to accept what is given. Hilary singles out the word "receive" in a text from Saint Paul: "We have not *received* the spirit of this world, but the Spirit which is of God" (1 Cor. 2:12). When we speak of God we speak of what we know and we know what we have received and we receive what is given through the Holy Spirit. Everyone has the facility to "apprehend God," says Hilary, but it is only when one receives the gift of the Spirit in faith that the "gift of knowledge" becomes our own: "Only in receiving can we know."[11]

Receiving, as Hilary understood it, was a matter of personal experience, but it also had an ecclesial dimension. For what one received were the words of the creed, the liturgical formula used in baptism, the Scriptures, the Eucharist. He mentions baptism explicitly and reminds his readers that when someone is baptized the exact words from the gospel (he is thinking of Matt. 28:19–20) were recited, that is, one is baptized "in the name of the Father and of the Son and of the Holy Spirit." These words and the actions that accompany them aid us in understanding God, for they designate God the creator, the only Son, and the "gift," that is, the Holy Spirit. What is received, indeed what stands at the center of the church's confession, is a belief not merely "in God, but in God as Father," and not merely in Christ but in "Christ as Son."[12]

What Hilary is getting at is that thinking about God begins with language that is given in the Scriptures and with convictions formed by the church's practice, most notably baptism in the name of the Father and of the Son and of the Holy Spirit. In his search for God Hilary first knew God through the beauty and order of creation, but only after he had come to know Christ did he realize that "*God* was in the beginning with God."[13] Behind Hilary's somewhat enigmatic language lies a truth that permeates all Christian thinking: the knowledge of the Triune God is grounded in Christ's coming in the flesh, what the early church called the economy. The Greek term, meaning order or arrangement, in theological discourse signified God's ordered self-disclosure in the biblical history reaching back to creation and culminating in Christ.

Hilary's book on the Trinity is thus an exercise in trying to understand the nature of God who is known in Christ. It is through the flesh of Christ that the soul is able to draw near to

God and know the "divine mystery."[14] The one God can be known through the things of creation, but it is only through the economy that one knows God as Father, Son, and Holy Spirit. All early Christian thinkers agreed on this point, but Hilary stands out because he not only appeals to the economy in his discussion of the nature of God, but also shows that the Resurrection is the defining event in the economy.

The first Christians, Hilary observes, were observant Jews who every morning recited the Sh'ma, the ancient prayer of the Jewish people: "Hear, O Israel, the Lord your God is one Lord. And you shall love the Lord your God with all your heart, and with all your soul, and with all your might" (Deut. 6:4). As faithful Jews the apostles believed that God is one. Because this is so, as the Sh'ma bears witness, what, asks Hilary, are we to make of Thomas's confession: "My Lord and my God"? How could Thomas have confessed Jesus, a human being, as "Lord" and "God," and at the same time continue to pray the Sh'ma? The Sh'ma clearly affirms belief in one God, yet Thomas addresses Christ as God. According to the gospels, says Hilary, Thomas had often heard Jesus say things such as "I and the Father are one" and "All things that the Father has are mine." Yet during Christ's lifetime these words apparently made little impact on him. It was only when Thomas knew the resurrected Christ that he grasped the meaning of what Jesus had said earlier.[15]

This is a precious passage. Hilary envisions a time at the very beginning of Christianity when Jesus' disciples were still observing Jewish traditions yet following Christ. During Christ's lifetime his followers did not grasp fully who he was. Even though some of his sayings imply that he had a unique relation to God, and he performed miracles and revealed his heavenly glory to his most intimate followers at his Transfiguration on the mount, his disciples did not have eyes to see who he was. They had sound theological reasons for their opacity. They knew by heart the words of the Sh'ma, "Hear, O Israel, the Lord your God is one Lord." Hence Hilary asks a question I am sure many other readers of the New Testament have asked themselves: How could a faithful Jew who had recited the Sh'ma since childhood, whose prayers were addressed to God the king of the universe, address Christ as God or Son of God, as the earliest Christians did? Hilary's answer is that the Resurrection of Christ transfigured everything. When Jesus came and stood among the disciples and put his finger in his side, Thomas said, "My Lord and my God!" When confronted by the risen Christ one does not say, "How interesting," but "My Lord and my God!"

The terms used by Thomas, *Lord* and *God*, are significant, and they allow Hilary to drive home his point. "Lord" and "God" are the terms that occur in the Sh'ma, yet here they are used not of God the creator of the world and king of the universe, but of Christ. Because of the Resurrection Thomas recognized that the one he knew, who had lived among them, was not just an extraordinary human being but the living God. "No one except God is able to rise from death to life by its own power," writes Hilary. But his argument runs deeper. He wishes to say not only that the Resurrection revealed something about Christ to his disciples, namely, that he is God; his more penetrating observation is that Resurrection caused them to think about God differently. Once Jesus was raised, writes Hilary, Thomas "understood the whole mystery of the faith," for "*now*," that is, in light of the Resurrection, Thomas was able to confess Christ as God "without abandoning his devotion to the one God." After the Resurrection he could continue to recite the Sh'ma because he had begun to conceive of the oneness of God differently. Thomas's confession "my Lord and my God" was not the "acknowledgment of a second God, nor a betrayal of the unity of the divine nature": it was a recognition that God was not a "solitary God" or a "lonely God." God is one, says Hilary, but not alone.[16]

This passage from Hilary's treatise *The Trinity* occurs within a discussion of the unity, that is, the oneness, of God. Hilary's opponents had argued that the defenders of the Council of Nicaea were inconsistent in their thinking about God. By using the words "God from God," as in the creed of Nicaea, they put into doubt the unity of God. God by definition cannot have an offspring. If Christ is "God from God," then there are two Gods and the Nicene theologians have abandoned belief in one God. Christ was divine by adoption, not God in the sense that God the Father and creator is God. In his defense of the divinity of Christ Hilary appeals to such biblical texts as "And the Word was God" and to biblical titles for Christ. But only when he comes to the "evangelical narrative"[17] does his argument take wing. By appealing to the Resurrection of Christ he grounds his interpretation of the Bible in the events recorded in the Scripture, that is, in the economy. The Resurrection is the key to Hilary's interpretation of the Scriptures and the reason for rejecting a strictly monistic view of God.

The economy allowed human beings a glimpse of the inner life of God. This fundamental insight drove Christian thinking about God. In a striking comment on Colossians 1:19, "In [Christ] all the fullness of God was pleased to dwell," Origen of Alexandria had said that through God's revelation in Christ we become "spectators" of the "depth of God." And in our day the theologian Wolfhart Pannenberg has written, "As God reveals himself, so he is in his eternal deity."[18] But it was Hilary, the fourth-century Latin theologian, who expressed most succinctly why the historical events of Christ's life, in particular the Resurrection, had altered the conditions under which reason worked. Thinking about God could no longer be carried on independently of what had taken place in the evangelical history. What others had left unspoken he stated explicitly: after Christ's Resurrection God's unity had to be conceived differently. Though one, Hilary affirmed, God was not a solitary being and in some mysterious way the life of the one God was communal.

The Divine Wisdom

The New Testament presents Jesus of Nazareth as a human being who lived the life of child, grew to maturity, was crucified in Jerusalem, executed by being hung on a cross, and raised to new life three days after his death. This portrait was indelibly part of Christian memory and Christian worship. But the writers of the New Testament not only told the story of Jesus, they also explained his significance by a treasury of titles, of which Christ, the anointed one, the Messiah, came to function almost as a name: not Jesus the Christ, but Jesus Christ. There were many others, among them "Word of God" (John 1:1), "wisdom" and "power" of God (1 Cor. 1:24), "firstborn of all creation," "image of the invisible God" (Col. 1:15), "the very stamp of God's nature" (Heb. 1:3), "Son of God" (Rom. 1:3), "Alpha and Omega." These titles referred to the concrete historical person, but they implied that the Jesus portrayed in the gospels existed in intimate fellowship with God. Among these titles, Word of God and Son of God were the most significant, Word of God because of its centrality in the prologue to the Gospel of John, "In the beginning was the Word," and Son of God because it appears in the account of Jesus' baptism in the Gospels. When Jesus came up out of the waters of the Jordan River the Spirit descended on him like a dove and a voice came from heaven, "Thou art my beloved Son; with thee I am well pleased" (Mark 1:10–11 and parallels). But Wisdom ran a close third, and its importance in the Old Testament opened up a rich vein of associations for thinking about the person of Christ and his relation to God the Father. In his treatise *First Principles*, Origen mentions Wisdom first in his list of titles for Christ.[19]

The term *wisdom* was normally used adjectivally as in the phrase *wise man*. *Wisdom* referred to a quality or characteristic of a person. Yet there were passages in the Old Testament, particularly in the wisdom books, that seemed to depict wisdom not simply as a divine attribute but as a divine being with its own proper existence. A key passage is found in the Wisdom of Solomon, a book that is part of the Septuagint and hence part of the Bible of the early church: "For wisdom is more mobile than any motion; because of her pureness she pervades and penetrates all things. For she is a breath of the power of God, and a pure emanation of the glory of the Almighty; therefore nothing defiled gains entrance into her. For she is a reflection of eternal light, a spotless mirror of the working of God, and an image of his goodness" (7:24–26). Here wisdom reflects the nature of God. Wisdom is also called "the fashioner of all things" (7:22), "an associate in [God's] works" (8:4), a member of God's heavenly council who exists from eternity (24:9). In these passages Wisdom is not simply an attribute displayed in God's activity in the world, for example, in creation, but a divine agent carrying out God's purposes for humankind. Another passage, Proverbs 8:22–23, said God had made Wisdom "the beginning of his ways for his works. He established me before time was, in the beginning before he made the earth."

Because the New Testament identified Christ with Wisdom (1 Cor. 1:24) and used phrases from the Wisdom of Solomon to refer to Christ, for example, "very stamp of God's image" (Heb. 1:3), the words of the Wisdom of Solomon, a book from the Old Testament, were understood to refer directly to Christ. The title Wisdom provided a secure foothold in the Old Testament, that is, in Israel's history, that spoke of the activity of Christ prior to the Incarnation. Read in light of the Resurrection those passages from the Old Testament that depicted the activity of Wisdom helped Christian thinkers to fill out what it meant to call Christ God. One of the works of Wisdom was the creation of the world, a view that was confirmed by the words of the psalmist, "All things were made by wisdom" (Ps 102:24). Hence early writers like Origen appealed to the title Wisdom to defend the biblical teaching that Christ was creator. Wisdom, he writes, was at the beginning with God and contained within herself "the beginnings and the causes and species of the whole creation."[20]

As we have seen, Hilary recognized that it makes a huge difference whether sayings of Jesus were heard before the Resurrection or after the Resurrection. Only after the Resurrection did Thomas (and others) know what Jesus meant when he spoke of his unique relation to God. In the same way it was only after the Resurrection that the followers of Jesus knew what to make of passages from the Old Testament on Wisdom. Wisdom leaped, as it were, out of the shadows into the clear light of day. Now

Christians were able to identify Wisdom with an actual historical person, with events that had taken place in time and space, and give Wisdom a name, Jesus Christ. As a consequence Wisdom acquired features that were not apparent before the coming of Christ, that is, before the economy, and reflection on the nature of Wisdom helped Christians to understand the mystery of God.

In the debate with Origen mentioned at the beginning of this chapter, Heraclides was very reluctant to say that belief in Christ implied that the church confessed two gods. He was not alone. When some of the faithful heard theologians like Origen talk about a second God or certain apologists mention ranks of deity, they believed something had gone awry. After all, in becoming Christians people thought they had been delivered from the worship of many gods to serve the one true God. Celsus had defended the veneration of a hierarchy of deities as pious and god pleasing: "The person who worships several gods, because he worships one of those which belong to the great God, even by this very action does that which is loved by him."[21] Only the pagans spoke of many gods, and language about two gods seemed to revert to the world Christians had left behind. Hence Heraclides' reluctance to answer Origen's question.

Tertullian, a contemporary of Origen, said that the rank and file among the Christians—he called them the "simple folk"— believed that in preaching "two or even three Gods" the church's belief in one God was compromised. "We hold," they said, "to the monarchy." *Monarchy* was the theological term to designate the belief that there was a single solitary God, and Monarchians were those Christians who adhered to the belief in the single (*monos*) rule (*arche*) of God. According to the Monarchians, Christ and the Holy Spirit were divine powers or emanations from God and had no independent existence. Tertullian's chief argument against the Monarchians was that in claiming to safeguard belief in the one God, they "take fright at the economy," that is, the evangelical history. They do not understand that "while they must believe in one God only, they must believe in him along with his economy." In his view, and in the view of all early Christian thinkers, thinking about God had to begin with the appearance of God in the person of Christ. As a result of "God's descent into human affairs," wrote Origen, we "have been able to perceive clearly the true conception of God's nature." The economy was the engine that drove trinitarian thinking.[22]

But the titles were also necessary because they offered images and a vocabulary to explain that the divinity of Christ did not compromise the unity of God. In his *Commentary on the Gospel of John* Origen discussed many titles, including light, door, way, shepherd, king, life, but Wisdom, Son, and Word proved to be the most fruitful for thinking about the relation of Christ to the Father. The term *logos* (word) occurs in the Septuagint version of Psalm 45:1 (44:2): "My heart uttered a good word." The word mentioned there and the word in the prologue to the Gospel of Saint John were taken to be the same word, that is, Christ the Word of God. In its conventional sense *word* designates "an utterance occurring in syllables," that is, a sound that disappears as soon as it is heard. Applied to Christ, this would mean Christ was only an emanation from God, the form that God took to reveal himself to human beings, the sound that is heard but soon fades and is heard no more. Origen, however, proposed that the term *word* should be interpreted in conjunction with the title Son, a term, he says, that implies "having life in itself." Though a son receives life from his mother, he exists as a human being independent of her. If the terms *word* and *son* are taken together it is obvious that "the word is distinct from God (the Father) and has its own existence." The Word of God must be understood as something that is *like* a human word but is not a human word. Consequently, it is possible to say that the Word of God has its own individuality and is to be distinguished from reason (*logos*), "which has no individual existence apart from us." The Scriptures, says Origen, teach that the Son is "other than the Father" and has his "own distinct individuality."[23]

Tertullian had come to a similar conclusion, although his reasoning follows a different course. Like Origen, he argued that the titles in the Scriptures should not be taken in isolation from one another. *Word* and *son* and *wisdom* had to be understood with reference to each another. The Scriptures speak of the same "power . . . now with the name of wisdom, now with the designation word." In answer to those who took Psalm 45 ("My heart has uttered a good word") to imply no distinction between God and his word, Tertullian cites texts that speak of Christ as the son. If the word spoken by the Father cannot be distinguished from the Father, it would seem that the son addressed in Psalm 2:7, "You are my son, this day have I begotten you," must be the same as the Father, which is absurd.[24]

Tertullian also provides an acute analysis of the term *word*, *logos* in Greek, *ratio* or *sermo* in Latin.[25] There is a sense, he says, in which reason in a human being can be understood to have its own existence. When a person deliberates silently within himself, something takes place that is similar to what takes place in God. At every moment of one's thinking reason is accompanied by a word (*sermo*): "Whatever you think takes the form of a word, and whatever you imagine is reason. It is necessary that you speak a word in your mind and while you speak it you have as conversation partner that word which has in it that same reason by which you speak when you think and by which you think when you speak."[26]

Tertullian's point is subtle. As human beings we think of ourselves as a single self, with our own individual consciousness, and we look at the world from the perspective of a unique subject. Yet, reasoning is always dialectical, it involves questioning, saying yes and and then saying no, a back and forth in the mind as words, ideas, and concepts challenge, criticize, or confirm each other. Such silent dialogue takes place within the mind; no word is spoken. In thinking, one becomes aware of an other within oneself which, paradoxically, is oneself. This other, of course, takes many forms depending on the topic and purpose of the deliberations, whether one is thinking alone or is in discussion with someone else. Yet the other is always present in the form of a question, an alternative, a doubt, a contrary proposal, or a complementary thought. The very term *deliberation* suggests that thinking is a kind of conversation that goes on within the self.

Because human thinking involves a back and forth within the mind, it is plausible, argues Tertullian, to speak of a kind of second person within us. Tertullian is not interested in establishing a truth about human psychology, though he wrote a large book dealing with the human soul, but in drawing an analogy between the human mind and God's nature. Human beings were made in the "image and likeness of God." If one can speak of a "partner in conversation" in the human mind, an "associate" if you will, "how much more completely . . . does this take place in God, whose image and similitude you are said to be. Even while silent one has in himself reason, and in reason word. . . . So I have been able with good reason to conclude that even before the world came into being God was not alone, for he always had in himself Reason, and with Reason Word, who came to be beside himself by activity within himself."[27] God does not live in solitude.

The Son Never Acts Alone

In the strict sense the argument that God was not a "solitary God" was not concerned with the doctrine of the Trinity. The debate focused on the relation of the Son to the Father. It remained for the next generation to take up the topic of the Holy Spirit. Although the book of Acts makes the outpouring of the Holy Spirit on Pentecost a pivotal event in the formation of the church (Acts 2) and hence of the economy, discussion of the status and character of the Holy Spirit trailed behind the debate about the Son. Unlike the early Christian Pasch (Easter) that was celebrated as an annual festival early in the church's history, the feast of Pentecost, the day on which the Holy Spirit was poured forth, emerged only slowly. In the earliest sources the term *Pentecost* designated not a single feast day, but the period of time after Easter, what Tertullian called "a most joyous space for Baptisms."[28] The season of Pentecost was viewed as a continuation of Easter and had no distinctive character of its own. Only in the fifth century did it emerge as a feast day in its own right. The earliest creeds mention the Holy Spirit, but not until the end of the fourth century, at the council of Constantinople, was a full article on the Holy Spirit added to the creed.

The belated recognition of the status of the Holy Spirit did not escape the church fathers. "Theology," says Gregory the

Theologian, "reaches maturity by additions." In the Old Testament the Father was proclaimed openly but the Son "obscurely." The New Testament revealed the Son, but only "gave us a glimpse of the deity of the Spirit." Only now, by which he means the time of the church, when "the Spirit has taken up residence among us, does he give us a clearer manifestation of himself." To which he adds, somewhat audaciously, that it would have been imprudent before Father and Son had been acknowledged to "burden us further with the Holy Spirit."[29] The truth arrives through time.

The presence of the Holy Spirit was evident in the church's life. In the *anaphora*, the central prayer in the Christian liturgy spoken over the bread and wine in the Eucharist, the bishop beseeched the Holy Spirit to descend on the gifts: "And we pray that you would send your Holy Spirit upon the offerings of your holy church; that gathering them into one, you would grant to all your saints who partake of them to be filled with the Holy Spirit." When a new bishop was consecrated, the other bishops laid hands on the candidate and prayed, "Pour forth now that power which is yours of your royal Spirit which you gave to your beloved servant Jesus Christ which he bestowed on his holy apostles. . . . And by the Spirit of high-priesthood give him authority to remit sins according to your commandments." Catechumens were baptized in the name of the Father and of the Son and of the Holy Spirit, and the liturgy began and ended with the invocation of the Holy Trinity. "The Spirit dwells among us, offering us a most clear display of himself," wrote Gregory.[30]

The role of the Holy Spirit in Christian worship and experience helped propel Christian thinkers to affirm that the Spirit, like the Son, is God. Yet some claimed that bishops like Gregory and his close friend Basil, who wrote a book on the Holy Spirit, "bring in an alien God [the Holy Spirit] not written about in Scripture." In response Gregory cites those passages in the New Testament that link specific actions in Christ's life with the work of the Spirit. "Consider the following," he writes: "Christ is born, the Spirit is his forerunner (Lk 1:35); Christ is baptized, the Spirit bears witness (Lk 3:21–22); Christ is tempted, the Spirit leads him up (Lk 4:2,14); [Christ] works miracles, the Spirit accompanies him (Mt 12:22,28); Christ ascends, the Spirit takes his place (Acts 1:8; 2:3–4)." In the Scriptures, Gregory argues, Christ's works are not presented as activities of the Son alone. God's revelation in Christ is confirmed and mediated through the presence of the Holy Spirit. Gregory of Nyssa wrote, "With regard to the divine nature . . . we do not learn [from the Scriptures] that the Father does something on his own without the cooperation of the Son, or that the Son acts on his own independently of the Spirit. Rather every divine action that has to do with creation and is designated according to our different conceptions has its origin in the Father, passes through the Son, and is brought to completion by the Holy Spirit."[31]

It is sometimes said that the doctrine of the divinity of the Holy Spirit is a deduction based on the logic of Christian thought about the status of the Son. But Christian thinking seldom proceeds by deduction; rather, it works off the language of the Bible and the *res,* the reality to which the Scriptures and Christian worship testify. To establish that the "Spirit is no stranger to the Son," Athanasius cited Romans 8:11: "If the *Spirit* of *Him* who raised *Jesus* from the dead dwells in you, he who raised Christ from the dead will give life to your mortal bodies also through his Spirit that dwells in you" (Rom. 8:11). Here the

Father and the Son and the Holy Spirit are involved in a single activity. Basil appeals directly to the formula used in baptism, "in the name of the Father and of the Son and of the Holy Spirit," as support for his argument that the Spirit is to be ranked with the Son and the Father.[32]

But the strongest argument in defense of the individuality of the Holy Spirit was that the Scriptures bear witness to two "sendings," the sending of the Son and the sending of the Holy Spirit. The pivotal text is Galatians 4:4: "But when the time had fully come, God *sent* forth his Son, born of a woman, born under the law, to redeem those who were under the law, so that we might receive adoption as sons. And because you are sons, God has *sent* the Spirit of his Son into our hearts, crying, 'Abba Father!'" (Gal. 4:4–5). In his treatise *The Trinity* Saint Augustine cites this passage to show that the sending of the Holy Spirit was no less historical than the sending of the Son. As certain things took place when Christ became man, so when the Spirit was sent, for example, to Christ at his baptism, or poured out on the church at Pentecost, something had taken place. As Augustine put it, "That which was hidden from eternity was made known in time." By Augustine's day Pentecost was a separate liturgical festival, and Augustine understood it as the celebration of an event no less historical than the birth of Christ. In a sermon preached on the day of Pentecost, he says, we are celebrating "the solemnity of a day so holy, that today the Holy Spirit himself came."[33]

For Augustine and other Christian writers the Holy Spirit was a datum of history and a fact of experience. The doctrine of the Holy Spirit took form as Christian thinkers, with the help of the Scriptures, learned to express in words and concepts what they knew. We are accustomed to think of exegesis as an enterprise of drawing out the meaning of a text by determining what the words signify. The interpreter begins with the words, that is, the signs, and seeks to discover the *res*, the subject matter about which the text speaks. But if the interpreter has no knowledge of the reality to which they refer, the meaning will always be elusive. How unsatisfying are the observations of an art critic if one has not seen the painting or a guidebook before one has visited the place. Only as the biblical texts on the Holy Spirit were read in the context of the church's life and worship did they disclose their meaning.

Yet the task of finding the right terms and formulations remained, and in this case Christian thinking was guided by particular words from the Scriptures: "poured out," "given," "abide in," and, most strikingly, "love." Besides passages such as Acts 2, "I will pour out my Spirit on all flesh," two texts stand out: Romans 5:5, "God's love has been poured into our hearts through the Holy Spirit which has been given to us," and 1 John 4:13, "We abide in him because he has given us of his Spirit." In these passages the biblical writers, says Augustine, wanted to say something about the unique character of the Holy Spirit, namely, that it is the Spirit "that make us abide in God and him in us." And because we can abide in God only through love, one can say that *love* is the proper term to depict what is distinctive of the Spirit. It follows then that the Holy Spirit is the "gift of God who is love." What is given enters into the life of the recipient and becomes his own and turns the recipient toward the giver. *Gift* and *love*, as used in the Scriptures, are relational terms and have built into them reciprocity and mutuality.

Augustine, however, wants to say more than that the gift of

the Holy Spirit creates a communion between God and the believer; he insists that "relation" is also characteristic of the divine life. For the Spirit is the "bond of love" and the "communion" between Father and Son, and the sending of the Holy Spirit not only reveals the Spirit's role in bringing human beings into fellowship with God, but also displays to us the love that unites the Father and Son in a divine communion. In some passages biblical writers speak not only of the work of the Spirit in the economy, but also of the Spirit within the life of God. A key text is 1 Corinthians 2:10: "The Spirit searches everything, even the depths of God. For what human being knows what is truly human except the human spirit that is within? So also no one truly comprehends what is truly God's except the Spirit of God." In his book on the Holy Spirit, written in the late fourth century, Basil interpreted this text (he cites it twice) along lines similar to those pioneered by Tertullian in his discussion of the word. He writes, "But the greatest proof that the Spirit is one with the Father and the Son is that He is said to have the same relationship to God as the spirit within us has to us."[34] As God is revealed in human beings, so is the life of God.

Hilary's phrase "not a solitary God" was felicitous. In its original setting it was a tentative effort to find a way of explaining why after the coming of Christ it was not possible to think of God as a solitary monad. What we believe in, wrote Hilary, is not merely God but "God as Father," and not merely in Christ but in "Christ as son of God." If God is Father, not only creator, and Christ is Son, not only redeemer, then the relation between them is an essential feature of the divine life. When the words *Father* and *Son* are spoken, said Gregory of Nyssa, the listener recognizes at once "the proper and natural relation they have to one another."[35] In the Old Testament the term *Father* appears only occasionally as a term for God, but in the New Testament it is used by Jesus more than 170 times. The New Testament intensifies the identification of God as Father and makes the divine relations constitutive of God. If God is not solitary and exists always in relation, there can be no talk of God that does not involve love. Love unites Father, Son, and Holy Spirit, love brings God into relation with the world, and by love human beings cleave to God.

Finding God and Seeking God

At the beginning of his great work *The Trinity* Augustine cites the words of Psalm 105, "Seek his face always." This verse also appears midway through the work at the beginning of book 9. There Augustine accents the word *semper,* always. He cites the text again at the beginning of book 15, the final book of *The Trinity,* this time in its entirety: "Let the hearts of those who seek the Lord rejoice; seek the Lord and be strengthened; seek his face always." And in the prayer that concludes the treatise he cites it once more, this time adding "passionately" (*ardenter*), "Seek his face always with burning desire."[36] In writing the book on the Trinity Saint Augustine was seeking something more than an intellectual understanding of the church's central teaching.

In the first book Augustine explains to his readers why he had undertaken to write such a long and complicated book. He knew that in dealing with the doctrine of the Trinity, a debate in which Augustine is still engaged, he would certainly not please everyone. Some of the things he said would be misunderstood; in some cases he would not express himself clearly, in others readers would deliberately misunderstand what he wrote. He was also aware of his own limitations; some things he wrote would have to be corrected. Hence he says, "Dear reader, whenever you are as certain about something as I am go forward with me; whenever you hesitate, seek with me; whenever you discover that you have gone wrong come back to me; or if I have gone wrong, call me back to you. In this way we will travel along the street of love together as we make our way toward him of whom it is said, 'Seek his face always.' "[37]

What was Augustine seeking and what did he invite his readers to seek with him? Augustine answers that he "wishes to enter into the presence of the Lord our God with all who read what I write." He is seeking "the unity of the three, of Father and Son and Holy Spirit." This quest, however, he reminds his readers, is unlike any other: "For nowhere else is a mistake more dangerous, or the search more laborious, or the finding more advantageous."

This is an enigmatic sentence. Augustine says that in a matter of such gravity one does not want to go wrong; presumably he means not fall into doctrinal error. When he refers to the labor that the search requires he has in mind the intellectual task that lies before him. *The Trinity* is a demanding book, for Augustine is seeking to express the mystery of the Triune God in words and concepts. "Let us seek to understand," he writes, "*that* the Father, Son and Holy Spirit. . . are a trinity of persons related to each other, and a unity of equal being, asking the help of him whom we wish to understand." "Finding" means understanding, and *The Trinity* is an intellectual effort to comprehend what the church confesses in the creed. Once we have understood, says Augustine, "we will seek to explain what we understand."[38]

Yet Augustine was seeking something more. *The Trinity* is

not an exercise of "faith seeking understanding" as that phrase is conventionally understood. Nowhere except here, he says, would "finding" be "more beneficial," in Augustine's Latin, "more bountiful." What Augustine is seeking is not a theological concept or an explanation as such, but the living God who is Father, Son, and Holy Spirit, the "Trinity that is God, the true and supreme and only God." If one asks, What does it mean to find the one God, Father, Son and Holy Spirit? the answer is not so obvious. Finding means more than simply getting things straight or discovering the most appropriate analogy in human experience for the Triune God. There can be no finding without a change in the seeker. Our minds, he says, must be purified, and we must be made fit and capable of receiving what is sought. We can cleave to God and see the Holy Trinity only when we burn with love.[39]

As we grow in understanding, says Augustine, we think we will reach an end to our search. But the psalmist says, "Seek his face *always*." David is not speaking about knowing God as we know other things, but about intimacy with God, delight in God, loving God, knowing even as one is known. As Saint Paul wrote, "If anybody thinks he knows anything, he does not yet know as he ought to know. But anyone who loves God, this person is known by him" (1 Cor. 8:2–3). As we come to know the God we seek, we discover that finding leads to further seeking. Maturity does not mean arriving, but "stretching out eagerly to what lies ahead" (Phil. 3:13). "Let us then," says Augustine, "seek as those who are going to find, and find as those who are going to go on seeking." With an uncanny eye for just the right text Augustine quotes the book of Sirach: "When a man has finished, then it is that he is beginning" (Sir. 18:7).[40]

When Augustine returns to the words of the psalm, "Seek his face always," in the final prayer, he says, "I have sought you intellectually" and "I have argued much and toiled much." But then he adds, "Give me the strength to seek you," for as "you have caused yourself to be found," you have given me hope of finding you "more and more," of remembering you, understanding you, and loving you: "When we do attain to you, there will be an end to these many things which we say and do not attain, and you will remain one, yet all in all, and we shall say one thing praising you in unison, even ourselves also being made one in you."[41]

Chapter 5

Not My Will But Thine

And [Jesus] withdrew from them about a stone's throw,
and knelt down and prayed,
"Father, if thou art willing, remove this cup from me;
nevertheless not my will, but thine, be done."

LUKE 22:41–42

THE EARLY CHRISTIANS, it is sometimes alleged, were given to squabbling over picayune points of doctrine. In the great debate over the doctrine of the Trinity in the fourth century, the issue seemed to turn on a single letter, the Greek iota, what Edward Gibbon called a "furious contest" over a diphthong. Was the Son of "like substance" with the Father, using a Greek word with an iota (*omoiousion*), or of the "same substance" with the Father, using a Greek word without an iota (*omoousion*)? Yet the iota signified a genuine, not contrived, difference over a matter of great moment, and the adoption of "same substance with the Father" instead of "like substance with the Father," no matter how subtle the linguistic resolution may appear to some, did make a lasting difference in the church's faith and life. By enshrining this formula in the creed of the council of Nicaea the church definitively confirmed its belief that Christ was fully God, not an exceptional human being.

As early as the second century Celsus, the critic of Christianity, had belittled Christians because they were divided into competing sects with divergent views. He was speaking of the division between orthodox Christians and Gnostics. In response, Origen made the eminently reasonable point that it was hardly a charge against Christianity that some Christians disagreed with other Christians. Differences, he pointed out, not just on "small and trivial things" but about "the most important matters" were, as any philosopher would recognize, a mark of intellectual seriousness.[1]

Nevertheless, it requires a surfeit of charity as well as refined theological perspicacity to savor the melancholy course of some disputes in the church's history. At no time was this more true than in the debate over the person of Christ that divided the church in the centuries following the council of Chalcedon in A.D. 451. In the fourth century the disputes over the doctrine of the Trinity called forth two councils, the council of Nicaea in 325 and the council of Constantinople in 381. But the controversy over the person of Christ commandeered the intellectual energies of Christian thinkers for several centuries and provoked the convocation of no fewer than four councils, and by some reckoning five. The conflict exploded early in the fifth century, resulting in the summoning of bishops to the council of Ephesus in 431, and did not come to a resolution (and then only for part of the church) until three more councils had been called, Chalcedon in 451, II Constantinople in 553, and III Constantinople in 680–

81. And there is good reason to regard the seventh ecumenical council, the second council of Nicaea in 787, which dealt with the veneration of icons, as yet another chapter in the early church's effort to interpret the relation between the divine and human in Christ.

It is not an edifying history. Few of the protagonists, whether bishops or monks or emperors (and empresses), come off looking good. Yet there were heroes as well as villains, and the issues plunged so deeply into the heart of Christian belief that they recur again and again even to this day, for example, in the tension between the Christ of faith and the Jesus of history. In its simplest form what drove the controversy was a question at the center of Christian life: If Christ was fully God, "of the same substance" with God the Father, as the councils had confessed in the fourth century, in what sense is he fully human? No one doubted that Christ was human. The gospels made this clear. Speaking of Jesus as a child, Luke wrote, "Jesus increased in wisdom and in stature" (Luke 2:52). Yet it was one thing to say, "the Word became flesh," that is, God became man, and quite another to find words to express what this means for the understanding of Jesus of Nazareth, the person depicted in the gospels.

No matter how tawdry the politics or unforgiving the polemics, in any account of the formation of the Christian intellectual tradition the church's meditation on the person of Christ in the long centuries after Chalcedon cannot be bypassed. It is, however, a large, complicated story that goes far beyond the ambitions of this book. Yet it extends an occasion to consider another way in which Christian teaching was formed by the evangelical history. One way to lay bare the nerve of the matter is to focus on a moment in the seventh century when the debate took a singular turn to center on an incident in the gospels, what in the early church was called the "agony of Christ,"[2] Christ's petition that the Father remove the cup of suffering from him (Luke 22:39–42 and parallels). In particularly acute form this passage highlighted the will of Christ ("not my will but thine be done") and invited Christian thinkers to ponder the nature of Christ's humanity in all its concreteness. Did Christ have a human will? or was his will the will of the eternal Son of God, that is, the divine will? The topic may appear arcane, yet in the debate Christian thinkers of the time, by attending closely to a single event in Christ's life, were able to express the nature of Christ's humanity more clearly than any had done earlier. This meant turning again and again to the same event, considering it ever more closely, viewing it this way, then that, being drawn as it were into the event itself. As reason penetrated more deeply into the evangelical history, its imaginative powers were unleashed. The monothelite (one will) controversy, as the dispute is called, was also a compelling human drama that pitted a monk and a pope against the emperor and tested the meaning of fidelity to Christ in ways that were reminiscent of the age of the martyrs. Unlike other disputes, this one is memorable not only for what was achieved but for the courage and steadfastness of those who achieved it.

Mary Mother of God

The monk was Maximus the Confessor, the pope was Martin I, and the emperor was Constans II, and each had a part to play. What Maximus the theologian accomplished could not have been done without the support of Martin, but it was the monk's keen, irresistible intelligence as well as his spiritual depth that give the tragic events enduring intellectual significance. Some perspective on the debate can be gained by briefly retracing developments at the very beginning of Christianity and how they led up to the dispute over the will of Christ.

Recall how Saint Paul opens his letter to the Romans: "Paul, a servant of Jesus Christ, called to be an apostle, set apart for the gospel of God which he promised beforehand through his prophets in the holy scriptures, the gospel concerning his Son, *who was descended from David according to the flesh,* and *designated Son of God in power* according to the Spirit of holiness by his resurrection from the dead, Jesus Christ our Lord" (Rom. 1:1–4). In this passage Paul sets, as it were, the boundaries in which Christians would think about the person of Christ. Jesus Christ was a human being born in the line of David and at the same time the Son of God, as his Resurrection from the dead bore witness.

Early in the church's history some Christians found either one or the other of these claims unpalatable. The docetists believed that Christ only seemed to be a human being, hence his human appearance was only apparent, not real. At the other extreme such groups as the Ebionites denied that Christ was divine, claiming he was only a noble human being like the ancient sages or prophets of old. But the central tradition of Christian thought affirmed that Christ was fully divine *and* fully human. The debate over the person of Christ that erupted in the fifth century was a genuine effort of thinkers who lived by the church's faith to clarify the relation between the divine and human in Christ. No doubt this is one reason the arguments were so intense and the name calling so intemperate.

One of the first signs of fissures at the highest level of the church's leadership appeared early in the fifth century when Nestorius, bishop of Constantinople, somewhat imprudently cast into doubt the term *theotokos*, bearer of God or mother of God, as an epithet for the Virgin Mary. He preferred the term *christotokos*, bearer of Christ or mother of Christ. Nestorius had a point. Though the term *theotokos* had been used by Christians, it had not yet gained wide currency. But Cyril, bishop of Alexandria, realized that the expression *mother of Christ* was inherently ambiguous and thought it should be avoided. *Mother of Christ* did not state unequivocally what the church believed, that in the person of Jesus of Nazareth the holy and ineffable God had been born a human being of the Virgin Mary. In his words, "Since the holy Virgin gave birth to God according to the flesh . . . we say that she is the mother of God."[3]

At the Council of Ephesus in 431 Cyril was able to vanquish his rival, the bishop of Constantinople, but his victory brought no peace, only greater discord. In its wake the council ushered in a decade of political maneuvering and theological negotiations. In 451, in hope of gaining agreement between the various parties, another council was convened at Chalcedon, a city across the Bosporus from Constantinople. By the time the bishops gathered for this council, however, Cyril had died, and his successor, Dioscorus, a much lesser man, lacked the political canniness and theological acuity to carry forward his mentor's policies. The Council of Chalcedon adopted a theological formula that seemed, at least to some, to compromise the teaching of the great bishop. We confess, the decree begins, "one and the same . . . Lord Jesus Christ, and we all teach harmoniously that he is the same perfect in godhead, the same perfect in manhood, truly God and truly man," and acknowledge that Christ is known "in two natures, without confusion, without change, without division, without separation."[4] This statement, formulated under pressure from the imperial court, was a pastiche of terms and phrases drawn from the chief protagonists in the dispute. Its purpose was to bring about unity, but it lacked conceptual cohesion and from the moment of its adoption spawned division. In the long view of history the nice symmetry of "perfect in godhead" and "perfect in manhood," and "one person . . . in two natures" has the feel of balance and proportion, but in the mid–fifth century the decree seemed partisan and one-sided. Chalcedon, alas, was to go down in history as a council of rupture and schism, not of union and concord. Instead of bringing an end to the conflict Chalcedon fueled an even more acrimonious debate that would dominate the church's intellectual energy and the empire's political life for more than two hundred years.

The ostensible difficulty lay in the meaning of the phrase "in two natures." Some had preferred the formula "from two natures" because it more clearly expressed the unity of the person of Christ. "In two natures" seemed to imply that in Christ there were two independent agents only loosely joined. Even though the decree spoke about "one person," to some it seemed to divide Christ into a divine nature that, for example, healed the sick and raised the dead and a human nature that hungered, thirsted, suffered, and died. The real difficulty was that the decree was formulaic and abstract. In what sense was the Christ of Chalcedon the man depicted in the gospels? In an effort to find fitting terminology to express the relation between the divine and human, the council fathers had little to say about the concrete reality of Christ's person, his human consciousness (or soul, in the language of the time), his human knowledge, his will, and his suffering. But it was precisely in the details, how the divine and the human were united in the actual life of Christ, that the most troubling issues lay hidden.

One of the persistent criticisms of the Christology of the early church is that the church fathers, particularly those who were associated with Alexandria in Egypt, were interested in the *fact* of the Incarnation, not in the things that were done by the incarnate Son of God during his sojourn on earth. What mattered was that the divine Son had been joined to human flesh, as in the oft-quoted axiom, "God became man that we might become God."[5] Through the union of God and man in the Incarnation human beings were brought into fellowship with God. Athanasius, the great defender of the divinity of the Son in the fourth century, had difficulty finding a place for a human consciousness, or soul, in his portrait of Christ. Although scholars still debate his teaching on this matter, the vagueness of his language suggests that the divine Word took the place of the human consciousness in Christ. He regularly speaks of Christ's human nature as "flesh" or "body." Athanasius surely believed that Christ was fully human, but when one examines his interpretation of certain events in Christ's life it appears that he conceives of the divine Son of God acting through a human body. What Christ actually experienced as man had but a small role to play in his thinking.

There was, of course, a reason for Athanasius's reluctance to follow out the implications of the gospel narrative. For Athanasius the great issue of the day was the relation of the Son to the Father, that is, whether Christ was fully divine. Like that of other defenders of the Council of Nicaea in the fourth century, his thinking about Christ moved in a vertical direction: Christ as divine, as the eternal Logos, as one with the Father. Though the "fact" of the Incarnation was at the center of his thought, the life of Christ as sketched in the gospels had not sunk deep into his thinking. Passages from the gospels appear often in his dogmatic and polemical works, but they are often "problem" texts thrust upon him by his opponents, as, for example, "Jesus increased in wisdom" (Luke 2:52), "Now is my soul troubled" (John 12:27), or "Of that day and hour no one knows, not even the angels in heaven, nor the Son, but only the Father" (Mark 13:32). The task of integrating the Christ of the gospels fully into the church's understanding of Christ was to fall to a later generation.

Glory in Suffering

Cyril of Alexandria, Athanasius's most faithful disciple and worthy successor as bishop of Alexandria, was a diligent commentator on the Bible, including the gospels. In conventional accounts of the history of Christian thought, however, Cyril is known chiefly for his controversial works against Nestorius. When introducing Cyril in his *History of Dogma,* Adolf von Harnack, the nineteenth-century historian of Christian thought, observed that Cyril knew only how to express his beliefs polemically, and he directs the reader to the three volumes of his polemical writings in the *Patrologia Graeca,* the corpus of Greek patristic literature.[6] What von Harnack failed to mention was there were ten volumes of Cyril's writings, and the seven that he ignored were all exegetical, commentaries on biblical books. Cyril wrote two large commentaries on the Pentateuch, a huge verse-by-verse commentary on Isaiah, another verse-by-verse commentary on the Minor Prophets; there are fragments of commentaries on the books of the Kings, the Song of Songs, the Psalms and Proverbs, and other Old Testament books. His writings on the New Testament include a full commentary on the Gospel of John, fragments of a commentary on the Gospel of Matthew, and a series of homilies on the Gospel of Luke. Cyril is not only a pivotal figure in the development of the church's understanding of Christ, but one of her most prolific biblical commentators. Though he was a vigorous polemicist who touched off the christological controversy by criticizing the teaching of his fellow patriarch of Constantinople, Nestorius, Cyril was much more than an ecclesiastical politician. Cyril's thinking was shaped by the Bible, the fruit of years of patiently expounding the Scriptures verse by verse. In his works one glimpses how the portrait of Christ presented in the gospels began to shape the church's understanding of Christ.

A particularly illuminating example of the subtle shift that was taking place can be seen in Cyril's exegesis of John 13:31–32: "*Now* is the son of man *glorified*." This text was perplexing because it identified Christ's suffering with glory. Jesus had said, "The hour has come for the Son of man to be glorified" (John 12:23). How can this be? According to the Scriptures, the Son of God, the second person of the Holy Trinity, is encompassed by glory. If the son of God is already crowned with glory, how can he be said to be glorified *now?* Texts of this sort received little attention in earlier commentators, and Athanasius seems to have avoided them. Cyril, however, does not balk at the identification of suffering with glory, and in his commentary on John plunges confidently ahead to meet the challenge presented by the words of the gospel. When Saint John uses the term *glory* in this context, says Cyril, it can only mean that Christ is glorifed as man, which, he adds, is something different from being eternally glorified as the son of God. Further, the evangelist indicates that this glory is greater than the glory associated with his miracles. Armed with this insight Cyril turns to the heart of the matter, that the significance of the passage is that Christ's glory is found in his suffering: "The perfect fulfilment of his glory and the fullness of his fame clearly lie in this, in his suffering for the life of the world and making a new way through his Resurrection for the resurrection of all."[7]

Schooled by the fourth evangelist, Cyril realized that suffering was not an unfortunate interlude in the life of Jesus. It is an integral part of God's plan and the necessary fulfillment of the Incarnation. Commenting on "the hour has come for the Son of man to be glorified," he says that after Christ had preached the gospel and done everything to bring men to faith he "desired to pass to the very crowning point of hope, namely the destruction of death. This could not be brought about in any other way than by life undergoing death for the sake of all men so that in him we all may have life. For this reason Christ says that he is glorified in death. . . . His cross was the beginning of his being glorified upon earth."[8]

As Hilary saw clearly, it was the Resurrection of Christ that led Jesus' followers to think about God in a new way. When Cyril writes his commentary on the Gospel of John, he sees another dimension to the Resurrection. The Resurrection was evidence that Christ was a unique kind of man. Christ, he writes, "presented himself to God the Father as the first fruits of humanity. . . . He opened up for us a way that the human race had not known before." Before Christ came into the world "human nature was incapable of destroying death," but Christ was superior to the tribulations of the world and "more powerful" than death. Hence he became the first man who was able to conquer death and corruption. By showing himself stronger than death, Christ extends to us the power of his Resurrection "because the one that overcame death was one of us." Then Cyril adds the sentence, "If he conquered as God, to us it is nothing; but if he conquered as man we conquered in Him. For he is to us the second Adam come from heaven according to the Scriptures." This is an extraordinary statement and to my knowledge unprecedented. Cyril asserts that Christ triumphed over death because of the kind of human being he was. His human nature makes Christ unique.[9]

By immersing himself in the gospels Cyril discerned that what set Christ apart was what he did as man. Though he was like us in every respect save sin, he was not an "ordinary man" or a "mere man," but the man come from heaven, the new Adam who showed humankind a way that no human being had trod before him. This insight into Christ's humanity allowed Cyril to bring the eternal Son of God into intimate relation with the Christ of the gospels, indeed, to see Christ as the divine Son in human form. As Cyril made his way through the events of Christ's life, two moments stood out, Christ's passion, his moment of "glory," and his Resurrection from the dead, when "human nature made a second beginning." Two centuries later Maximus, building on this foundation, would hold up a single incident of Christ's passion, the "agony" in the garden of Gethsemane, to show another aspect of the uniqueness of the man Jesus of Nazareth. Though Maximus was a much more speculative thinker than Cyril, the evangelical history was no less formative in his thinking.

The Church Divided

Maximus the Confessor did not write commentaries on the gospels. Although he was a penetrating reader of the Scriptures with a keen eye for the deeper meaning of the text, his exegesis is found in brief expositions of biblical passages. Within a very short period, 642–46, Maximus wrote three commentaries on the agony of Christ. His ideas came hot from the forge as they were being hammered out in his mind. He attacked the issue before him not by stepping back to create a leveling idiom of abstract categories, but by allowing the facts of Christ's passion to mold his imagination.

The account of Christ's agony in the Gospel According to Saint Luke reads as follows: "And he came out, and went, as was his custom, to the Mount of Olives; and the disciples followed him. And when he came to the place he said to them, 'Pray that you may not enter into temptation.' And he withdrew from them about a stone's throw, and knelt down and prayed, 'Father if thou art willing, remove this cup from me; nevertheless not my will, but thine, be done.' And when he rose from prayer, he came to the disciples and found them sleeping for sorrow, and he said to them, 'Why do you sleep? Rise and pray that you may not enter into temptation'" (Luke 22:39–46).

This passage had been interpreted many times by Christians, but in Maximus's day and in the monothelite controversy one interpretation especially was on the minds of bishops and theologians, that of Gregory Nazianzus, the mellifluous bishop from Asia Minor who lived in the late fourth century. He was known as Gregory the Theologian to Byzantine Christians. One of Maximus's most important books, *Difficulties,* is a discussion of disputed passages from the writings of Gregory. In his theologi-

cal orations delivered against the critics of the Council of Nicaea, Gregory had discussed the agony of Christ in some detail.
This was not a text of his own choosing. It had been imposed on
him by the Arians in conjunction with another text from the
Gospel of John: "I have come down from heaven, not to do my
own will, but the will of him who sent me" (John 6:38). Taken
together these two passages from the gospels seemed to support
the Arian claim that Christ's will was different from that of the
Father, hence the Son was not of the "same substance with the
Father." When these passages on the will were joined with other
passages from the gospels, for example, "the Father is greater
than I," they implied that Christ was subordinate to the Father.

Gregory had little interest in what the text says about Christ
as a human being; what occupies his attention is what it says (or
does not say) about the relation of the divine Son to the Father.
In his view the passage is speaking of the eternal relation of the
divine *Logos* to the Father. It is inconceivable, he says, that the
Son would not know whether he would drink the cup of his
passion or that his will would be opposed to the will of the
Father. Hence when Christ says, "Not my will but thine," he is in
fact saying that his will is the same as that of the Father. Because
there is "one godhead," says Gregory, "there is one will." "The
passage does not mean that the Son has a distinct will of his own
besides that of the Father."[10]

For Gregory the agony of Christ presented a problem to be
solved, and in this he belongs to the same spiritual milieu as
Athanasius of Alexandria. He approaches the person of Christ
vertically, that is, his assignment was to establish the unity of
Christ with the Father. He assumed, of course, that Christ was
fully man; what this meant for the actual human life of Jesus

Christ, however, remained a matter of secondary importance. The idea that Christ could have a will that was fully human, hence other than the divine will, yet not opposed to the will of God, was beyond his ken. So things would remain until Maximus was forced by the unfolding theological and political drama of his day to look at the agony of Christ with fresh eyes.

The theological debate over the wills of Christ took place in a volatile, charged environment. By the time Maximus was born the church in the East was rent over how to conceive of the unity of the person of Christ. In the generations after Chalcedon the emperor, the patriarch of Constantinople, and other patriarchs and bishops sought without success to find a formula to clarify the decree of Chalcedon and unite the contending parties. The first effort made by the emperor Zeno at the end of the fifth century went nowhere, and a century later even the great Justinian (d. A.D. 565), for whom the religious unity of the empire was a key feature of his political program, failed to unite the defenders and critics of Chalcedon. During his reign divisions that had festered for generations spawned an actual schism that persists to this day among the churches of the East.

At the beginning of the seventh century, as the empire was buffeted by economic troubles within and mounting threats from without, the emperor Heraclius and the patriarch Sergius joined in yet another effort to end the deepening divisions. In contrast to earlier efforts, this time the approach was explicitly theological. Emperor Heraclius, guided by his resourceful if not theologically acute patriarch, proposed that one way of affirming that the "two natures" in Christ were united in one person was to speak about a "single activity" or "single energy." Though

Christ possessed a divine and a human nature, it could be acknowledged there was a single activity in the things he did.

To test the political traction of the idea of a single energy in Christ, Patriarch Sergius sought the advice of a number of learned bishops from regions at odds with the Chalcedonian policy of Constantinople, notably Egypt. When his proposal met little opposition, bishops in Egypt thought the doctrine of one energy could be the basis for reconciliation between Chalcedonians and non-Chalcedonians. In 633 at a festive celebration in Alexandria a detailed theological agreement between the two parties was proclaimed from the pulpit of the cathedral.

But trouble lay ahead. At the time the agreement was being adopted, Sophronius, an elderly and respected monk from Palestine who was shortly to become patriarch of Jerusalem (it was his unhappy task to hand over the city to the conquering Muslim armies in 638), happened to be in Alexandria. He was given a copy of the document and did not like what he read. So respected was his voice that as soon as he wrote Sergius to register his disapproval, Sergius issued an "authoritative opinion" that backed away from the formula of one energy. This document, known as the *Psephos*, attempted to finesse the matter by ruling the term *energy* out of the discussion. To avoid confusion and misunderstanding, it decreed that neither the phrase "one energy" nor "two energies" should be used. "One energy" was too similar to "one nature" and seemed to call into question the teaching of Chalcedon on the "two natures." As for "two energies" Sergius had this to say: "Moreover the expression 'two energies' scandalizes many because it has not been used by any of the saints or eminent teachers of the mysteries of the church.

Further it would have as consequence that one would confess 'two wills' contrary to one another as if on the one hand the divine Word had willed to accomplish the saving passion, and on the other hand his humanity being in opposition had resisted his will."[11]

When Sergius says that the Word "willed to accomplish the saving passion" he had in mind passages like 1 Timothy 2:4: God "wills all men to be saved and to come to the knowledge of the truth." In line with ancient tradition Sergius affirmed that the divine Son in common with the Father and the Holy Spirit willed the saving passion and hence the redemption of mankind. In his passion Christ is acting out the will of the Holy Trinity, but there is no suggestion that as a human being he willed his passion. What was accomplished in his suffering was the fulfillment of the divine will from eternity. Like Gregory Nazianzus, Sergius could not conceive of a human will of Christ that was other than the divine will yet in harmony with it. If one posits two wills, he writes, then one introduces the idea of "two beings who will things that are contrary." In other words, the idea of two wills seemed to be a throwback to the thinking of Nestorius, whom Cyril had opposed and the council of Ephesus condemned. At this point Maximus enters the discussion.

The Agony of Christ

Maximus was born in Constantinople in 580 and educated in the great capital. Historical information on his early years is meager and contradictory, and it is not until he is thirty years old that he comes to historical notice as a secretary at the court of Emperor Heraclius. For a man of his intellectual gifts and spiritual intensity, however, life at the court was distracting and unsatisfying.

He seems to have served there only for a short time, resigning his position in 614 to enter a monastery at Chrysopolis, a city across the Bosporus from Constantinople. He remained at Chrysopolis for approximately six years and then moved to the monastery of Saint George at Cyzicus on the southern shore of the Sea of Marmara, a little east of Chrysopolis. His first works come from this period in his life. Among them is a beautiful little essay entitled *On Love*, which, youthful in thought but profound in feeling, reveals a man of deep humility and fervent piety. One reason Maximus is so appealing as a thinker is that he combines intellectual fireworks with emotional force.

As Maximus was taking his first steps in the religious life in the monasteries close to Constantinople, the Persians, always a threat on the eastern border of the Roman Empire, had begun to conquer the provinces east of the Mediterranean (present-day Jordan, Syria, Turkey). They occupied Jerusalem in 614, terrorizing the Christian population and carrying off the True Cross as booty. Their ultimate goal was the capital in Constantinople, and as their armies drew closer to the city and Persian ships patrolled the lanes that led from the Aegean into the Sea of Marmara, Maximus and the monks of Saint George fled to Cyprus, then to Crete, and finally made their way to Carthage on the coast of North Africa far to the west. By 630 he was settled in Carthage, the city of Augustine's youth, and was to remain there for almost a decade and a half. One wonders whether he came to know the writings of the great Latin bishop while there.

Several years after arriving in Carthage, probably 633, Maximus received a copy of Sergius's *Psephos* brought from Constantinople. His initial response was positive, and it appears he had not yet begun to think carefully about the matter. In an essay on the Incarnation written about this time, however, he does explore the idea that will is an essential feature of Christ's human nature. Through his birth from the Virgin he has become one with us, yet he was without sin: "Because of sin we often rebel against God and our will fights against God. Our will is inclined one way, then another. In Christ, however, being by nature free from all sin, since he was not a mere human being but God incarnate, there is nothing [in his will] contrary to God." And then he adds a provocative interpretation of a puzzling verse from the Gospel of John. When Jesus said, "The ruler of this world is coming, but he will find nothing in me" (John 14:30), he meant that he would find none of the things that display the "contrariness of our will that debases our nature."[12]

For earlier writers, the words of Jesus' petition, "Father, if thou art willing, let this cup pass from me" (which seemed to imply that the Christ could act in opposition to the will of the Father), were understood as hypothetical. Maximus, however, asks whether the second part of Christ's prayer, "Not what I will, but let your will prevail," makes sense if the words "let this cup pass from me" were not spoken in earnest. At the same time he notes that the most significant feature of the account is that Christ did drink the cup. What Christ says is, "Not what I will," but "Let your will prevail." Do the words of Jesus, asks Maximus, express "shrinking back" from what lay before him, that is, refusal to drink the cup? or do they represent a supreme act of courage and assent? For Maximus, Jesus' words express neither resistance nor fear but "perfect agreement and consent." As a man, acting in freedom, Christ submitted to the will of God by conforming his human will wholly to God's will, and in this way demonstrated "the supreme agreement of his human will to the divine will which is at the same time his own will as well as that of the Father." It follows, then, that "in the one who has two natures there are two wills and two energies that conform to each nature. There is no contrariety whatsoever between the two, though the distinction between the two is preserved."[13]

Christ's humanity, then, is most evident in the agony in the garden:

> If the Word made flesh does not himself will naturally as a human being and accomplish things in accordance with his human nature, how can he willingly undergo hunger and thirst, labor and weariness, sleep and everything else common to man? For the Word does not simply will and accomplish these things in accordance with the transcendent and infinite nature he shares with the Father and the Holy Spirit. . . . For if it is only as God that he wills these things, and not as himself being a human being, then either the body has become divine by nature, or the Word has changed its nature and become flesh by abandoning its own divinity, or the flesh is not at all in itself endowed with a rational soul, but in itself completely lifeless and irrational.[14]

Note that Maximus uses almost the same formulation about Christ's will as Cyril did about the Resurrection. Cyril had said, "If he conquered as God, to us it is nothing," and Maximus says, "If it is only as God that he wills these things," then his flesh is "lifeless and irrational." In short, if Christ does not have a human will he cannot be fully human.

The will, that is, self-determination, is the characteristic feature of our human nature, and freedom its supreme token. Hence, if one is to be faithful to the Council of Chalcedon, Maximus argued, Christ had to have had a human will as well as a divine will: "The Word himself shows clearly that he has a human will just as by nature he has a divine will. For when he became man for our sake, he pleaded to be spared death, saying, 'Father, if it be possible, let the cup pass from me' (Matt. 26:39). In his way he displayed the weakness of his own flesh. Those who saw him recognized that his flesh was not imaginary, but in fact he was a genuine human being."[15]

Of course Maximus does not suggest that Christ's human will could have been set in opposition to the will of the Father. Yet he gives full weight to both parts of his petition, the request that the cup be removed *and* the decision to drink the cup and act in accord with the will of the Father. So fully did Christ's will conform to the divine will that his will can be said to be godlike: "It is clear that his human will is wholly deified, in that it is in harmony with the divine will, for it is always moved and formed by it. His human will is in perfect conformity with the will of his father when as a man he says: 'Let not my will but thine be done.' "[16]

In Maximus's hands Christ's act of will became a decisive moment in the history of salvation. It had long been affirmed, following the Scriptures (God "wills all men to be saved" [1 Tim. 2:4]), that the eternal Son of God, in concert with the Father and the Holy Spirit, had willed the salvation of humankind. But Maximus now discerns that at the moment of his agony in the Garden of Gethsemane, Christ the man willed the salvation of the world. He cites the word from 1 Timothy to highlight the distinction between the divine will from eternity (which was, of course, also the will of the divine Son) and Christ's human will in action during his passion. The words "not my will, let yours prevail" were said "in a human fashion" by Christ to his God and Father. This leads Maximus to the triumphant affirmation that Christ by his obedience as man "willed and carried out our salvation."[17]

It is often said that the divine plan of salvation depended on Mary's free assent to the word of the angel. The work of salvation is a work of God, but it could not be carried out without the cooperation of human beings. After Mary heard the word of the angels she said, "Let it be to me according to your word." This fiat, this "let it be done," made possible the Incarnation of the eternal Son in the womb of the Virgin. Maximus proposes that there is another fiat in the gospels, another "let it be done," the agony of the man Christ, in which Christ, by accepting his suffering and death, wills the salvation of mankind. Just as the plan of salvation required Mary's "yes," so it also needed Christ's "yes," for it was only through Christ's passion and death that the world's salvation could be accomplished.

The acceptance of the cup of suffering was Christ's free act. That salvation which the eternal Son had willed "in union with the Father and the Holy Spirit," Christ now wills as a man, and in this way shows himself to be a new kind of human being. The human will is not less human but more human because it is in harmony with the divine will. Like Cyril, Maximus wishes to say that Christ showed us a "wholly new way of being human." Christ's life, writes Maximus, was "new, not only because it was strange and wondrous to those on earth, and was unfamiliar in comparison to things as they are, but also because it carried within itself a new energy of one who lived in a new way."[18]

The Martyr and the Confessor

As Maximus was working out his understanding of the wills of Christ, large events shattered the world in which he had been born. To him the catastrophes in Syria and Palestine seemed to portend the end of the world.[19] By 640 the Muslim armies had swept across most of the lands east of the Mediterranean, cutting off the eastern provinces of the empire from Constantinople and threatening the capital itself. At the same time hopes of a resolution of the theological divisions had collapsed. Instead of unity, monergism (one energy) and its corollary, monothelitism (one will), provoked new divisions. Nevertheless, the authorities in Constantinople issued another statement of faith (the *Ekthesis*) that affirmed the two natures were united in a single will. The emperor Heraclius died in 641, after repudiating the *Ekthesis*, and was succeeded by Constans II, who not only accepted it but tried to impose its teaching on the empire. What Maximus had debated as an exegetical and theological problem became a deadly game of imperial politics. The losers would be in peril of their lives.

Now the scene shifts to Rome, where Pope Theodore (642–49) had begun an aggressive defense of the doctrine of two wills, setting him in open opposition to the emperor in Constantinople and to the patriarch of Constantinople. In the meantime the emperor had issued a new decree called the *Typos*, which imposed heavy penalties on anyone who asserted either the doctrine of two wills or two energies. Theodore was succeeded by Martin I (649–53), who was equally uncompromising against the proponents of one will in Christ. Elected in July, in October he called a council in the Lateran basilica in Rome to discuss the matter. It was attended in the main by bishops from Italy and

Africa, but among its company were several leading Greek clerics and monks from the East and Maximus, who had come to Rome from Carthage. Maximus not only gave intellectual leadership, he was the key figure in gathering patristic references in support of the decree and in editing the acts of the council, which were in Greek. Maximus was neither a bishop, nor priest, nor even a deacon.

The decree issued by the Lateran Council begins by citing the text from the Council of Chalcedon on the two natures, then says, just as we acknowledge in him "two natures united without confusion and division, so also we acknowledge two wills in accordance with the natures, divine and human, and two energies in accordance with the natures, divine and human, and in complete certainty confirm and without reserve affirm that one and the same Jesus Christ, our savior and God, is truly by nature perfect God and perfect man—with the exception of sin—and that he willed and carried out as God and as man our salvation."[20] Earlier decrees had considered the mystery of Christ in ontological terms, but now Christ is also understood historically and existentially. Lateran 649 is not simply a reassertion of Chalcedon; it deepens the understanding of Christ by interpreting the Incarnation in terms of the actual events of Christ's life.

As soon as the council was adjourned Pope Martin sent its results to Constantinople with a covering letter urging the emperor to accept its decisions. The emperor was not amused. At once he sent his chamberlain Olympus as exarch to Rome with orders to arrest the pope. But Martin was able to marshal support and hold off the emperor's soldiers. Several years later, however, Constans dispatched a new exarch to Rome, again to arrest the pope. He found Martin ill in the Lateran basilica, where he had taken refuge. His soldiers entered the church "carrying their lances and their swords and their bows strung with their shields," says Martin. The pope was handed an imperial order that he had been deposed, was arrested, and within days was taken in chains to a ship and sent to Constantinople. He arrived in Constantinople in September, still ill, and, after being detained for three months, was charged with treason against the emperor. To humiliate him further the emperor forced him to stand in a courtyard with the people jeering while his pallium, the two strips of lamb's wool marked with six black crosses worn over the shoulders by the pope, was removed. Then he was led through the city in chains to be kept in prison before being exiled to Cherson, a town in the Crimea. What made his suffering particularly bitter was that his own church in Rome also abandoned him. Though he wrote letters requesting aid and supplies, they ignored his request. In the end they bestowed on him the ultimate humiliation, electing his successor before he died. On September 16, 655, Martin died from starvation, cold, and mistreatment.

The heartrending tale of the deposition, humiliation, imprisonment, and exile of Pope Martin by the emperor, his abandonment by the church of Rome, and his faithfulness to the end have commended him to later generations as a martyr. In fact, he was the last pope to receive that title. At the hands of imperial officials Maximus suffered an even crueler fate. Not only was he imprisoned and exiled for refusing to submit to the demands of the emperor, he was brought back from exile to be tried a second time. This time his right hand was cut off and his tongue ripped out and he was banished to exile in the Caucasus on the eastern shore of the Black Sea. His foes did not want him ever to speak or write again. Because of his courage, vision, and sheer doggedness in proclaiming the church's faith even at the cost of exile and death, in Christian memory he came to be known as Maximus the Confessor.

Maximus's theological insight and boldness raised a conventional theological dispute to transcendent heights. He defended a doctrine that was not enshrined in ancient sources and had been given precise formulation only in his own day at a council called by the reigning pope. There had been no official teaching on the matter of Christ's will, and Maximus's views took form only during the course of the controversy. Yet Maximus knew that what he taught was faithful to the apostolic faith, and once he grasped that truth there was no turning back. "I have no teaching of my own," he said at his trial, "only the common teaching of the Catholic Church. For I did not promote any formula that could be considered my own teaching."[21]

Chapter 6

The End Given in the Beginning

Since the creation came into being at the beginning
through God's power, the end of every thing that exists
is inseparably linked to the beginning.

GREGORY OF NYSSA

FEW PASSAGES FROM the Bible have resounded more thunderously down the centuries than the account of the creation of the world and of human beings in the opening chapters of the book of Genesis, and no words from those pages are more arresting than the first: "In the beginning God created the heavens and the earth." By comparison, other accounts of creation—Plato's *Timaeus*, Lucretius's *On the Nature of Things*, Ovid's *Metamorphoses*—have had but slight influence on thinking about how the world came to be. Like minor figures in a drama they have their entrances and exits, but Genesis stands always at center stage reciting lines that remain fresh and sparkling no matter how often they are heard. The stately sequence of days with the rhythmical and repeated refrain "Let there be . . ." stirs even the indifferent listener.

Years ago I used to visit a very elderly woman to talk, read the Scriptures, and pray, and each time I arrived at her home she unfailingly asked me to read the first chapter of Genesis. At the time I could not understand why, yet as I read the passage again and again with her, the nobility of its language and the hypnotic predictability of the narrative seemed to create a strange and wondrous peace. As Mrs. McCluhan was coming to the close of her life she sensed more clearly than I that where we are tending is hidden in where we are from.

Saint Augustine grounded his critique of Manichaean dualism in the refrain in Genesis that sounds after each kind of thing is created: "And God saw that it was good." In the biblical account the words, "And God saw that it was good" occur no fewer than six times in the course of a few paragraphs. After the creation of light, the biblical writer says for the first time, "And God saw that the light was good." Then after each day's work the phrase is repeated: after the creation of the earth, after the creation of plants and fruit-bearing trees, after the creation of the sun and the moon, after the creation of fish and birds, and after the creation of cattle and creeping things and beasts of the earth. Each day God looked at what he had made and "saw that it was good." Finally, after God had created human beings, he looked at everything he had made, and "Behold, it was very good. And there was evening and morning, a sixth day." From this unforgettable phrase "God saw that it was good," Saint Augustine derived the maxim that whatever is is good.[1]

But it was the word "beginning" in the first words of the chapter, "In the beginning God created . . . ," that most captivated Christian commentators on Genesis. And nowhere is this fascination displayed with more limpidity and artistry than in a series of homilies preached on the first chapter of Genesis by Basil, bishop of Caesarea, in the latter half of the fourth century. Basil's *Hexaemeron* (the work of creation in six days) is a profound meditation on the creation of the world as depicted in the book of Genesis as well as one of the most beautiful and polished literary works of Christian antiquity, a quintessential example of the rhetorical skills of a mature, experienced orator in the golden age of patristic literature. It quickly won admirers. Twenty years later Ambrose drew on Basil's homilies while preparing his sermons on the *Hexaemeron*, and Augustine consulted them before writing his *Literal Commentary on Genesis*. In less than a century they were translated into Latin by Eustathius, a Christian scholar in North Africa.

Basil was a man of many parts. As bishop he took an active role in the defense of the faith of Nicaea, and as a theologian he wrote the first treatise on the Holy Spirit in the church's history. As pastor he built hospitals for the sick and hostels for the poor, supporting them with an extensive network that remained after his death. He composed several rules, that is, guidelines for ordering a monastic community, that are still in use today, and he wrote a charming little essay on solitude that sets forth in simple, well-crafted prose the case for withdrawal from the world. He was a tireless letter writer, and almost four hundred of his letters are extant.

Basil grew up in a large Christian family of five boys and five girls with deep Christian roots. His grandparents suffered during the persecutions at the beginning of the century, and one of his grandmothers taught the children sayings she had learned from the sainted Gregory the Wonderworker, a holy Christian teacher who had lived in the previous century. Such continuity within Christian families over several generations helped spark the flowering of Christian intellectual life in the late fourth century. As a recent student of Basil has observed, "Remarkably few of the well-known Christians of Basil's generation leap onto the historical stage straight from a completely pagan milieu. Christians had been breeding Christians for a long time."[2]

Of the ten children, Basil, the eldest boy, and his younger brothers Gregory (of Nyssa) and Peter became bishops, and the eldest, his sister Macrina, was renowned for her strength of character, holy life, and learning. Her life, written by her brother Gregory, is one of the first lives of a sainted Christian woman, and from the way Gregory depicts her in his book *On the Soul and Resurrection* she was admired for her theological acumen as well as her piety. In the treatise it is Macrina who instructs Gregory about the Resurrection, not the bishop Gregory who teaches Macrina. She has been called the fourth Cappadocian, a Christian teacher who could hold her own with her learned and accomplished brothers and Basil's friend Gregory Nazianzus.

According to Gregory, Basil's homilies on the six days of creation were preached "before a crowded church" filled not only with educated folk but also with workers and artisans, housewives, and a noisy group of young people. It is an improbable scene, the old bishop (the homilies were probably preached a few years before Basil's death) speaking on cosmology, a topic more suited to the classroom than the pulpit, to a congregation more interested in being entertained or getting on with the day's business than in being instructed on how the world came to be.

According to Gregory there were moments when the minds of Basil's hearers wandered and the congregation was unable to "follow the penetrating subtlety of his thoughts." Yet Basil held their attention by sticking to a "straightforward interpretation of the Scripture" and only sprinkled in comments on the views of the philosophers as he saw fit. His goal, says Gregory, was to lead his hearers from the "creation of what is visible and the beautiful things in the world to the knowledge of the Creator of all things."[3]

Basil took the phrase "in the beginning" as a kind of chapter title for what follows and employed it as a recurring refrain throughout the first homily: "'In the beginning God created the heaven and the earth.' I am stupefied when I consider this thought. What shall I say *first*? How shall I *begin* my address?" Echoing the word "beginning" in his words "first" and "begin," Basil plays on the meaning of the word *arche* in Greek. "It is," he writes, a "fitting beginning [*arche*], for one who intends to speak of the formation of the world must set forth the 'principle' [*arche*] that prevails in the order of visible things." In Greek *arche* does not simply mean "beginning," that is, "when"; it can also signify the principle that gives coherence to the whole. Without preliminaries Basil directs his hearers to that principle. The account in Genesis shows that the world did not come into being "spontaneously as some have imagined" but rather was "brought about by God." If one is to understand what is seen with the eyes one must first have eyes to see what the eye cannot see: "Anyone who does not . . . enjoy fellowship and intimacy with God is unable to see the works of God." The study of cosmology begins with the things of the spirit, one reason Moses is such a reliable guide. He is the only man "whom God found worthy to behold Him face to face," and after fleeing Egypt and taking refuge in Ethiopia, Moses spent forty years "contemplating the things that are."[4]

Human beings can search the heavens, measure the distances of the stars, observe their revolutions, says Basil, but unless they recognize "that God is the creator of the universe" they will see nothing as it truly is.[5] If the world is cut free from its creator, it loses its natural axis. The starting point, says Basil, must be that an "intelligent cause stands behind the birth of the world."[6] When it is recognized that the intelligibility of the world is derived from something beyond itself, everything comes into focus. Creation displaces cosmology. When the Scripture says, "In the beginning God created the heaven and the earth" it rules out any form of naturalism. The world is not random or disordered, it came into being not by chance or spontaneously, but by God's wisdom and love.

But the term *arche* does mean "beginning," and beginning implies time. Genesis places the term *beginning* at the head of the account, says Basil, so that no one would think that matter existed before it was formed into the world we know. He is thinking of the traditional Greek understanding of creation, that a demiurge or craftsman formed the world out of shapeless matter. The text that had the greatest influence on ancient views of the origin of the world was Plato's dialogue the *Timaeus*. In it Plato says that the demiurge "took what was visible and what was not at rest but in discordant and disorderly motion and brought it from a state of disorder to one of order." In Genesis, however, "beginning" means that creation was a single divine act in which matter was created as well as knitted together. Matter does not exist without form. "What a beautiful order," Basil writes. "The author of Genesis first sets forth the beginning, so that it might not be supposed that the world had no beginning." By adding the word "created" Moses shows that creation is not "composite," as though "matter" came from one place and its "shape and form from God." Moses does not say "God worked" or "God formed," but "God created." In these few sentences Basil sets forth the Christian teaching that the world was created "out of nothing" by a free and gratuitous act of God: "The creator of the universe, whose creative power is not bound by one world but transcends all bounds, brought into being the vast extent of the visible world solely by the movement of his will."[7]

Beginning also implies end, not only in the sense that the world will come to an end, but that its creation was directed to a "useful end." Creation is the work of God's wisdom, of "artistic reason," not a matter of "arbitrary power" or chance. There is no more challenging doctrine in the Bible than this, that creation is purposeful. Basil recognizes, too, that creation is also an ongoing work of God, and the world is providentially ordered by God's guiding hand. Creation affects things at every later moment. In the beginning God said, "Let the earth bring forth vegetation, plants yielding seed according to their own kind" (Gen. 1:11), and we "still see this happening at the present time," says Basil. As understood by the church fathers Genesis describes the coming into being of a living system that has within itself the capacity for growth and development. God not only formed man from the dust of the earth, says Augustine, but also "provides for the ordinary development of new creatures in appropriate periods of time." Basil echoes the same sentiment in a comment on a verse in Psalm 116 (114:6), "The Lord preserves the little ones": "How could the embryo in the mother's womb . . . be nourished or able to move . . . being unable to breathe," he asks, "if it were not preserved by God's care?" Creation implies ordered novelty and change over time.[8]

Basil shows in addition that creation is the work of the Holy Trinity. When the Scripture says that the world came about by a divine command, "Let there be," this does not refer to the organs of voice or the movement of air, but to God's will, the divine intelligence, or Word of God, the eternal Son of God. Holy Scripture teaches not only that God "willed the creation" but that "he brought it into being with the help of an associate." Further, when the text of Genesis says, "spirit of God," it does not mean the "movement of air." The term *spirit of God* refers to the Holy Spirit, and Basil offers a charming interpretation that he learned from a Syrian whose language, he reminds his congregation, was closer to the original Hebrew of the book of Genesis than the Greek translation he was using. The Holy Spirit is like a bird that covers her eggs with her body and by her body's warmth imparts the vital force that will give them life. In Genesis the Holy Spirit plays an "active role in creation" because the Spirit gives water the power to produce living things.[9]

Although Basil's homilies exemplify how Christian thinking about the origin of the world was shaped by the account of creation in Genesis, the form of the book—homilies delivered before a noisy, restless congregation—imposed constraints on the discussion. Afterward, some (intellectuals no doubt) were apparently dissatisfied with his effort. Shortly after Basil's death his younger brother Gregory of Nyssa wrote a companion treatise entitled *Apology on the Hexaemeron*. In this work Gregory seeks to answer Basil's critics, but it is clear his aim is more ambitious. He wishes to explore certain of the philosophical and cosmological questions in greater depth. Though Gregory begins his essay with high praise for his brother's accomplishment, between the lines one detects signs of sibling rivalry. Gregory is pleased to address the topic without having Basil looking over his shoulder, and he seizes the opportunity to move out from behind the commanding figure of his older brother. Had Basil been alive it is unlikely he would have countenanced his little brother discoursing on a subject he had treated only a few months earlier.

Gregory was a more penetrating thinker than Basil and gave greater attention to philosophical difficulties posed by the biblical narrative. He thought his brother had not adequately dealt with the central problem presented by the account in Genesis, that creation is depicted as taking place over a series of days. What needs to be explained, says Gregory, is how one can make sense of a narrative of the coming into being of the natural world that is *sequential*. For we know by observation and experience that all the individual parts of the world are interconnected. Just as one cannot have life without warmth and water, and birds cannot fly without air, so there cannot be day and night without the light of the sun. It is impossible for one part of nature to be created before the other parts. To put it somewhat whimsically, if everything is not in place certain wild animals would go hungry while waiting for their prey to be created. The idea of a sequential creation is unintelligible to reasoned inquiry, whether the inquirer be a Christian bishop or a Greek philosopher. The church fathers knew that the account in Genesis could not be taken literally.

To deal with this conundrum, Gregory, like Basil, begins with the first words in Genesis. The Greek translation used in the churches, the Septuagint, was made in the second century B.C. In the second century A.D., however, Aquila, a convert to Judaism, had produced a more literal translation. In his version, instead of "In the *beginning* God made the heavens and the earth," the opening phrase was rendered, "God made the heavens and the earth *summarily*." Gregory takes "summarily" to mean simultaneously or at once. Whether the words are read "in the beginning" or "summarily," says Gregory, they convey the sense that "everything was created together" or instantaneously. Here Gregory echoes the views of Philo the Jewish philosopher, who had developed a similar understanding of creation. Gregory puts it this way: "I understand the *beginning* of creation to mean two things. First that in an instant God assembled together the starting points and the causes and the qualities of all things, and second that at the first impulse of his will there was a confluence of the essence of each of the things that exist individually, heaven, ether, stars, fire, air, sea, earth, animals, plants. Each was perceived by the divine eye, and each identified by the Word of his power, which, as Susanna says, 'sees all things before they come into being'" (Daniel 13:42 Septuagint). In God there is a "confluence of will and power," hence what God wills is the same as what happens: "Without any interval of time God's work was joined together with his will. For his power is identical to his will. . . . At creation everything that is God's, his will, his wisdom, his power, and the individual existence of things, is conceived simultaneously."[10]

If the world came into being at a single moment, as Gregory believed, what does one make of the narrative in the first chapter of Genesis, that things were created one by one over the course of several days. He suggests that the succession of days, with the creation of the sun and moon on one day, plants on another, and

animals after that, is to be understood to refer to the connected-
ness of all things, as we might say, to the ecological structure of
the natural world. By presenting a sequence of actions Moses
wants to display the interdependence of the natural order:
"Since the necessary ordering of nature required that things
come to be in a logical fashion, Moses, giving as it were a
philosophical account of nature, was able to explain in the form
of a narrative how each thing came to be. And thus he could, in a
manner befitting God, imagine God speaking the various specific
commands for each thing that came to be." In other words,
Moses presents in a historical narrative what are in fact necessary
natural interrelations.[11]

Within the central argument of Gregory's treatise on the
Hexaemeron there runs a subsidiary theme. Because *logos* inheres
in things, what we see in the created world can be known and
understood: "[God] made all things in wisdom," wrote the
psalmist (Ps. 104:24). Hence the world is purposeful and intelligible. If the world had come to be by chance there would be no
possibility of discovering order in its structure. This is why
David said, "The heavens declare the glory of God" (Ps. 19).
Though "the heavens neither babble nor converse and their
voices are not heard," they nevertheless proclaim that the world
came into being by God's wisdom and was ordered by reason. In
Gregory's interpretation the narrative in Genesis presents a coherent philosophical account of creation.

On the Making of Man

Shortly after Basil's death, Gregory wrote another treatise on
the first chapter of Genesis, *The Making of Man*, this one dealing with the famous text, "Let us make man in our image and

likeness" (Gen. 1:26). His ostensible reason for writing the book was that Basil's homilies had not reached verse 26 and hence had not provided an "investigation of man." Gregory, however, was not one to be content with completing someone else's work. As in his treatise on the *Hexaemeron* Gregory had a larger agenda in mind. He thought it was time for a thorough presentation of the church's teaching on man. Earlier Christian thinkers had dealt with occasional questions concerning human beings, most notably freedom of the will and the soul, but Gregory was the first to deal systematically with the Christian doctrine of man in its fullness.

What is unusual about this treatise, in comparison to other early Christian writings, is that at the outset Gregory sets down the method he intends to pursue. Like Basil, indeed, like all Christian thinkers in the early church, he assumes his discussion will proceed on the basis of an "interpretation of Scripture." And the treatise can be read as commentary on the biblical verse, "Let us make man in our image and likeness." But there is more here than an exposition of the biblical account of the creation of Adam and Eve. Gregory says his aim is to "fit together" what he learns from the Scripture with "conceptions that are drawn from arguments based on reason."[12]

In dealing with the person of Christ or the Holy Spirit, Christian thinkers drew primarily on the Scriptures and the knowledge of Christ and the Spirit gained by participating in the church's life and worship. But in addressing the creation of the world and the nature of man they could not appeal to the Scriptures alone; they had to give a hearing to Greek and Roman philosophers who had written on man and to the scientific and medical knowledge at their disposal. Gregory's discussion will be based on arguments from reason and science as well as on passages from the Holy Scriptures. He draws, for example, on Aristotle's idea of the threefold partition of the soul into the vegetative, animal, and intellectual faculties.[13] At the same time he shows that the Bible speaks of a threefold faculty in man and refers specifically to the words of Saint Paul, "body, soul, and spirit" (1 Thess. 5:23). In discussing the relation between mind and body in human beings he draws directly on the thought of the physician and philosopher Galen.

Gregory does not, however, set up reason as an independent source of truth. In his view reason's role was to aid in understanding what is revealed in the Scriptures. The truths of the Scriptures are not isolated dictums standing apart from everything else; what is written there needs to be interpreted in light of other sources and ideas. Just as Gregory had expounded the sequential account of the creation in light of what he knew about the workings of nature, so in this treatise his goal is to arrive at an understanding of man that is coherent and fits what "appears contrary" to the Scriptures into a unified conception.[14] The truth about man is not a private dogma of Christians, but a truth for all reasonable persons.

As much a rhetor as a philosopher, in the opening sections of *The Making of Man* Gregory gives the impression he is as interested in pleasing his readers with the felicity of his prose as he is in persuading them of the cogency of his arguments. When he turns to his first topic, the creation of man after the creation of the world, he begins with an extended simile:

It is not right that the ruler should appear before his subjects. Hence his kingdom was first prepared and only af-

terward did the ruler appear. After the maker of all had
prepared a royal dwelling place (the earth and islands and
sea and the heavens covering everything like a roof) for
the future king, and a great horde of wealth was stored in
the palace (and by wealth I mean the whole creation, the
plants and trees, everything that has sense and breath and
life . . .), only then does he bring man into the world to
behold its wonders. . . . As he enjoys these things he acquires knowledge of the one who gave them, and by the
beauty and majesty of things he sees he finds traces of the
power of the maker who is beyond speech and thought.[15]

As soon as Gregory has finished the simile of the king he
introduces a second simile, that of a host preparing a feast for
guests. Only after the host has decorated his house, prepared the
couches for dining, and set the table does he welcome his guests.
In like manner God first prepared a "habitation" adorned with
"beauties of every kind," then "brought in man" and allowed
him to "enjoy what was there." If "there was no one to share it"
the world would be incomplete.[16]

Gregory, however, is not simply parading his rhetorical skills;
he knows where he is heading, and he exploits the term *enjoy* to
introduce his central point. In the scriptural passages that use the
word *enjoy* ("God who richly furnishes us with every good thing
to enjoy" [1 Tim. 6:17]), the term refers to delight in the created
world. But Gregory takes the term *enjoy* to signify the enjoyment of God as well as the "good things of the earth." Only
man, whose nature was "more divine" than that of the things, is
able to "enjoy God." Here was a theme so large in its propor-
tions and so cumulative in its effect that it lurks behind every-

thing the church fathers say about human nature, about sin, about redemption, about hope, about human destiny: "What food and drink are to the body, the means by which natural life is preserved, that for the soul is to gaze upon God." Everything else in nature finds its completion in the things that have been made, but human beings find their fulfillment in God. In Augustine's unforgettable words, "You have made us for yourself, and our heart is restless until it rests in you."[17]

When Gregory introduces the passage on the creation of man in Genesis, he calls the reader's attention not only to the words "image and likeness," but also to what precedes them. God said, "*Let us make* man in our image and likeness." Although the world is very great, says Gregory, it was made, as it were, "in an offhand manner" by a "simple command." But when God came to man, he "took counsel before making him." God said, "Let us make man." "What a marvel," says Gregory. "A sun is made and no deliberation precedes. In the same way a heaven. Nothing in creation is equal to these. Something so great is made by a word alone and the text says nothing about when or how or anything about them. So too with every other thing, the air, the stars . . . the sea, the earth, the animals, the plants. . . . It is only when God comes to make man that the maker of all approaches the task circumspectly, preparing materials beforehand for the business of making, and likens his form to an archetypal beauty."[18]

The Christian understanding of man has much in common with earlier Greek ideas: that human beings have free choice, that reason and speech set them apart from animals, that they are social beings. But the biblical doctrine of the image of God set Christian thinking on a different course, as critics of Christianity recognized. Celsus had censured Christians for their belief that man was made in the image of God. "God," he wrote, "does not resemble any other form at all." For the Greeks, man was a "microcosm," a "little world . . . composed of the same elements as the cosmos." Gregory has no quarrel with this, but he believed it was the wrong place to begin, for it misses what is distinctive about human life. What is so great, he asks, about being "an imprint and likeness of the world, that is, of the heavens that go round and round, of the earth that changes, of all the things that they contain which are doomed to pass when that which embraces them is gone?" If human beings are like the things of this world, they are as ephemeral as the grass that flourishes in the morning and in the evening withers: "Remember how much more you are honored by the creator than the rest of creation. He did not make the heavens in his image, nor the moon, sun, the beauty of the stars, nor anything else you see in creation. You alone are made in the likeness of that nature which surpasses all understanding. . . . Nothing in creation can compare to your greatness."[19]

According to the "church's teaching," writes Gregory, what is distinctive about human beings is not that they are like the created world, but that they are made in the "likeness of the one who formed the world." We know ourselves by looking at the face of God. Though human beings have life like plants and sensory activity like animals, they also have the capacity to know God: "When you hear that the Divine Majesty is exalted above the heavens, that its glory is inexpressible, its beauty ineffable, and its nature inaccessible, do not despair of ever beholding what you desire. It is indeed within your reach, for your Maker has endowed your nature with this wonderful quality. God has imprinted on it traces of the good things of his own nature, as one impresses a design on wax." The likeness to God makes man mysteriously different from all other things that are.[20]

Gregory finds evidence of man's uniqueness in the relation between the mind and the body. The mind is "incorporeal" and "intellectual," yet it is able to communicate through the senses. By playing the vocal chords as a musician plucks a string, the mind is able to indicate "movement within." The human voice, says Gregory, is a combination of a flute and a lyre, a wind instrument and a stringed instrument, for air is forced through the trachea, which in turn causes vibrations in the mouth that create the tone and amplify the sound. In this way the mind "makes music of reason." Not only is the mind able to communicate with the external world, it can also receive impressions from outside itself through the senses. There is a vast inner capacity "into which everything that is heard flows." More remarkable, the senses are distinct and convey different impressions, yet the mind is able to sort them out, assigning each its proper place so that they impart knowledge. When one senses honey with its golden color, its aroma of flowers, its pungent sweetness, the senses know that it is not several things, but one, honey.[21]

For Gregory all this is a matter of wonder. That God is ineffable, beyond our powers of comprehension and understanding, was axiomatic for Christian thinkers. "Who has known the mind of the Lord?" asked Saint Paul (Rom 11:34). God's thoughts are not our thoughts, God's ways are beyond our comprehending. But, Gregory asks, who has understood his own mind? Let those who reflect on the nature of God ask themselves whether they "know the nature of their own mind." The mind of man was no less a mystery than the nature of God. We do not know ourselves, said Augustine, for "there is something of the human per-

son that is unknown even to the 'spirit of man which is in him.' "
The mystery of the human mind is evidence that human beings
are created in the image of God: "Because our mind is made in the
likeness of the one who created us, it escapes our knowledge.
That is why it is reasonable to think that the human mind accu-
rately resembles God's superior nature, portraying by its own
unknowability that nature that is beyond our comprehension."[22]

Among the divine qualities the maker impressed on our nature, the most important, says Gregory, is freedom. The measure
of man's uniqueness is the "gift of liberty and free will." In an
almost Jeffersonian phrase Gregory says that human beings are
"free by nature," and in another place, "by nature equal." Gregory was one of the few church fathers to condemn slavery explicitly. It is a betrayal of human nature, he writes, "for man
whose nature is free and possesses free will . . . to be condemned
to slavery." Society's laws on slavery "overturn God's law for
human beings" by "dividing human nature into slavery and
ownership and making human nature at the same time slave to
itself and master of itself."[23]

More often, however, Gregory speaks of human freedom as
moral freedom, the freedom to become what we were made to
be. Freedom, as he puts it, is the "royal exercise of the will," but
will is much more than choice, than deciding to do one thing in
preference to another. It is an affair of ordering one's life in
terms of its end, freedom oriented toward excellence (the original meaning of *virtue*) and human flourishing. As we grow in
virtue we delight in the good that is God. Hence freedom is
never set forth in its own terms, but rather is always seen in
relation to God. Because human beings were made in the image
of God, our lives will be fully human only as our face is turned

toward God and our actions formed by his love. Freedom is as much a matter of seeing, of vision, as it is of doing. We know ourselves as we transcend ourselves, and we find ourselves as we find fellowship with God. Happiness, the happiness that gives fullness to life, will be ours only as our will conforms to God's will. And that finally is found in Christ.[24]

In one place in *The Making of Man* Gregory presents human nature in light of what it becomes in Christ: "The man who was shown forth at the first creation and the one who will be at the completion of things, are the same. For they equally carry the divine image." Even in an essay dealing with the creation of human beings Gregory discovered he could not discuss the nature of man independently of what human nature became in Christ, the man who is the perfect image of God. Again and again in his writings Gregory stresses that the archetypal image of God is the one "born of the virgin." In an Easter sermon he said, "On this day was created the true man, who is according to the image and likeness of God." For Christian anthropology it is a matter of capital importance that in Christ human nature appeared in its original and authentic form.[25]

For this reason it is not surprising that at one point in the treatise Gregory introduces three qualities of human beings drawn directly from the New Testament. The first is logos, or reason, which he takes from John 1, "In the beginning was the Word." The second is "mind of Christ," which comes from Saint Paul, who wrote that one who has received the gifts of the Spirit of God "has the mind of Christ" (1 Cor. 2:16). The third is love, which Gregory derives from the Gospel of John, "By this all men will know that you are my disciples, if you have love for one another" (John 13:35) and the first epistle of John, "'God is love' (1 John 4:7), the fount of love." If love is absent, says Gregory, "the imprint of the image is altered."[26] Almost imperceptibly Gregory here changes the tone of the discussion to depict human nature in light of what it has become in Christ. Christ, as the image of God, figures not only in the restoration of human nature but also in any full account of its creation. Completion and beginning are seen as complementary, in his words, "The end is given in the beginning." Creation is promise as well as gift, and it is only in seeing Christ that we know what was made in the first creation.[27]

Garments of Skins

Promise was needed because mortality had entered the world, and Gregory says the obvious: human beings, as our daily experience bears witness, are most unlike God and show few signs that they are made in God's image. For Gregory the inexplicable contrast between what the Scriptures say about man in Genesis and the stubborn facts of human life was the starting point for talking about sin. How is it, he asks, that the man we know, someone who is "mortal, driven by unruly passions, soon to die," can be the image of a "nature that is uncontaminated, pure and exists forever." What a contrast between the "misery and wretchedness of human nature" and the "happiness of the divine life!" While God dwells in bliss, man is miserable. So different is the life of a human being from God that it seems what is made in the image of God must be "one thing" and what we experience in life "something else." Even the Scriptures, he once mused, seem to contradict what is written in Genesis. For the words "all things are futile" in the book of Ecclesiastes seem an "indictment of creation."[28] How can God be the creator of futility?

Any full account of the "making of man" had to deal with man's unmaking, the fall and the intractability of evil in human life. Midway in the treatise Gregory turns his attention to man's experience in light of his origin and discusses, albeit briefly, the misery of human life. Gregory can speak about the consequences of sin in language no less vivid than that of Saint Augustine: "Because of the guile of him who sowed in us the weeds of disobedience, our nature no longer preserves the stamp of the divine image; it has been transformed and made ugly by sin. Our nature freely chose to act in accord with the evil one. For this reason human nature has become a member of the evil family of the father of sin." Human nature is "enfeebled" and "enervated by evil," and man does not "return from evil to good as easily as he turns towards evil." Human beings are "prone to sin," and sin is "present in us when we are born, for it is written, 'in sin my mother conceived me.' "[29]

Like other early Christian thinkers, Gregory was fascinated by the enigmatic reference to "garments of skins" at the very end of the narrative of creation in Genesis: "And the Lord God made for Adam and for his wife garments of skins, and clothed them" (Gen. 3:21). Moses is speaking, says Gregory, in veiled language, and "skins" should not be taken in its plain sense. When Adam and Eve were "stripped of happiness," they were clothed in garments of skins, that is, subject to death and at the mercy of "unruly passions." All who follow Adam wear the garments of skins. "Adam is, as it were, living in us," says Gregory and "after being stripped of our magnificent garments" we have been clothed in garments of skins. Among human beings no one can be found who "is able to live one day without stain." All human beings "share a common nature with Adam and participate in his fall. For, as the apostle says, 'in Adam we all die.' Therefore, the repentance appropriate for Adam is suitable to all who have died with him." So pervasive is sin that "it arises when we come into existence" and "grows with us."[30]

Sin is always positioned between two certain truths, that human beings, on the one hand, are created in the image of God and, on the other, are destined for life with God. In the thinking of the church fathers, the reality of sin does not eradicate the image that lies hidden beneath the filth that obscures it. Hence when speaking about sin, they preferred metaphors that had to do with defacing or damaging or tarnishing the image: scraping off what was impressed on a coin, disfiguring the beauty of the image, making it ineffective, becoming diseased. After the fall certain aspects of the image remained, for example, reason and freedom, though reason was darkened by sin and human freedom was captive to the passions. The image is "always there," says Augustine, "even if it is worn away almost to nothing."[31]

If human beings are made in the image of God and are destined to be like God, the present condition of humankind is unnatural, an aberration from our true life. One biblical text often paired with Genesis 1:26 was 1 John 3:2: "Beloved we are God's children now; it does not yet appear what we shall be, but we know that when he appears *we shall be like him,* for we shall see him as he is." In commenting on Genesis 1:26, "Let us make man according to our image and likeness," Didymus the Blind, a contemporary of Gregory who lived in Alexandria, observed that "like" in 1 John echoes the word "likeness" in Genesis. "In the passage, 'Let us make man according to our image and likeness,'" Didymus wrote, "God speaks of two kinds of becoming." We are first made in God's "image," and only later are we made in his "likeness." "By advancing to perfection the image becomes the likeness of God which Saint John sets forth when he writes, 'Beloved, we are God's children now; it does not yet appear what we shall be, but we know that when he appears we shall be *like* him' (1 John 3:2). We are already made according to the image of God and we hope to become God's likeness."[32] The words of Genesis encompass the entire mystery of salvation.

Bodies Are Not Ornaments

Human beings have bodies, and Gregory addresses the relation between the physical and spiritual aspects of human life, between the soul and the body. He realizes, of course, that "image of God" does not refer to the body. Yet he thinks it significant that man is not bent to the ground like other animals and stands upright "looking to heaven and to things above." At the same time he rejects any notion that the soul had a life of its own before its life in the flesh. The soul and body were formed together and have a "common" or "single beginning" in the "will of God." It is a theme repeated again and again in early Christian literature. In the words of Maximus the Confessor, "Soul and body are indissolubly parts of the whole human species." To drive home his point he wrote, "The body, after its separation from the soul [at death], is not simply called body, but the body of a man, indeed the body of a certain man."[33]

Although Christian thinking on the body is formed by the account in Genesis, of equal if not greater importance is belief in the resurrection of the body. In the form of the "Nicene" creed adopted at the Council of Constantinople, the final clauses read, "We look forward to the resurrection of the dead and the life of the world to come." Christian thinking about human beings oscillates between the beginning and the end, origin and goal. The hope of resurrection led inevitably to the question of whether the body was part of the definition of the self. The bodily resurrection of Jesus was, of course, a matter of biblical history, but it took time for Christian thinkers to draw out the full implications of the Resurrection for Christian anthropology. For one thing there were texts such as 2 Corinthians 5, "away from the body and at home with the Lord." The story in Luke in which Jesus' body passed through walls also seemed to suggest a different view. And then there was that puzzling chapter 15 of 1 Corinthians. The metaphor of the seed implied that the raised body would be transformed into something as different as the plant is from the seed. Furthermore, bodies were always changing and subject to decay. Which body would be raised? the body of the youth, the middle aged, or the old? In spite of very real intellectual challenges, Christian thinkers affirmed without qualification that in the absence of a body a soul is not a person.

The question of the body was not simply a matter of theological debate. It touched on that most sacred of human tasks, how one is to care for the bodies of those who have died. One of Augustine's least known, yet most fascinating, writings is a treatise entitled *On Caring for the Dead*. It was written in response to a letter he had received from Paulinus, bishop of Nola in southern Italy, concerning a widow who wanted to bury her son at a shrine where the famous Saint Felix was buried. Would it benefit her son, Paulinus asked, to be buried next to Saint Felix? Augustine answers her question in the negative, but, as one reads on in the treatise, it is apparent that Augustine recognized there was something to the widow's wish. For the body is not simply an external or incidental covering for the soul, something that can be disposed of and forgotten. Gregory of Nyssa had the relics of martyrs buried alongside his parents. When one sees the bones of a holy person it is as though the person "were fully present." As the ring or garment of a loved one is treated with love and affection, so we should care for the bodies of our loved ones as though they are the person. Bodies are not "ornaments," says Augustine, that are "fitted from without." The body belongs to the "very nature of man." Why is this so? "Care for the bodies of our dead is an affirmation of our firm belief in the resurrection."[34]

In an enigmatic passage in his *Literal Commentary on Genesis* Augustine suggested there could be no full vision of God without the body. Some had apparently claimed that the beatific vision would be given only to the soul, but Augustine asks, "If the spirits of the departed can be admitted to the highest blessedness without the body, why must they be reunited with their bodies in the resurrection?" Augustine acknowledges that the angels are able to behold God without bodies, but that is not the case with human beings. "For some mysterious reason," he writes, or "simply because it possesses a kind of natural appetite for managing the body," the soul needs the body. "As long as it is not joined to the body," it is not fully itself and it yearns to be united with its body: "Only when the soul . . . again receives this body . . . will it have the perfect measure of its being." The direction Christian thought would take on the relation between the soul and body first appears in antiquity, but the view that the beatific vision was possible only when the soul rejoined the body was more fully explored in medieval times. Saint Bonaventure, a contemporary of Thomas Aquinas in the thirteenth century, put it this way: "The person is not the soul; the person is a composite of soul and body . . . and unless there is soul and body there can be no perfect joy."[35]

The Christian doctrine of the Resurrection shaped Christian understanding of the human person and in turn formed the culture of the West. What Christian tradition bequeathed to our civilization was not, as some suppose, gnosticism or shame over the body, but the psychosomatic unity of the human being. There is no self that is not embodied.

In his *Homilies on the Hexaemeron* Basil of Caesarea said that any consideration of how the world came into being must begin with the God who created the world. Before writing about what could be seen, Moses had spent years learning to see things as they are. Human beings, as Origen wrote, were born with a desire to search out the cause of things and the purpose for which they were made. But it was only as one looked beyond what could be seen that it was possible to discern the reason that inheres in things. For the early Christians the knowledge of the world began with the knowledge of God, and God could be known only in faith, the subject of the next chapter.

Chapter 7

The Reasonableness of Faith

Nothing would remain stable in human society if we determined to
believe only what can be held with absolute certainty.

SAINT AUGUSTINE

THE CENSORIOUS CHARGE that Christian thinking relies on
faith, not reason, is as old as the church itself. As early as the mid
second century the physician and philosopher Galen complained
that it was pointless to engage Christians in discussion because
they never give arguments for what they believe. They only
make appeals to "God commanded" or "God spoke." In *True
Doctrine*, written about the same time, Celsus echoed Galen's
accusation: "Some Christians," he wrote, "do not even want to
give or to receive a reason for what they believe, and use expressions such as 'Do not ask questions, just believe' and 'Your faith
will save you.' Others quote the apostle Paul. 'The world's
wisdom is evil and foolishness a good thing.' "[1]

In the late eighteenth century this ancient reproach was given new life by the French *philosophes*. Scorning any appeal to authority and tradition, they believed the time had come, after centuries of Christian hegemony, to liberate reason from its bondage to religious faith and, in the words of Thomas Jefferson, to "burst the chains" of "monkish ignorance." Reason, which had long been yoked to tradition and custom, could now be autonomous and begin with a clean slate purified by the cleansing acid of critical reason. Only when free of the fetters of accumulated beliefs and practices could the human mind reach its full potential.

With its dogmas, its authoritative Scriptures, its bishops and pope, the church, it seemed, stood astride the path to enlightenment. Christianity, said Edward Gibbon, had "debased and vitiated the faculties of the mind" and ushered in an age of darkness, extinguishing the brilliant flame of the intellect kindled by the ancient Greeks. By undermining confidence in the power of reason, Christianity had smothered the spirit of questioning and investigation. "Truth was finally made hopeless," wrote one modern interpreter of classical thought, "when the world, mistrusting Reason, wary of argument and wonder, flung itself passionately under the spell of a system of authoritative Revelation, which acknowledged no truth outside itself, and stamped free inquiry as sin. . . . The intellect of Greece died ultimately of that long discouragement which works upon nations like slow poison."

One suspects that the author of this last comment has let his imagination and his rhetoric, not to say his prejudices, roam at will, untethered from sources or facts. It represents only passing acquaintance with early Christian literature and little knowledge of the dialogue between Christianity and Greek and Roman thinkers that lasted for six centuries. One of the most remarkable features of intellectual life in the Roman Empire is not only that the church attracted gifted thinkers from the society but also that their writings became the object of serious criticism by the best philosophical minds of the day, among them Galen in the second century and Porphyry in the third. The persistence of argument and debate between Christians and pagans over the course of several centuries lays to rest the view that Christianity undermined confidence in the power of reason. Christian thinkers could not be summarily dismissed. Henry Chadwick, the distinguished historian of the early church, once remarked that in his day Augustine of Hippo was the most intelligent man in the Roman Empire.

No one can read Celsus's *True Doctrine* and Origen's *Contra Celsum* and come away thinking that Celsus, a pagan philosopher, appealed to reason and argument and Origen relied solely on authority and faith. Like their critics, Christian thinkers welcomed debate, appealed to evidence and experience, used reason to weigh, judge, interpret, and explain what was held to be true. And they did this not only in books written to outsiders, but also in essays and treatises written for other Christians. Thinking was part of believing. To cite again the passage from Saint Augustine quoted in the introduction to this book, "No one believes anything unless one first thought it believable. . . . Everything that is believed is believed after being preceded by thought. . . . Not everyone who thinks believes, since many think in order not to believe; but everyone who believes thinks, thinks in believing and believes in thinking."[2]

A century before Augustine wrote these words, Origen, one

of the church's boldest thinkers, had defended his critical examination of Christian teachings and inquiry into "first principles"
by appealing to the universal desire of human beings to search
out the cause of things:

> A desire to know the truth of things has been implanted in
> our souls and is natural to human beings. . . . When our
> eye sees the work of a craftsman, especially if the object is
> well made, at once the mind burns with desire to know
> what sort of thing it is, how it was made and for what pur-
> pose. Even more, indeed incomparably more, does the
> mind burn with desire and ineffable longing to know the
> design of those things which we perceive to have been
> made by God. This desire, this love, we believe, has been
> implanted in us by God. For as the eye by nature seeks
> light and sight and our body instinctively craves food and
> drink, so our mind nurtures a desire, which is natural and
> proper, to know the truth of God and to learn the causes
> of things. Moreover we have not been given this desire by
> God in such a way that it should not or cannot be satisfied.
> For if the love of truth were never able to be satisfied, it
> would seem to have been implanted in our mind by the
> creator in vain.[3]

Faith, however, is a defining term in Christian discourse.
Christianity did introduce something new to intellectual life,
namely, that faith is the portal that leads to the knowledge of
God. Whether one opens the Bible to the story of Abraham,
whose faith was reckoned to him as righteousness, or turns to the
words of Isaiah, "If you believe you will understand" (in the
Greek and Latin versions of Isaiah 7:9), or hears Jesus' invitation

to his followers to believe, or studies the epistles of Saint Paul, who said that gospel is the power of God for salvation "to every one who has faith," in the Scriptures faith is a distinctive mark of a genuinely religious person. The Christian confession begins with the words "I believe," *credo* in Latin, hence is called a creed; a common expression to designate the Christian religion is the Christian *faith*; and the Christian people are called the *faithful*. Why did early Christian thinkers insist that when it came to God and the things of God reason begins with faith?

Trustworthy Witnesses

As every reader of Augustine's *Confessions* will remember, when he was a student in Carthage he had attached himself to the Manichees, a dualist sect that originated in Persia and had by his day spread into the Roman world. Augustine was attracted to their intellectualism and their confident dismissal of authority. "I fell among these people," he wrote, "for no other reason than that they declared they would put aside all awesome authority, and would by pure and simple reason bring to God those who were willing to listen to them." They "pressed no one to believe until the truth had been discussed and elucidated."[4] The Manichees were proud of their emancipation from tradition and boasted they had no need to defend their teachings by appeals to authority or to sacred scriptures. For them reason was sufficient. "We require no testimonies [from the prophets] about our Savior," said Faustus, one of their leaders.

As Augustine came to know the Manichees better, however, he discovered that although they talked a great deal about intellectual prowess, they fell silent when faced with hard questions.

When Faustus came to Carthage, Augustine asked for a private interview to lay his doubts before him, but Faustus offered few answers, and Augustine went away sorely disappointed, even disillusioned. He found Faustus to be poorly educated, "ignorant of the liberal arts," and possessed of a thoroughly conventional mind.[5] The Manichaeans were more adept at deriding and ridiculing the beliefs of the Catholics than they were in offering convincing arguments for their own teachings. Within months of talking with Faustus, Augustine had quit their company and sailed to Rome to seek wisdom elsewhere.

Yet Augustine would not forget the Manichees or his friends who still belonged to the sect; several of his early treatises dealt with their teachings. These works cover theological topics, for example, the Manichaean doctrine of God and the world, the nature of evil, free will, subjects that were part of the stock repertoire of Christian apologetics. But the Manichees also prompted Augustine to address issues that had been discussed only intermittently and unsystematically in early Christian literature. One of these was the place of faith in Christian thinking, and with it the role of authority.

Honoratus was a friend of Augustine's from his student days at Carthage. Although initially cool to the Manichees, at Augustine's urging Honoratus had become a member of the sect, and now some years later, after Augustine had abandoned it, he maintained ties to the group. In 391, shortly after he had been ordained, Augustine wrote a treatise on the Manichees and dedicated it to Honoratus. From the way the argument proceeds it appears that Augustine took up questions that he and Honoratus had discussed when Augustine was an adherent of the sect. The treatise has the provocative title *De Utilitate Credendi,* usually translated as "On the Usefulness of Believing," but it might also be rendered "On the Reasonableness of Believing."

The significance of the title becomes clear in the first two paragraphs. Nothing is easier, writes Augustine, than to claim "that one has discovered the truth." Yet it is more difficult to attain the truth than haughtily to assert one possesses it. The Manichees had manifestly not found the truth, but they persisted in belittling faith and exalting reason: "They mischievously and rashly reproach those who accept the authority of the Catholic faith before they can perceive the truth (which only the pure heart can behold), and by believing are fortified and prepared to be enlightened by God."[6] Religion, however, is not a deduction from what one knows. If one begins with proofs and resolves to hold only what can be proven, one will never have done with beginning.

Augustine's thinking, like that of other Christians in antiquity, began with the facts of revelation, God's disclosure in Christ as narrated in the Scriptures. The creed asserts that God is known through a specific historical person who lived at a particular time and place: "He was crucified for us under Pontius Pilate, and suffered, and was buried and rose again on the third day." Little historical summaries are sprinkled through Augustine's writings. Here is a passage chosen at random from a sermon on Psalm 19: "[Christ] was born, he grew, he taught, he suffered, he rose, he ascended." Through these events God was made known, hence the truth of Christianity was dependent on things that took place long ago in "one particular region of the earth" and "in time." It cannot, however, be established as certain and beyond doubt that the events on which Christian faith rests took place. As John Henry Newman once observed, "It is the same fault to demand demonstration of an historian as to be content with probabilities from a mathematician."[7]

What we know of past events depends on the testimony of those who have witnessed them. Historical events are unique and singular, and one cannot run an experiment to verify whether what is reported is true. When someone says that Cicero killed those who had conspired against him, an event that happened hundreds of years before Augustine's time, it is not proper, says Augustine, to say, "I *know* it"; rather, one must say, "I *believe* that wicked conspirators were once put to death by the virtuous Cicero."[8] Belief, that is, faith, is a constituent part of historical knowledge.

Augustine distinguishes between historical knowledge, which depends on the veracity of the witness, and mathematical knowledge, which is certain and demonstrable. That seven times seven is forty-nine is indubitable and known by anyone who takes the trouble to learn the times tables. But the knowledge of an event that happened in the past, as well as of an event that takes place in one's own time at a place distant from oneself, is always indirect and dependent on someone else's word. The term *believe* signals that one is speaking about knowledge that is probable, not certain. When Augustine wrote his treatise *On the Usefulness of Believing*, he avoided the term *knowledge* for historical "knowledge," but later, when he reviewed his writings as an old man, he changed his mind, not about the nature of historical knowledge, but about the appropriateness of the word *know*. Although the proper term for historical knowledge is *belief*, he recognized that in common usage we use the term *know* for historical as well as for mathematical knowledge.[9] At the same time he wished to maintain the distinction between the two senses of the word.

The distinctive feature of historical knowledge is that it is based on the "testimony of witnesses worthy of trust," one reason *martyr,* the Greek word for witness, is a hallowed word in the Christian lexicon. A martyr is one who bears witness to the Resurrection of Christ by his life as well as his words, and the first martyrs had known Christ and seen him alive after his death. The term *witness (martyr),* however, was also used for those who bore witness to the Resurrection by their words. At the beginning of the Acts of the Apostles when the apostles gather to choose a replacement for Judas, they require that he be someone "who accompanied us during all the time that the Lord Jesus went in and out among us" and was a *"witness* to his resurrection" (Acts 1:22). Likewise, in his long speech in the second chapter of Acts, Peter says that he and the other apostles are witnesses that "God raised up Jesus" (Acts 2:32).

The Inevitability of Authority

Historical knowledge requires witnesses, and witness invites faith, or confidence in the word of the one who bears witness. Augustine, however, also introduces the term *authority* into his discussion of faith. We owe our beliefs to authority, he says. What does he mean? In our vocabulary, authority is often associated with coercion, with power and force, with the ability to enforce laws or impose regulations that exact obedience from us. We speak of submitting to authority and of obeying authority and assume that authority has to do with bending the knee or, in the case of ecclesiastical doctrines, sacrificing the intellect. In Augustine's day the term *authority* carried overtones that differ from our usage. In the Latin language *authority* (*auctoritas*) derives from the term *auctor,* the word for author, and in its original sense referred to the person who guaranteed the validity or authenticity of a will or some other legal document. Authority referred to that quality of a person, for example, a magistrate or testator, that makes it possible to act on the basis of what someone has said. In this sense authority is a common, indeed indispensable, aspect of human life and society. For what we accept and act on as true often depends on the integrity and reliability of someone else. "In practical life," says Augustine, "I cannot see how anyone can refuse to believe altogether."[10]

To illustrate his point Augustine gives an arresting example. A child cannot know with absolute certainty who his father is unless he believes what his mother tells him. Such information cannot be known by reasoning, that is, by a process of deduction from principles or by weighing of evidence. The only way one's father can be known with certainty is "by believing the authority of the mother." For only the mother can know who the father is, and the child must rely on the word of the mother, that is, must believe the mother. Of course with DNA testing this no longer holds true in legal matters, but in the relation between children and parents Augustine's experience is ours. Without faith, that is, without confidence in the truthfulness of others, in Augustine's language, without authority, "the sacred bond of the human race" would be shattered: "Nothing would remain stable in human society if we determined to believe only what can be held with absolute certainty."[11]

The absence of authority in society not only severs the fragile bond of trust that binds people together, it makes learning impossible. How, for example, is a person to learn a foreign language without hearing it spoken by a native speaker? or how can one learn to play the violin without having one's fingers trained by a skilled teacher? I am often reminded of this simple truth when I set out on a Saturday morning to fix something around the house, relying solely on my reason. More times than not I fail to anticipate the difficulties that await me and make stupid mistakes that could have been avoided had a practiced carpenter or electrician or plumber been at my side. Autonomous reason, I have learned, is not the way to keep the house running smoothly.

Augustine, of course, is thinking about how one comes to know God in Christ, but he realizes that there are similarities between learning a trade or raising children and knowing and loving God. If faith in authority is necessary to learn to plow a field, "how much more so in religion." By bringing up these kinds of examples, Augustine wishes to say that the knowledge acquired by faith is not primarily a matter of gaining information. The acquiring of religious knowledge is akin to learning a skill. It involves practices, attitudes, and dispositions and has to do with ordering one's loves. This kind of knowledge, the knowledge one lives by, is gained gradually over time. Just as one does not learn to play the piano in a day, so one does not learn to love God in an exuberant moment of delight. If joy does not find words, if it does not exercise the affections and stir the will, if it is not confirmed by actions, it will be as fleeting as the last light out of the black west. The knowledge of God sinks into the mind and heart slowly and hence requires apprenticeship. That is why, says Augustine, we must become "servants of wise men."

In their smugness the Manichees thought they could reason their way to God without entrusting themselves to those who know and love God. They even refused to rely on the authority of the Bible, ridiculing biblical writers for speaking of a six-day creation, concocting the story of Jonah in the belly of a whale, and claiming that Joshua had stopped the sun in its course. How can one believe the other things written in these books, they said, when they present such absurdities to us? In response, Augustine gives the Manichees an elementary lesson in how to read a great work of literature.

The first task of a serious interpreter is to give oneself to the author. It was a point T. S. Eliot learned when studying Indian philosophy: "You don't really criticize any author to whom you have never surrendered yourself. . . . You have to give yourself up, and then recover yourself, and the third moment is having something to say, before you have wholly forgotten both sur-render and recovery." The student begins by putting himself or herself in the hands of a teacher who knows and loves the work. For the Manichees, however, in an ancient version of the modern hermeneutics of suspicion, the first step was to attack the text with critical questions, "tearing to pieces books which they do not understand," thinking that criticism would lead to under-standing. But, says Augustine, the only way to understand Virgil is "to love him." Without sympathy and enthusiasm, without giving of ourselves, without a debt of love, there can be no knowledge of things that matter. Even though at the outset we may be unable to explain what is to be gained from reading Virgil, we expect to profit from reading him, says Augustine, because "our elders have praised him."[12]

By making authority a necessary part of knowing, Augustine shifts the question away from What should I believe? that is, What teachings should I accept? to the question Whom should I believe? that is, Which persons should I trust? In another early treatise, *On True Religion,* he says there are two ways by which the soul is led to God, by authority and by reason: "Authority invites belief and prepares man for reason. Reason leads to understanding and knowledge. But reason is not entirely absent from authority, for we have to to consider *whom* we are to believe."[13] Here Augustine puts in religious terms what he had said about reading a work of literature. The place to begin is not with the truth or falsity of certain teachings, but with the persons whose lives are formed by the teachings. In matters of religion it is reasonable to begin by following. Augustine is not speaking about blind obedience or leaping into the dark or submitting to someone else's dictates: he is speaking about placing one's confidence in men and women whose examples invite us to love what they love.

Faith in What Can be Seen

Christian thinking is inescapably bound to the witness of others. From those who have gone before we learn to use language in a distinctive way, to perceive the relation between seemingly disparate aspects of Christian teaching, to know what is peripheral and what essential. Those who have gone before teach us how to use such words as *God, Spirit, hope, grace, sin, forgiveness,* and as we grow accustomed to using them we conform our lives and thoughts to those who have gone before. Memory is essential for Christian thinking, and like all memory it is particular and privileges certain moments and events in the Christian past, certain books and ideas, certain terms, and most of all certain persons. It begins with what has been received. Recall the words of Saint Paul: "Now I would remind you brethren, in what terms I preached to you the gospel, which you *received*, that Christ died for our sins . . . that he was buried, that he was raised on the third day . . . and that he appeared to Cephas, then to the twelve" (1 Cor. 15:1–5). One of the most distinctive features of Christian intellectual life is a kind of quiet confidence in the faithfulness and integrity of those who have gone before. In the debate with the Donatists over baptism Augustine observed that even though earlier thinkers did not address the specific questions that arose in his day and in some cases held views that varied from his (Cyprian on rebaptism, for example), the matter under dispute was "tried" by them even though it was not known to them. We are sustained by the saints and trail our thoughts behind the truths of others.

In his work *Sic et Non* (Yes and No) in which he set forth differing views of the church fathers on matters of faith and morals, the medieval theologian Peter Abelard said that one should not judge them rashly. For the Scripture says, "The holy ones shall judge the nations." "We do not," wrote Abelard, "presume to accuse them of lying or condemn them with errors. For the Lord says: who hears you, hears me; who rejects you, rejects me. When we consider our weakness we believe that we lack more grace in understanding than they did in writing, for of these it is said, 'Not you who speaks, but the Spirit of your Father who speaks in you.' "[14]

Authority in Augustine's view does not impose or coerce, it enlightens. Its appeal is to the understanding, not to the will. A good teacher does not strong-arm students or make appeals to status or position ("I am the teacher!"), but earns confidence by experience, knowledge, insight, and, finally, truth. A teacher who repeatedly says, "Believe me" without explaining why things must be so soon forfeits his authority and blocks the path to understanding. In the middle ages Thomas Aquinas put it this way: "If the teacher determines the question by appeal to authorities only, the student will be convinced that the thing is so, but will have acquired no knowledge or understanding, and he will go away with an empty mind."[15]

But Augustine has something more in mind than the relation of student to teacher or disciple to master. He is thinking quite specifically of the nature of Christian revelation and of the God who is disclosed in the Scriptures. In the Bible there are occasions when God is revealed directly to an individual, for example, to Jacob in a dream and to Moses on Mount Sinai. But these are exceptions known only to God and to those to whom he revealed himself. More often in the Scriptures God is known through events that took place in history and the testimony of those who saw and heard the wondrous things that had happened. For this reason, says Augustine, we need "to consider what *men* or what *books* we are to believe in order that we may rightly worship God."[16]

For Christians, however, historical knowledge is not the primary object of faith. "I believe in *God* the Father Almighty," says the creed. Faith lives from its object, the God known in Jesus Christ. This can be seen most vividly in the way the opening lines of the first epistle of John depict *what* witnesses of Christ saw. The letter begins this way: "That which was from the beginning, which we have heard, which we have seen with our eyes, which we have looked upon and touched with our hands, concerning the word of life—the life was made manifest, and we saw it, and testify to it, and proclaim to you the eternal life which was with the Father and was made manifest to us—

that which we have seen and heard we proclaim also to you so that you may have fellowship with us; and our fellowship is with the Father and with his Son Jesus Christ" (1 John 1:1–3). Like Peter and James in Acts of the Apostles, Saint John bears witness to what he has seen and heard. He even adds the graphic word "touched." What he saw and heard and handled was a human being, Jesus of Nazareth, who could be seen with the eyes, whose voice was heard, and whose body could be embraced. In bearing witness to the deeds and words of Jesus of Nazareth, John speaks of things that are not dissimilar to the report that virtuous Cicero killed those who conspired against him.

If, however, one takes a closer look at the passage it is apparent that something else is at work there. Even the structure of the first sentence is odd. When John says that he bears witness to what he has heard and seen and touched, the object of those verbs is not something that can be heard or seen or touched. At the point where he says *what* he heard and saw and touched, he abruptly shifts away from the body of Jesus and says that what he saw was life. And then he adds that this life was eternal and "with the Father." In the phrase "that which was from the beginning," he had alerted the reader to what was coming, but only as the sentence unfolds does it become clear what he means. In looking at Jesus, John saw the eternal Word of God. He saw Jesus with the eyes, but what he saw with the eyes was not all there was to see. For what he saw, the eternal Word of God, cannot be seen with the eyes.

In his homilies on First John, Augustine noticed the unusual wording of this passage. When Saint John says that what cannot be seen with the eyes was handled, he is, of course, referring to the Incarnation of Christ, but, says Augustine, the "Word did not begin then." The Gospel confirms this when it says, "In the beginning was the Word and the Word was God." Hence the phrase "word of life" in the epistle of John has reference to "Christ," not to the "body of Christ which was handled by hands." By becoming flesh, the life that had previously been seen only by the angels can now be seen and heard and handled by human beings. That means, says Augustine, that "the reality that can be seen by the heart alone" can now "be seen by the eyes that it might heal hearts." How clever of Augustine to add the word "hearts." Only because the eye sees the Word made flesh can the eye see what the eye cannot see and the heart love what is not seen. Before Christ's coming, says Augustine, we had the means to see the flesh, that is, to see Christ as a human being, but we did not have the means "to see the Word." After his coming, we can "*see* the Word."[17]

In bearing witness to what happened, the apostles did not simply narrate a past event, as one might, for example, tell others about having seen with one's own eyes the Rose Bowl Parade on New Year's day. What was seen and handed on to others was the Word of Life who was with God in the beginning. Though the Word of Life had existed prior to the Incarnation, it was only when he took on our nature that we could "see" the Word and "behold" his glory. In the church's language the word for this kind of seeing, this kind of knowing, is faith. Without faith there is no seeing and hence no genuine knowledge of God.

Origen grasped this point with typical insight in his commentary on John 2:22: "After he was raised from the dead, his disciples remembered that he had said this; and they *believed* in the Scripture and the word that Jesus had spoken." In his exposition Origen first cites the words spoken to Thomas in chapter 20,

"Blessed are those who have not seen and yet have come to believe." Then he asks: How could it be that those who have not seen and have believed are more blessed than those who have seen and believed? If that were the case, those who came after the apostles would be more blessed than the apostles, which is clearly impossible. The apostles saw *and* believed, for even those who knew Christ in the flesh needed faith to know him.

Origen reminds his readers that doubting Thomas is not the only model of faith in the Scriptures. Faith is more than believing what was not seen with the eyes. Jesus said to his disciples, "Happy are your eyes for they see and your ears for they hear" (Matt. 13:16). His saying suggests that those who have *seen* with the eyes are happy, not just those who believed without seeing. Was not Simeon happy, asks Origen, when he saw the Christ child and "held God's salvation in his arms." Did he not say, "Lord, now let your servant depart in peace for my eyes have your salvation" (Luke 2:29–30). Origen concludes that "faith complemented by vision is far superior to faith through a mirror."[18] The disciples who saw Jesus alive after his death knew him by faith *even though* they could see him with their eyes.

There can be no knowledge of God without faith, for faith is the distinctive way we know God. "Faith," writes Origen, "in the strict sense is embracing with one's whole soul the object of faith at baptism."[19] Even after the Resurrection of the dead there will be faith, indeed, only then will there be perfect faith because faith in this life is always incomplete. Hence we can say of faith what Paul says of knowledge, "Now we believe in part." When the "perfection of faith comes," that which is partial will disappear, for faith will then be complemented by vision. What Origen is driving at is that faith in God is a disposition of the soul by which one enters into the life of God. Hence when God is seen face to face faith will not be expendable, for what gives faith its distinctive character is not so much the way one knows, but who one knows, the living God. This is a point of capital importance. The knowledge of God draws life from its object. "It is . . . the things believed, not the act of believing them, which is peculiar to religion," John Henry Newman wrote.[20]

Where There Is Love There Is Seeing

Though the knowledge of God is intimate and personal it does not come to us directly; it is always mediated, usually through another human being. Whether this be a mother teaching her child the Lord's Prayer, a bishop expounding a passage from the gospels, a missionary explaining the words of the Apostles' Creed, or someone telling a friend how her life has been changed by Christ, the truth that Christians confess is transmitted through other persons, through the Christian community, the church. There is no way to Christ without *martyrs,* without witnesses.

In Christian speech a witness is not a reporter. The mother who talks to her child of Christ does not simply pass on what she has heard, she speaks about what she knows, the Word of Life. The witnesses of Christ's Resurrection not only told people what they had seen, but also spoke of what had happened to them because of what they had seen. They spoke about Christ in them, not only about the person they had known during his sojourn among them and who had appeared to them alive after his Resurrection. When Saint Paul gives a list of witnesses to the Resurrection in 1 Corinthians 15 he mentions only followers of Christ. Indeed, he begins with those who knew him best. In the second century Celsus challenged the veracity of the Resurrection of Jesus on the grounds that all the witnesses were disciples. Why did Jesus not appear, he writes, "to those who had treated him despitefully and to those who condemned him and to everyone everywhere?"[21] It is a reasonable question, and Origen took it with utmost seriousness.

Origen's answer is that Jesus appeared only to those who were capable of knowing what they were seeing. When Christ came into the world he did not simply display himself to men and women as an actor on a stage, "he also concealed himself." God's voice is not "audible to all." Someone who is "hard of hearing in his soul" will not hear God speaking. Christ said, "Let him who has ears to hear, hear" (Matt. 11:15). Consequently, to know the risen Lord is not only to give an account of something that happened in the past. It is an interior knowing that transforms the knower. In meeting Christ alive after his death, Thomas said, "My Lord and my God!" Once one has known the living Lord life will never be the same. It is not enough, Origen explained, to say, "Christ was crucified": one must say with Saint Paul, "I am crucified with Christ." Likewise it is not enough to say, "Christ is raised." One who knows Christ says, "We shall also live with him" (Rom. 6:10). The witnesses to Christ's Resurrection are not reporters who tell of the interesting things that happened one morning in Jerusalem. Without persons who see and believe, God's mighty deeds are only ancient prodigies and wondrous tales.[22]

Martyrs always speak in the first person. When Polycarp was brought before the authorities he said, "Eighty-six years I have served him, and he never did me any wrong. How can I blaspheme my King who saved *me?*"[23] All Christian witness is in the first person, a truth I learned in training lectors to read the lessons in the liturgy. When I began to work with lectors I thought the most important thing was to read slowly and loudly. But then I began to realize that pace and volume were insufficient. Often the readers did not understand what they were reading. This led me to spend time with them studying the meaning of the passages to be read. But then I sensed that understanding was not enough. The readers had to learn to speak not in the voice of Paul or Isaiah but in their own voice—using, of course, the words of Paul or Isaiah. The text must pass through the life of the lector so that it becomes a living word in the present, not a recitation of what someone said long ago. Only then can the lesson be heard by the congregation as the Word of God. As Saint Paul wrote to the Thessalonians, "The word of God which you heard from us, you accepted not as the word of men, but as what it really is, the word of God, which is at work in you believers" (1 Thess. 2:13).

In chapter 1 we saw that Origen distinguished between knowing sensible objects, for example, a tree, and knowing God. To see things in the world, it is necessary only for the eye to fix on the object. Whether the object is a tree or a stone or a river is immaterial, for the act of knowing is similar. But in the case of God there is no object out there, no thing that awaits our perception. The characteristic term in the Scripture to speak of God in relation to human beings is that God appeared. The accent is always on what God does, and when God appears the response of human beings is not, as in the case of things, "Yes, I see it," but wonder, adoration, obedience, and love.

For Augustine, as for Saint Paul and Saint John, obedience and love are closely aligned with faith. At one point toward the end of his treatise *On True Religion*, he says, "Rational life . . .

does not owe its excellence to itself, but to the truth which it willingly obeys." As in many of Saint Augustine's formulations it is a single striking word that catches the reader's attention. In this case it is the little word *obey,* a term that had not figured large in the treatise or in the companion treatise *On the Usefulness of Believing.* Yet, like *faith,* it is an honored biblical word, one that is sometimes coupled with faith in the Scriptures, as in Paul's phrase, "the obedience of faith," used in the first sentence of the letter to the Romans (1:6) and repeated in the final sentence (16:26).

In modern parlance *obedience* and *understanding* seem to have little to do with each other, but Augustine took them to be complementary. Obedience, as the Latin root of the word indicates (*oboedire,* from *ob* and *audire*), is a way of hearing, of hearkening to someone. In a memorable passage in his *Tractates on the Gospel of John* Augustine wrote that it was the "obedience of believing" that made possible understanding. He was commenting on the words of Jesus in the *Gospel of John,* "If a man is willing to do [God's] will he knows whether the teaching is from God" (John 7:17). Faith, as Augustine understood it, is an affair not only of beliefs, but also of things that rouse the affections and move the will to act, with real, not "notional," assent, to use Newman's phrase. One of the difficulties in dealing with the Manichees, Augustine discovered, was that they did not want to understand. Before he could make them "understand divine things," he must first make them "desire to understand."[24] Love must precede argument.

In the sermon on John 7 Augustine cites one of his favorite texts from Isaiah: "If you do not believe, you shall not understand" (Isa. 7:9, Latin). Isaiah is speaking of the kind of faith, he explains, that the Lord meant when he spoke of being willing to do God's will. Faith is not only a matter of trust or confidence: it has to do with the knowledge that draws one deeper into what is known. It is like seeing a light. One cannot see a light without being enlightened, without sharing the light. Believing in God, says Augustine, does not only mean one believes that something is the case, but that one loves God: "By believing we love him, by believing we esteem God, by believing we enter into him and are incorporated in his members. This is why God asks faith of us."[25] Faith throws open the door that leads to the knowledge of God.

"It makes a great deal of difference," said Augustine in one of his sermons, "whether someone believes that Jesus is the Christ, or whether he believes in Christ. After all, that he is the Christ even the demons believed, but all the same the demons didn't believe in Christ. You believe in Christ, you see, when you both hope in Christ and love Christ. If you have faith without hope and without love, you believe that he is the Christ, but you don't believe in Christ. So when you believe in Christ, by your believing in Christ, Christ comes into you, and you are somehow or other united to him and made into a member of his body. And this cannot happen unless hope and love come along too."[26]

The Manichees thought that the way to God was to step back, to pose critical questions, to seek external warrants for belief. But in matters of religion the way to truth is not found in keeping one's distance. It is only in loving surrender that we are able to enter the mystery of God. In the words of Richard of Saint Victor, the twelfth-century theologian and spiritual writer, "Where there is love, there is seeing."[27] Faith, then, is the way of reason. By putting itself in service of truth, faith enables reason to exercise its power in realms to which it would otherwise have no access. It is only in giving that we receive, only in loving that we are loved, only in obeying that we know. As John Donne put it in his famous poem "Three Person'd God," "For I / except you enthrall mee, never shall be free, / Nor ever chaste, except you ravish mee."

[handwritten notes:]

Critrum — knowl.

TS Eliot ⟍ Gerstner

indicia — dad

Chapter 8

Happy the People Whose God Is the Lord

The Holy Scriptures of the Hebrews say, "Happy is the people whose
God is the Lord" (Ps. 144:15). It follows then that a people alienated
from that God [of the Hebrews] will be miserable.

SAINT AUGUSTINE

READING THE SCRIPTURES as an old man Saint Augustine
was drawn to the historical books of the Bible. As a young priest
he had studied the epistles of Saint Paul, and as a bishop he
preached a series of sermons on the Gospel of John, on the first
epistle of John and on the Psalms. In the last years of his life,
however, he found himself rereading the history of the kings
of Israel recorded in the books of Samuel and Kings. What
impressed him most in these books, Peter Brown observes in
his biography of Augustine, "was the manner in which the hidden ways of God had caused the most reasonable policies to
miscarry."[1]

The dream that human beings, guided by reason, tempered by

virtue, and moved by good will, could build a lasting city in this world inspired men and women in ancient times no less than it animates people in our own day. For many this hope seemed to have been realized in the institutions of the Roman Empire. No other political order had been successful in embracing so many peoples in so many countries under one system of government. Even today one gazes in wonder and admiration at the ruins of Roman cities stretching from one end of the Mediterranean world to the other, in Tunisia (ancient Roman Africa) on the southern coast of the Mediterranean, in Turkey (ancient Asia Minor) on the northern coast, and in Syria far to the east. It is astonishing that these cities were once part of a single rule and a common culture. Ancient Rome was unique. It could not only boast of having brought peace and prosperity, stability and the rule of law, but also claim universality and aspire to finality. Its capital was Roma Aeterna, the eternal city that would endure long after others had fallen. As Virgil, the celebrated poet of Rome, had sung, for the Romans the gods

> Set no limits, space or time
> But make the gift of empire without end.[2]

As long as there is civilized life, Rome, it seems, would endure.

As a boy Augustine had committed Virgil's verse to memory. Raised in the certainty that the city of Rome, the empire, the institutions and conventions that ordered the rhythms of society, the Latin language and Roman culture had been there for centuries, Augustine lived with the quiet confidence that the world that was in place would last indefinitely, a belief he held till his death. Augustine could no more conceive of Rome passing away than Americans can imagine our way of life and institutions fading into oblivion or being displaced by another form of government, another language, another way of life. In one of his sermons he referred to the "city that had given us birth according to the flesh," to which he added, "Thanks be to God."[3]

Yet he lived at a time when the institutions he cherished were threatened. In 410, when Augustine was in his late fifties, Rome was sacked by a Gothic army that had marched down into Italy from the barbarian north. To the horror of its inhabitants and the disbelief of citizens all over the empire the invaders looted and plundered the eternal city, and with impunity. Rome had stood for a thousand years; never before had it been overrun by a foreign army. People were stunned, fearful, incredulous. Although Constantinople in the East had claimed the title New Rome, the old Rome, the historical capital of the empire, held their affections and sustained their memories. Rome represented civilized rule, an ancient way of life, culture, and law, the things that make social and civic life possible. "If Rome can perish," wrote Jerome, "what can be safe?" His sentiments were Augustine's.

The sack of Rome was the immediate occasion for Augustine's most ambitious work, the *City of God*. Written during the two decades after the sack of Rome, the *City of God* occupied Augustine's thinking for fifteen years. The first three books were finished in 414, when he was sixty, but the last book was not completed until 426, when Augustine was in his early seventies. Yet the entire work was conceived according to a comprehensive plan, and Augustine remained true to his original conception until the final page.

The *City of God* stands apart from other early Christian treatises. For one thing, it is very long, more than a thousand pages in English translation. Augustine referred to it as "this huge work." For another, it ranges over topics so diffuse and varied that it can almost serve as a handbook of Christian thought. Whether the subject is Christ, creation and fall, sexuality, biblical exegesis or history, political philosophy, human passions, love, prophecy, Incarnation, sacrifice, miracles, suicide, or Christian hope, one will find a discussion in its pages. What makes the *City of God* invaluable, however, is that it is the first treatise to deal in depth with the relation of Christianity to social and political life. In the second and third centuries several apologists had touched on such questions, and Melito (d. 190), bishop of Sardis in western Asia Minor, suggested that there was a convergence between the rise of the Roman Empire and the appearance of Christianity. In the fourth century Eusebius, the first historian of Christianity and biographer of the first Christian emperor, Constantine, had addressed the challenge of relating Christianity to the new political situation in which the Roman emperor was a Christian.[4] But Augustine wrote on a much larger scale and with a keener appreciation that the sacred history of the Bible did not simply continue without interruption in the history of the church. The *City of God* reflects the growing maturity of Christian thinking and provides an occasion to examine how one Christian thinker thought about the community of Christians, the church, in relation to the society in which he lived.

Although the *City of God* was occasioned by the sack of Rome, it is much more than a response to that catastrophe. As the early sections make clear, the book was an apology in defense of Christianity to those who "prefer their own gods to the founder of the city of God." In the first five books Augustine addressed Romans who believed that worship of the traditional gods ensured happiness in this life, and in the second five books, particularly beginning in book 8, he turns to a more formidable foe, the Platonists (whom we call Neoplatonists), who shared with Christians belief in one God but did not think worship of the one God excluded veneration of lesser gods. Even though Christianity was now the official religion of the Roman Empire, there were many critics among the intellectual class. Augustine's book was addressed to such critics as well as to Christians whose faith had been shaken by the assault on the ancient and venerable city. Something like the *City of God* would probably have been written even if the Goths had not sacked Rome.

The *City of God* can be read as a Christian response to Plato's *Republic,* though Plato's work does not figure large in it. In a revealing passage early in the work Augustine alludes to the program of the *Republic.* There Plato had sketched out a rational ideal of a perfect commonwealth, in Augustine's words, "what kind of city *ought* there be." The use of the term *ought* is noteworthy. Augustine emphasizes that Plato had set forth his thinking on what an ideal city would look like. One might have expected Augustine in response to outline his ideal city, contrasting the city of God with the kind of commonwealth envisioned by Plato. But Augustine does not present a model city, a society human beings should strive to build in this world. His city of God is not an ideal but an actual city, a living community to which one belongs. In a telling phrase in one of his letters, he refers to the city of God as a city one enters, that is, a society of which one becomes a part. Though the life of the city of God is oriented toward the future, it is a social and religious fact. In the very first sentence of the *City of God* Augustine says that he has taken upon himself the task of "defending the glorious city of

God against those who prefer their own gods to the Founder of that city."[5]

The *City of God*, then, is not the defense of an idea or a set of beliefs (though much of the book is, of course, a defense of ideas and beliefs), but rather a defense of a community that occupies space and exists in time, an ordered, purposeful gathering of human beings with a distinctive way of life, institutions, laws, beliefs, memory, and form of worship. The most characteristic feature of the city of God is that it worships the one true God. Augustine never defines this city outright, but it is closely identified with the church. The *City of God* was written, he tells us, against philosophers who attack "the city of God, that is, [God's] Church." Wherever the church is, he says, there will be "God's beloved City." The City of God is more than the church because it includes the angels and the saints who have gone before, but there can be no talk of the city of God without the church.[6]

Yet the *City of God* is not a book on the doctrine of the church, at least not in any conventional sense. In his writings against the Donatists, a schismatic group in North Africa, Augustine developed a theology of the church. But his aim in the *City of God* is to interpret Christianity to the Romans, and with that goal in mind to explain how this new community, this other city, relates to the city in which Christians reside. Christ's coming joined people in a more enduring fellowship than the institutions or associations of civil society. Hence Augustine rests his argument not on political theory but on an understanding of the nature of the community whose founder is Christ. The political philosopher Sheldon Wolin wrote, "The significance of Christian thought for the Western political tradition lies not so much in what it had to say about the political order, but primarily in what it had to say

about the religious order. The attempt of Christians to understand their own group life provided a new and sorely needed
source of ideas for Western political thought. Christianity succeeded where the hellenistic and late classical philosophies had
failed, because it put forward a new and powerful idea of community which recalled men [and women] to a life of meaningful
participation."[7]

The Life of the Saints Is Social

Christian thinking about the city of God begins with the Bible. To
introduce the theme of his book Augustine cites three passages,
all from the psalms: "Glorious things are spoken of you, O city of
God" (Ps. 87:3); "Great is the Lord and greatly to be praised in
the city of our God" (Ps. 48:1); and "There is a river whose
streams make glad the city of God, the holy habitation of the Most
High. God is in the midst of her, she shall not be moved" (Ps.
46:4–5). All three of these passages are speaking about Jerusalem,
the ancient city in Palestine, the city of Jewish history, and the city
where Jesus was crucified and raised from the dead, a place one
can locate on a map. But for Augustine the phrase "city of God"
in the psalms also carried another meaning: it designated a company of men and women and angels who are united in their love of
God. His book is about this city; yet to depict this city Augustine
speaks about another city, "the city of this world," the earthly city,
the social and political community that exercises dominion over
human beings. The two cities must be discussed in tandem because "in this present transitory world, they are interwoven and
mingled with one another." The citizens of the city of God are
also citizens of the earthly city, and, conversely, many of the
citizens of the earthly city belong to the city of God.[8]

In the course of his book Augustine refines these initial definitions by introducing the notion of ends, the goal toward which
each city is directed. By *end* Augustine means that larger purpose
that sustains the life of a city. In setting forth the ends of the two
cities, Augustine begins with definitions that were well known to
Roman political thinkers. He draws on Varro, a Roman philosopher, and Cicero the great Roman statesman. In book 2 he cites
Cicero's *De Republica,* in which Cicero defines *community* not as
just any association of human beings, but one "united in association by a common sense of law and a community of interest." Yet
in book 19, his most detailed discussion of the ends of the two
cities, Augustine starts at another place. The end toward which
all human life is directed is peace. "Anyone who joins me," he
says, "in an examination, however slight, of human affairs, and
the human nature we all share, recognizes that just as there is no
man who does not wish for joy, so there is no man who does not
wish for peace." Even when men go to war their aim is to
achieve peace. All our "use of temporal things," he writes, "is
related to the enjoyment of earthly peace in the earthly city."[9]

For Augustine peace is not simply external peace, the peace
that exists between peoples or kingdoms that share a common
boundary. In his view the term also applies to the relations
among members of a family, to the bonds of trust between
citizens in a city, to the laws that make it possible for members of
society to carry on their activities without discord or fear or
danger. Peace means order within society: it presupposes law,
and it requires justice. Peace without justice, he writes, "is not
worthy even of the name of peace."[10]

All the components of society, whether the family, the neighborhood, civic associations, or legal and political institutions, are

directed to a common end, securing and preserving peace. Augustine writes, "Now a man's house ought to be the beginning, or rather a small component part of the city, and every beginning is directed to some end of its own kind, and every component part contributes to the completeness of the whole of which it forms a part. The implication is quite apparent, that domestic peace contributes to the peace of the city—that is, the ordered harmony of those who live together in a house in the matter of giving and obeying orders, contributes to the ordered harmony concerning authority and obedience obtaining among the citizens."[11]

In this passage Augustine is speaking of the peace for which the earthly city strives. *Peace,* however, was not simply a word borrowed from the lexicon of political thought. It was also a key term in the Bible, and it was used in the Psalms of the city of God. The passage that caught Augustine's attention was in Psalm 147, a psalm that speaks about Jerusalem, that is, the city of God: "Praise the Lord, O Jerusalem! Praise your God, O Zion! For he strengthens the bars of your gates. . . . he makes your borders [*fines*] peace" (147:12–14). This psalm teaches us, says Augustine, that the end of the city of God is peace, playing on the term *fines* (plural of Latin for *end*), which also meant borders or frontiers. To which he adds, drawing on a traditional etymology of the name Jerusalem, "Jerusalem means city of peace."[12]

Because peace as end applies equally to the earthly city and to the city of God, it is the pivotal term in Augustine's understanding of both cities. No word, he says, falls more "gratefully upon the ear, and nothing is desired with greater longing." At one level, then, the ends of the two cities are the same. At first this seems puzzling because Augustine has insisted throughout the

book that the two cities have different ends. To clarify the difference he introduces another biblical text, this one from Saint Paul,
that speaks of the end of the city of God as "everlasting life."
Paul writes, "But now that you have been set free from sin and
have become slaves of God, the return you get is sanctification
and its *end*, eternal life" (Rom. 6:22). Augustine will not, however, give up the term *peace* so he settles on the formulation that
the end of the city of God can be called "peace in life everlasting" or "life everlasting in peace." What sets the city of God off
from other communities is that it seeks "the end that is without
end," the supreme good, that "good whereby good is brought to
final perfection and fulfilment."[13]

This peace for which the city of God yearns is a "perfectly
ordered and harmonious fellowship in the enjoyment of God," a
peace of "enjoying one another in God." Notice that Augustine's language is social, not individualistic. He does not say
"fellowship with God," but enjoying one another in God or, as
one translator has it, a "*mutual* fellowship in God." Augustine's
controlling metaphor for the new life that God creates is not, for
example, being born again, but becoming part of a city and
entering into its communal life. When the Scriptures speak of
peace they do not have in mind simply a relation between an
individual believer and God; in the Bible peace is a gift that
human beings share in communion with God. In a hymn to the
church in an early writing Augustine said, "You unite together
citizens to citizens, nations to nations, indeed the whole human
race . . . so that all are joined together not simply as a social
organization but as a family"[14]

Christianity is inescapably social. The philosophers, Augustine writes, had taught that the "happy life is social," that the

virtuous man wishes for others what he wishes for himself. Augustine agrees, but adds, "We insist on that even more strongly than they. . . . How could that City have made its first start, how could it have advanced along its course, how could it attain its appointed goal, if the life of the saints was not social?" Peace can be realized only in community and enjoyed only when all the members of the community share in that good. As always, Augustine rests his discussion on an apt scriptural text, this one from the Psalms: "Blessed is the *people* whose God is the Lord" (Ps. 144:15). In a thought-provoking passage late in the work he says that when the city of God reaches the "peace of God" (Phil. 4:7) there will no longer be enmity, no longer discord, and there will be such mutual trust that "the thoughts of our minds will lie open to mutual observation." This is why the apostle Paul said, "Pass no premature judgments" and added that when the Lord comes "He will bring to light the things now hidden in darkness and will disclose the purpose of the heart" (1 Cor. 4:5).[15]

Things Pertaining to This Life

Everything that Augustine says about the heavenly city *and* about the earthly city is related to peace. But peace, as Augustine understands it, can never be fully realized in this life, for the peace that human beings are able to build among themselves is always fragile, unstable, ephemeral. Accordingly, the Scriptures offer no promises concerning peace on this earth. In the Bible peace is always a matter of hope, and the peace for which the city of God yearns can only be the work of God, not of human hands. According to the prophet Habakkuk, the goal for which we hope cannot be seen with our eyes: we seek it "by believing." "The just man lives on the basis of faith" (Hab. 2:4). If we are to reach this end "we must be helped" by God, who is that very good we seek.[16]

It is possible for some human beings to find a measure of peace in this life, Augustine observes, yet we need only look around to see the miseries that afflict human life: "The attitudes and movements of the body, when they are graceful and harmonious, are reckoned among the primary gifts of nature. But what if some illness makes the limbs shake and tremble? What if a man's spine is so curved as to bring his hands to the ground, turning the man into a virtual quadruped? Will not this destroy all beauty and grace of body whether in repose or in motion?" Strive though we may to secure a safe haven in life, we cannot avoid being "tossed about at the mercy of chance and accident."[17]

What is more troubling, human beings discover they cannot find peace even within themselves. The more we strive for virtue and holiness, the more we discover refractory forces within ourselves that war against our best efforts. What stands in the way of a virtuous life is not what comes from outside, for example, the evils of society or the iniquity of fellow humans, but our own passions and turbulent desires. Even when we seem to achieve a measure of tranquility in our lives, we learn that virtue does not make us immune from pain and sorrow. Human life offers no lasting peace, whether peace among nations, peace within the city, peace in the home, or peace in the inner chambers of the soul. In this life perfect happiness is illusory.

Christians, however, belong to a community of hope whose end lay outside of history. As Saint Paul wrote, "It is in hope that we are saved," and Augustine commented, "It is in hope that we are made happy." As he was fond of putting it, the church is the city of God on pilgrimage "in this condition of mortality and it lives on the basis of faith." In a beautiful phrase depicting the future hope, Augustine says that the "angels await our arrival."[18]

It would seem, then, that the church has little stake in the effort to build a just society. Were the *City of God* to end at this point it would hold much less interest than it does. What gives the book its allure and abiding significance is that Augustine knew efforts to achieve peace on this earth, though fragile and destined to fail, must be undertaken. He illustrates this point with one of the most familiar, yet compelling, stories in the book. What shall we say, he asks, about a judge whose office is to determine the fate of men and women who come before him, knowing all the while that he cannot see into the minds of the people he judges? How can he be certain that his judgments are just? Will he not on occasion condemn an innocent person out of ignorance?

What is the judge to do, asks Augustine? In the absence of indisputable evidence, should he refuse to judge? Augustine writes, "In view of the darkness that attends the life of human society, will our wise man take his seat on the judge's bench, or will he lack the heart to do so?" To which Augustine replies, "He will sit. For the claims of human society constrain him and draw him to this duty; and it is unthinkable to him that he should shirk it."[19]

The claims of human society constrain him! What are these claims? If the ends toward which Christians strive are a matter of hope, and peace is a work of God, on what basis does Augustine defend the action of the judge?

For the first two hundred years of the church's history Christianity was a minority religion in the Roman Empire. The sociologist Rodney Stark, on the basis of statistical projections drawn from random references in the ancient sources, suggests that by the year 200 there may have been only two hundred thousand Christians in an empire of sixty million. By the year 300, however, the number may have risen to more than six million. When Augustine was born in midcentury the total may have reached thirty million; and the numbers were growing.[20] Christians were no longer outsiders. The emperor was a Christian, and Christians were well represented in imperial and provincial offices, on city councils, and in the military.

During the early history of the church the task of running the cities and the empire was someone else's responsibility. In the early third century, Origen thought that Christians should not hold public office. In his view they served their cities best by offering prayers for those in authority and training people to lead lives devoted to God. By our prayers, he writes, "we contribute to the public affairs of the community."[21]

In the fourth century, with the conversion of the emperor Constantine to Christianity and the steady growth of the church, the relation of Christianity to the society underwent a gradual but momentous transformation. Constantine introduced laws that made Sunday a day of rest, thereby creating a new calendar and reordering the life of society to make space for Christian worship. He advanced legislation that discouraged the exposure of infants by indigent parents and saw to it that the public fisc would provide food and clothing to rear abandoned children. He built churches, not only in the new Christian city of Constantinople and the old capital, Rome, but also in Jerusalem, a city that would acquire potent symbolic significance in the public consciousness. As these new buildings displaced the temples built by former emperors the plan of cities began to reflect the presence of Christianity in the life of the empire. The most prominent public building became the church, and to this day one will find a church on the central public square of European cities.

Priests had been a familiar feature of life within the Roman Empire, but Christianity introduced a new kind of priest, the Christian bishop. By contrast to pagan priests, the bishops were not functionaries of the state. Political authorities had no say in their selection. The responsibility of Roman priests had been chiefly cultic, but bishops exercised oversight (the meaning of *episcopos*, the Greek word for bishop) over the community, taught, for example, through preaching and writing, and presided over the church's worship. Most bishops were well educated and were expected to provide spiritual leadership and give a moral example. Unlike the older religious institutions of the empire, the church thought of itself as a single corporate body with a common identity, exemplified in the calling of church councils and in the extensive correspondence between bishops. As leaders of an alternate society—another city, if you will—the bishops became players in the social and political life of the empire.

By Augustine's day, Christians did not have the luxury of contributing to the commonweal solely by their prayers. Without the participation of Christians, the cities would lack qualified people to serve as magistrates, judges, civic officials, teachers, soldiers. Among some of Augustine's most interesting letters are those written to civil and military officials who were Christians, men who were no less engaged in preserving the peace of the earthly city than their fellow citizens. They too had a stake in the rule of law, in stability, in order, in civic concord, in good relations with the peoples who lived on the borders of the Roman Empire, in short, in earthly peace.

A few examples from Augustine's correspondence illustrate the point.[22] Augustine had a warm relation with Boniface, a Roman general and Catholic Christian who had spent his life in military service. Late in Augustine's life Boniface had been stationed on the southern border of the province of Africa with a small force of soldiers charged to protect the frontiers of the empire from hostile tribes threatening the stability of the region. When Boniface's wife died he considered giving up "all public business . . . to retire in holy retreat," that is, to become a monk. One would have thought that Augustine, who had encouraged others to enter a monastery, would applaud Boniface's decision, but instead he strongly urged him to stay at his post. Decisive leadership was needed to prevent the "ravaging of Africa." As a Christian it was Boniface's responsibility to ensure the safety of the society, not to retire from public life and devote himself to a life of prayer.

In another letter, this one written in 422 or 423, when Augustine was almost seventy years old, he wrote to his friend the bishop Alypius of Thagaste, Augustine's hometown, about a problem close to home. Slave traders had invaded the province and moved about in gangs in military dress terrorizing the populace in rural and sparsely populated areas and forcibly carrying off children and some adults to be sold as slaves. These slave traders had become so numerous, Augustine says, that they were emptying the province of able people and selling them as merchandise across the sea. Augustine tells Alypius about a young girl who had been abducted from her home by night in the presence of her parents and brothers.

What makes the letter so revealing is that Augustine took care to ground his opposition to the slave traders in Roman law, and at the same time, as a Christian bishop he complained that the punishment for the offense, flogging with leather thongs, was too harsh. Hence it was not being enforced. Further, he thought the law was not specific enough because it was vague about the more serious offense of these traders, selling persons who were supposed to be free and in effect making slaves of them. Augustine even appends a copy of the law in his letter to Alypius, though he suggests that what is needed is a revised law that included a financial penalty.

As citizens of the heavenly city, Christians knew that the yearnings of the human heart could be satisfied only in God and the hope for peace would be realized only in fellowship with God. Yet, in this life, when the city of God is on pilgrimage, Christians were full citizens of the communities in which they lived. Like other citizens they cherished law, stability, concord. But these goods were not possible without coercion, and Augustine recognized that in this fallen world human beings could not live together without some form of coercion. This is the reason, he writes, for "the power of the king, the power of the sword exercised by a judge, the talon of the executioner, the weapons of the soldier, the discipline of a lord, and the firmness of a good father. All these have their methods, their causes, their reasons, their usefulness. While these are feared, the wicked are kept within bounds and the good live more peacefully among the wicked."[23]

The Scriptures promise a peace in which there will no longer be the "necessary duty" of ordering society by coercion.[24] Until we arrive at this state of peace, however, the citizens of the two cities hold certain things in common; they differ in how they use these things. That is, Christians view the laws, political institutions, social practices and customs in light of a fuller, more perfect order, never as ends in themselves. All political institutions are provisional, and the city of God brings no grand projects to completion.

Yet, as the examples above indicate, the city of God must "make use of earthly and temporal things." For this reason Augustine says that there is a "coming together of human wills," an agreement whereby the citizens of the city of God join with the inhabitants of the earthly city "about things pertaining to mortal life." In Augustine's mind this conjunction is always prudential, limited "to the giving and obeying of orders . . . about things pertaining to mortal life." The city of God views the peace brought about by the laws and institutions of the earthly city in relation "to the heavenly peace" that is truly peaceful. The customs and practices of society can be embraced as long as they do not misshape the souls of the faithful or detract them from their ultimate goal of fellowship with God and with one another in God.[25]

Although citizens of the city of God participate in the life of the earthly city, indeed, love and cherish its institutions and way of life, they have no ultimate stake in them: "She [the city of God] takes no account of any difference in customs, laws, and institutions by which earthly peace is achieved and preserved." Here Augustine seems to imply that the city of God has *no* interest in the affairs of the earthly city. Yet he adds one qualification, and it is this qualification that gives the book its punch. The city of God, he writes, "neither annuls nor abolishes" the institutions of the society in which she lives "*provided* no obstacles are put in the way of the form of devotion that teaches the one supreme and true God is to be worshipped." The sentence is unexpected. But a few paragraphs later Augustine supports the argument with a citation from the book of Exodus: "Whoever sacrifices to any god save to the Lord alone will be destroyed" (Exod. 22:20). At the very point in the discussion where Augustine has drawn a thick line between the earthly and heavenly city he says that city of God *does* have an interest, indeed, a religious interest, in the affairs of the earthly city—for even the earthly city must honor and venerate the one true God.[26]

A Just Society Serves God

In book 2 of the *City of God* Augustine had cited a passage from Cicero's *De Republica* about the nature of political communities. The passage reads as follows: a people is defined as a multitude "united in association by a common sense of law and a community of interest." The term used for "law" in this definition is *jus*, the word from which the Latin term *justitia* comes and from which we derive our English word *justice*. Augustine explains that Cicero understood this definition to mean there can be no political community (*res publica*), no common weal, no state "without justice." For where there is no "true justice there can be no *jus*," no law, no equity, no right.

A republic cannot be simply a community of interest; it must be bound together by *jus*, by law or justice. A society united only on the basis of a common interest could just as well be a mob or a gang of pirates. Where there is no justice, only brigandry, lawlessness, and exploitation, there is no commonwealth. But justice has to do not only with the relation of human beings to one another. It also has to do with the justice due God. What kind of justice is it, Augustine asks, that turns human beings away from the worship of the true God? How can someone say that it is unjust for someone to take an estate away from a person who has bought it and give it to someone else, and at the same time say that God is not to be given his due worship? If one does not serve God there can be no true justice. A commonwealth that does not serve God cannot be a genuine republic.

Augustine is not speaking here about god in general, about an abstract, amorphous deity. His book is not a defense of a form of deism; the God of which he speaks is the God of the Bible. Some of his critics had asked, Who is this God you talk of and how is it that this is the "only one" to whom the Romans owe obedience? Augustine shows some impatience at the question. At this time in history, he says, it shows some obtuseness to ask "who this God is." Then he reminds his readers that the one God is well known from the history of Israel (which he has recounted in the *City of God*), from the revelation in Christ, and from the church. Hence the answer to the question, Which God? can only be, "The same God whose prophets foretold the events we now see happening. He is the God from whom Abraham received the message, 'In your descendants all nations will be blessed.' And this promise was fulfilled in Christ, who sprang from that line by physical descent." And, Augustine adds, he is the same God who is acknowledged by Porphyry, the "most learned of philosophers." The God of Abraham and Isaac and Jacob, the God to whom justice is due, is not the private deity of Christians or of Jews, but the one God who created all things and also elected Israel and appeared in Christ. This God commanded that worship be offered "to no other being whatsoever but to himself alone."[27]

The first biblical text to be cited in the opening paragraph of the *City of God* is Habakkuk 2:4, "The just person shall live by faith." In Augustine's Latin this text reads, "Justus vivit ex fide."

The same passage is cited at the beginning of book 19, the most concrete examination of relations between the city of God and the earthly city. What draws Augustine to this text is that it links the justice that is a mark of a genuine commonwealth with the justice due God—exemplified by the just person who lives by faith. Justice, Augustine says again and again, can be found only where God is worshiped. As a just person lives on the basis of faith, so the "association of just men" also lives by faith. Where this justice, the justice due God, does not exist there is no commonwealth.

Augustine then proposes another definition of a commonwealth. "A people," he writes, "is the association of a multitude of rational beings united by a common agreement on the objects of their love." The question, then, to be asked of any political community is, What does it love? This is a characteristically Augustinian and, one might say, uniquely biblical way of putting things. In the words of Jesus, "Where your treasure is there will your heart be also" (Matt. 6:21). A person is what one loves, and what a community loves makes it the kind of community it is. If this definition is applied to Rome, says Augustine, it is clear that Rome is a people and its corporate life is indubitably a commonwealth. But it is a very inferior kind of commonwealth because it does not render worship to the one true God. Because Rome does not give God his due, it is a city "devoid of true justice."[28]

Why is this so? Augustine's answer is that the good for which all human beings yearn, the final end of human life, the highest good, is God. It is only in God that human beings find fulfillment and perfection. If they have no sense of God, they have no sense of themselves. Although it may appear that a political community can form its people in virtue without venerating God, over time its life will be turned to lesser ends, to vice rather than to virtue. For virtue is not simply a matter of behaving in a certain way; it has to do with attitudes and sentiments as well as deeds, with loves as well as with duties and obligations. A society based on lies, for example, will not long endure. If the soul and spirit do not serve God, and reason does not bring the body and its impulses "into relation with God,"[29] a people will not be virtuous. Without the good that is God one cannot have other goods. Only in honoring and serving God can human communities nurture genuine virtue. A just society, then, must be one that "serves God."[30]

Augustine's *City of God* defends a fundamental truth about human beings and about society. Only God can give ultimate purpose to our deepest convictions, for example, the dignity of the human person, and provide grounds for communal life that transcend self-interest. A society that denies or excludes the principle that makes human beings human, namely, that we are created to love and serve God, will be neither just, nor virtuous, nor peaceful. The point is twofold. All human life, not just religious life, if it is to be fully human, is directed toward that good which is God, the summum bonum, the desire of all human hearts, and the Lord of all. Second, life directed toward God is always social. Virtue cannot be pursued independently of other human beings. Out of goodness and love God calls men and women to serve him and love one another as citizens of a city, the city of God. It is as a people, not as individuals, that they are blessed. The peace for which the city of God yearns will be found "in the enjoyment of God" and in a "mutual fellowship in God."

Augustine offers no theory of political life in the *City of God*.

But he shows that God can never be relegated to the periphery of a society's life. That is why the book discusses two cities. He wants to draw a contrast between the life of the city of God, a life that is centered on God and genuinely social, and life that is centered on itself. Augustine wished to redefine the realm of the public to make place for the spiritual, for God. As Rowan Williams, the archbishop of Canterbury, has observed, the *City of God* is a book about the "optimal form of corporate human life" in light of its "last end." In Augustine's view, "It is life outside the Christian community which fails to be truly public, authentically political. The opposition is not between public and private, church and world, but between political virtue and political vice. At the end of the day, it is the secular order that will be shown to be 'atomistic' in its foundations."[31] A society that has no place for God will disintegrate into an amoral aggregate of competing, self-aggrandizing interests that are destructive of the commonweal. In the end it will be enveloped in darkness.

Some have argued that in the *City of God* Augustine makes place for a neutral secular space where men and women of good will can come together to build a just society and culture on the basis of "things relevant to this mortal life." Here there could be a joining of hands of the city of God and the earthly city to cultivate the arts of civilization. For Augustine, however, a neutral secular space could only be a society without God, captive of the lust for power, the *libido dominandi*. He was convinced that in this fallen world there could be no genuine justice or peace without the worship of God. Where a people has no regard for God, there can be no social bond, no common life, and no virtue.

Augustine is defending neither a naked public square nor a disembodied theism. His theme is the worship of the one true God and of the community that worships and serves this God. The city of God is—I repeat—a book about the church and the God of the Bible. It is only in relation to the church and its destiny that Augustine takes up questions concerning the earthly city. Near the end he writes,

> The reward of virtue will be God himself, who gave the virtue, together with the promise of himself, the best and greatest of all possible promises. For what did he mean when he said, in the words of the prophet, "I shall be their God, and they will be my people"? Did he not mean, "I shall be the source of their satisfaction; I shall be every-thing that men can honourably desire; life, health, food, wealth, glory, honor, peace and every blessing"? For that is also the correct interpretation of the Apostle's words, "so that God may be all in all." [God] will be the goal of all our longings; and we shall see him for ever; we shall love him without satiety; we shall praise him without wearying. This will be the duty, the delight, the activity of all, shared by all who share the life of eternity.[32]

Like other early Christian apologists, Augustine realized that it was not enough to make abstract appeals to transcendent reality, to the god of the philosophers, to a deity that takes no particular form in human life. As Newman once remarked, "General religion is in fact no religion at all."[33] The god of theism has no life independent of the practice of religion, of those who know God in prayer and devotion, who belong to a community of memory, who are bound together in common service and share a common hope. Only people schooled in the religious life can tell the difference between serving the one God faithfully and bowing down to idols. For Augustine, defense of the worship of the true God could only take the form of a defense of the church, the city of God as it exists on pilgrimage.

The church is a social fact as well as an eschatological sign. It draws its citizens into a shared public life with its distinctive language, rituals, calendar, practices, institutions, architecture, art, music, in short, with its culture. Though it joins with others to promote the good of society in which it lives, its end is with the heavenly company of angels. "With us," says Augustine, "they make one city of God." That part of this city "which consists of us, is on pilgrimage," and "the part which consists of the angels, helps us on our way." The church is not an instrument to achieve other ends than fellowship with God. It serves society by being unapologetically itself and by bearing witness to the justice that alone makes human community possible, the justice due God. The greatest gift the church can give society is a glimpse, however fleeting, of another city, where the angels keep "eternal festival" before the face of God:

> It is we ourselves—we, his City—who are his best, his most glorious sacrifice. The mystic symbol for this sacrifice we celebrate in our oblations familiar to the faithful. . . . It follows that justice is found where God, the one supreme God, rules an obedient City according to his grace, forbidding sacrifice to any being save himself alone. . . . Where this justice does not exist, there is certainly no "association of men united by a common sense

of right and by a community of interests." Therefore there
is no commonwealth, for where there is no "people,"
there is no "weal of the people."

By offering itself to God as a living sacrifice, the church's life
foreshadows the peace for which all men and women yearn, the
peace that God alone can give.[34]

Chapter 9

The Glorious Deeds of Christ

Give me, page, my quill
that I may sing
a sweet and tuneful song
of the glorious deeds of Christ.
He alone shall be my Muse's theme,
Him alone shall my lyre praise.

PRUDENTIUS

WALKING INTO THE private library of a provincial Gaulic landowner, a Christian bishop in the fifth century felt he had wandered into the towering shelves of a bookseller. The books were arranged in sections, light reading and devotional works in one area and works of distinguished Latin stylists in another. Among the manuscripts were to be found writings not only of Horace and Varro, but also of Christian authors, Prudentius and Augustine. The bishop, Sidonius Apolinaris, expressed no surprise at seeing the writings of two Christians, and one, Prudentius, a poet, among works of literature.[1] Sidonius allows us a precious glimpse of a significant new development in Christian intellectual life.

Before the fifth century few books written by Christians would have been considered literary. There were works of biblical interpretation, essays on theological topics, tracts in defense of the faith, countless sermons, a few works of history, lives of holy men and women, a large body of letters, and other sundry writings. Some Christian writers, for example, Clement of Alexandria and Gregory Nazianzus, had literary ambitions; but most Christian writings were didactic in the broad sense of that term, not literary, that is, works of the imagination to be read for pleasure at one's leisure. Christians wrote to instruct and edify the Christian people and to explain and defend the faith. The genre that epitomized belles lettres in antiquity, poetry, was practiced by very few Christians.

It comes as something of a surprise, then, to learn that a Christian poet, Prudentius, was found on the bookshelves of a wealthy Gaulic aristocrat, and even more, that Sidonius paired him with the great Latin poet Horace. Christianity was beginning to create its own distinctive culture. As Christian intellectual life matured, Christians sought to give expression to their faith in art and architecture, law and politics, and the writing of history and poetry. The first Christian poet was Prudentius. His remarkable achievement offers an occasion to consider one of the ways the new Christian culture presented a public face to society. In Prudentius's verse the love of Christ and love of the Muses embrace, as beauty of language and dignity of form become a vehicle befitting the story of God's sojourn in this world. In comparison to the figures treated thus far he is little known, but he is a pivotal figure in early Christian intellectual life and in the literary and cultural history of the West. Prudentius stands at the beginning of a tradition of Latin literature that stretches without interruption from the fourth century to Dante and beyond.

Aurelius Prudentius Clemens was born into a Christian family in Roman Hispania, present-day Spain, in the northeast province of Tarraconensis, modern Calahorra, in A.D. 348. As a child of the provincial aristocracy he received a traditional education, which meant he studied Latin grammar, rhetoric, then law. When his studies were completed he pursued a career as an advocate, and then, like many others of similar background, he moved to a position in the civil administration. Advancing swiftly, he soon found himself the governor of a province, a post he held on two occasions. Later he was invited by the emperor to become part of the imperial court in Milan, most likely as a secretary in the *scrinia memoriae,* the office that kept records of the sovereign's words and actions. There he remained for some two decades until he retired and returned to Spain to devote himself wholly to poetry.

Prudentius's public career, though distinguished, was in many respects conventional for someone with his background. By his day many Christians from the best families followed a similar path. What sets Prudentius apart is that he was a poet and, more, saw himself as a poet by profession. Some bishops had written poetry, chiefly for didactic or liturgical purposes, but Prudentius was not a priest who dabbled in poetry in his spare time or wrote hymns to be sung in church. He was a layman who thought of himself as having a vocation as poet. In his words, "If I cannot give praise to God by my works, let my soul praise God with my voice."[2]

In a preface to a collection of poetry written near the end of his life he says he wished to be remembered only for his poetry. Others may offer God a "pure and innocent life" or "gifts of holy thoughts," but Prudentius offers his verses:

> Swift iambs I present
> To which I join the quick-revolving trochees,
> For I own no sanctity
> Nor gold to ease the pauper's wants and misery.
> Come what may, I will rejoice
> That feeble lips of mine have sung Christ's praises.

The Earliest Christian Poetry

Christian poetry begins with the Bible. The first verses were psalms and canticles drawn from the Old Testament and used in Christian worship. But even in the apostolic age Christians had begun to compose original works with a distinct poetic structure. Bits and fragments of Christian poems and hymns are scattered throughout the New Testament. Here is a hymn on the mystery of Christ found in 1 Timothy:

> He was manifested in the flesh,
> Vindicated in the Spirit,
> Seen by angels,
> Preached among the nations,
> Believed on in the world,
> Taken up in glory (1 Tim. 3:16).

In the original Greek all the verbs are in the same tense and mood and also in the same person and number. Hence all the endings are the same (*efanerothi, edikaiothi, ofthi,* and so on), and each verb, except for the first, stands at the beginning of the line, as translated here. The lines have a formal structure; they are not simply a series of sentences.

The earliest hymns outside of the New Testament were prose poems, that is, poems without meter, often imitating biblical models. A good example of this genre (though it comes from somewhat later) is the Te Deum, a Latin hymn praising God and celebrating Christ's victory over death:

> You, the glorious
> choir of the apostles,
> You, the admirable
> company of the prophets,
> You, the white-robed
> army of martyrs
> do praise.

As can be seen from these few lines, the hymn employs a strict parallelism in the fashion of the prophets and psalms: "the apostles . . . the prophets . . . the martyrs do praise you." The language of the hymn is drawn from the Latin translation of the Christian Bible, not from the vocabulary of Latin poetry. In its early stages Christian liturgical poetry was almost wholly untouched by the literary traditions of the Greco-Roman world.

Some Christian poets attempted to rewrite the narratives of the Bible in traditional verse. By using measured meter and poetic vocabulary they hoped to provide Christians readers with religious poetry in familiar dress. Aeneas and Dido gave way to Abraham and Joseph and Jonah. One poet, Juvencus, rewrote the Gospel of Matthew in hexameter verse. To write about Christian themes in classical verse, however, proved more difficult than it seemed. All imaginative writing requires a context of familiar associations and allusions, and in the case of Latin poetry all these points of reference were pagan. As a consequence Christian poets shunned the language of the Bible and employed a vocabulary that would resonate in ears schooled in Latin verse. A few examples: An early Christian poem based on the story of Jonah uses the Latin term *vates* (seer) in place of the biblical word "prophet"; instead of *martyr,* the biblical term for "witness," he uses *testis;* and in place of "angel" he chose "herald" (*nuntius*). Even more revealing, the poet avoids the term "resurrection," using instead "diverted from witnessing death" (*mortis testis abactae*). The biblical term "temple" was replaced by a pagan term, "shrine" (*adytum*), and "ask" (*rogare*), a good Latin word, took the place of the biblical "pray" (*orare*). Minor though these changes appear, they were as unsettling to Christian readers in antiquity as it would be to use the term "cult" today to refer to Christian worship, as in, "This Sunday I plan to attend the cult at First Baptist."

These early Christian poets won few readers. Their poems sounded like servile imitations of the real thing. In this period secular poetry itself lacked vitality. Like exercises in a Latin grammar, it was bookish, carrying the stale odor of the classroom. Prose proved a more versatile instrument to adapt to Christian needs, and the liveliest writing in this period can be found in the stirring accounts of the faith and courage of the martyrs.

The Making of Hymns

The first Christian poet to achieve genuine success was Ambrose, bishop of Milan in northern Italy in the fourth century. Born in A.D. 339 in Trier, where his father was praetorian prefect, Ambrose moved to Rome with his mother after his father's death. After passing through elementary school he was put under the tutelage of a grammarian who gave him a thorough training in classical verse. Ambrose had to learn by memory passages from the great Latin poets, notably Virgil. He was taught to analyze their techniques and to imitate their style. His sermons and speeches, for example, his oration at the funeral of his brother Satyrus, are the work of a well-trained, gifted stylist. Preaching was the one area in which Christians could display their literary skills.

When Ambrose was catapulted into the office of bishop in Milan, the city was deeply divided between orthodox Christians and Arians, the party that rejected the teaching of the Council of Nicaea. During Holy Week in 386, when the Arians, supported by the mother of the young emperor Valentinian, sought to gain control of one of the churches in the city, the faithful occupied the church and kept guard over it to prevent them from claiming it as their own. To encourage the people and to prevent them from "succumbing to depression and exhaustion," as Saint Augustine, who was living in Milan at the time, reports,[3] Ambrose composed hymns to be sung by the congregation antiphonally, that is, one side singing a stanza, the other responding with the next stanza. Before Ambrose introduced this practice it had been the custom to have trained soloists sing parts of the service in a kind of chant, half-recitation, half-song, with the congregation joining in at the end. Ambrose's compositions achieved their goal, and the Arians charged him with "beguiling" the faithful with the "strains of his hymns."[4]

Because he was well schooled in Latin verse, Ambrose sensed

that if Latin hymns were to take hold in the minds and hearts of the faithful they had to be genuinely poetic in the classical sense, yet thoroughly biblical and Christian in vocabulary and sentiment. One reason the prose hymns had not become popular was that they were divorced from Latin literary traditions. Ambrose's solution was to write metric hymns, relying on the traditional Latin practice of measured lines but complemented with a new emphasis on accent. He also strove for simplicity and brevity. Ambrose's hymns were written to be memorized. There were no hymnbooks in antiquity, and indeed few people in the congregation could read.

Ambrose's hymns employ what is called iambic dimeter: an iambic foot of short / long in a line of two equal parts ($\cup - \cup - / \cup - \cup -$). Each line has eight syllables, each stanza has four lines, and all hymns include eight stanzas. The entire poem is only 256 syllables. The final stanza took the form of a trinitarian doxology. Though the meter was traditional, the form of the whole was Ambrose's innovation. Here is the opening stanza of one of his hymns, first in Ambrose's Latin and then in a nineteenth-century English version that retains the meter:

Splendor paternae gloriae
de luce lucem proferens
lux lucis et fons luminis
diem dies inluminans.

[O Jesu, Lord of heavenly grace,
Thou brightness of thy Father's face,
Thou fountain of eternal light
Whose beams disperse the shades of night.][5]

Whether one recites these lines in Latin or English, it is easy to see what Ambrose was about and how magnificently he succeeded. The line is short, the meter simple, and the hymn is easily memorized. Yet the language is dignified. It is also biblical and bears distinct Christian overtones. The phrase "light of light" (*lux lucis*) is reminiscent of Psalm 36, "in your light we see light," and is close to the wording of the Nicene creed, "light from light" (*lumen ex lumine*)," which had been adopted by the church several generations earlier. Once this hymn had been sung a few times, the simple as well as the learned, had it by heart. Ambrose's hymns also touched the affections as well as the intellect, something that angered the Arians but moved Augustine when he heard them sung. As the sounds of Ambrose's hymns flowed into my ears, he wrote, the "truth . . . was distilled into my *heart*."[6]

Poetry for Recitation

Ambrose and Prudentius were contemporaries, Ambrose being ten years the elder. Prudentius knew and admired Ambrose's hymns and consciously went about his work with Ambrose's compositions before him. Yet when one looks at what Prudentius wrote it is clear that as a poet he was about something quite different. His was a grander and more expansive vision of Christian poetry. The most obvious difference is that Prudentius was not a liturgical poet, although some of his poems were composed for hours of prayer during the day. His poems were written not to be sung in church, but to be read aloud in the living room or salon or used as a basis for reflection in the quiet of one's study. Some are more than a thousand lines long. Ambrose wrote exegetical works, moral essays, doctrinal treatises, orations, and poetry, that is, hymns are only a small part of his literary output. By contrast Prudentius wrote only poetry, and his poetical corpus is more varied in content, form, and meter.

A listing of his works illustrates the point. He wrote a collection of poems for various times of the day, the *Cathemerinon* (Daily Round) poems to be read at the beginning of the day, at evening when the lamps are lit, and at bedtime, as well as poems to be read at meals and during times of fasting. Several of the longer poems treat doctrinal themes, for example, *Apotheosis* on Christ's triumph (1,100 lines) and *Hamartigenia* on the origin of evil (1,000 lines). He wrote an apologetic poem titled *Against Symmachus* (a Roman senator) in two books, one of 650 lines, the other of 1,100. He also wrote a collection of fourteen poems on martyrs, *Peristephanon* (Crown of Martyrdom). Finally, he composed the first Christian epic, a long, allegorical poem called *Psychomachia* whose title is best translated "spiritual warfare." The poems are introduced by an autobiographical preface and end with an epilogue, suggesting that Prudentius wanted his work to be viewed in its entirety as a poetic oeuvre, like the collected works of Horace.

The first poem of the Daily Round, a "hymn for cockcrow," is modeled on Ambrose's morning hymn *Aeterne rerum conditor* (Framer of the earth and sky). Prudentius uses the same iambic meter employed by Ambrose, and the poem contains verbal reminiscences of Ambrose's hymn. But the differences are apparent at once. For one thing Prudentius's poem is much longer: Ambrose's hymn has eight stanzas, Prudentius's twenty-five. Were it to be sung in church today, the clergyman would announce beforehand, "We will sing the first two stanzas and the final stanza." Ambrose begins with an address to God the creator, "Aeterne conditor" using a good biblical word, *Conditor* (Maker) (Heb. 11:10):

Framer of the earth and sky
Ruler of the day and night

Prudentius begins with the crowing of the cock, using a classical word, *ales* (winged bird), that does not occur in the Bible to symbolize Christ:

The winged messenger of day
welcomes dawn's approach.

A few lines later, describing birds whose singing awakens the sleeper, he echoes Virgil. Prudentius writes of the "loud chirping of birds under eaves [*sub ipso culmine*]," and Virgil wrote of the "birdsong under the eaves [*sub culmine*] in the mild morning light."[7] But what gives the poem its distinctive character is its more elaborate symbolism, for example, the cock as symbol of Christ; its leisurely pace, which allows for development of themes; the use of connectives such as "for," "moreover," "thence," "to be sure"; its vocabulary, for example, the unusual term "forgetfulness" (*oblivio*) to designate sin; its metrical variations, anapests ($\smile \smile -$) in the midst of iambs ($\smile -$); and the absence of a Trinitarian doxology in the final strophe. Prudentius has written a poem, not a hymn.

Every poet depends on readers who can savor form as well as content, and Prudentius's readers took delight in his metrical virtuosity and the verbal allusions to Virgil and Ovid and Horace. But what makes Prudentius's poetry memorable and enduring is that he successfully wedded traditional forms to a new content. In the "hymn for every hour of the day" he writes,

Give me, page, my quill
that I may sing
a sweet and tuneful song
of the glorious deeds of Christ [*gesta Christi insignia*].
He alone shall be my Muse's theme
Him alone shall my lyre praise.

Prudentius will sing of the "glorious deeds of Christ," the wondrous things that had taken place and continue to take place
because of Christ's coming into the world. As is fitting for
poetry, the theme will be "deeds," things that were done and
seen. What earlier Christian thinkers had explained and defended with arguments, that in the man Jesus of Nazareth human
beings had "seen" the living God, Prudentius presents in verse:

Of wonders done and confirmed we sing.
The world bears witness,
the earth denies not what it *saw*
God in person showing men his holy way.[8]

The subject of Christian poetry is Christ, his suffering, death,
and Resurrection:

Lift my soul your tuneful voice
Let the tongue be swift to praise.
Tell the victory of the passion,
Trumpet the triumphant cross.[9]

Prudentius, however, knew that the story of Christ comprised
not only what is written in the gospels, but also the story of the
heroes of the Bible, Abraham and David and Jonah and Judith,
and the tales of Christian martyrs whose noble deaths had been

celebrated in prose. As Christian artists would recognize, the church's history and experience are also the story of Christ. One of Prudentius's most original compositions, his series of poems on the Christian martyrs, the *Crown of Martyrdom,* includes fourteen poems on Spanish martyrs, on martyrs from the city of Rome, on Peter and Paul, on the female martyr Agnes, and on Saint Lawrence. One of these poems is only 18 lines, another runs to more than 1,100 lines. The meters are intricate and varied, and Prudentius moves surely from one metrical challenge to another with skill and imagination. The seventh poem in the series, in honor of Quirinus, a martyr from Siscia in present-day Serbia, is written in a rare form of glyconic meter that has no parallels.

Although the *Crown of Martyrdom* comprises individual poems written at different points in Prudentius's life, Prudentius invites the reader to see them as a whole. In the preface to his collection of poetry he refers to them as *carmen martyribus* (song to the martyrs), and in the poems the martyr appears as a new kind of hero, one befitting the new Christian Rome that was coming into being in the late fourth century. Like ancient Rome, the new Christian Rome has its founding heroes, but they were martyrs, not military heroes, and they vanquish their foes not by strength of arms but by faith in Christ. Augustine had drawn attention to the parallel between the martyrs and Roman heroes, but he thought it inappropriate to use the term *hero* for martyrs.[10] Prudentius unapologetically makes the martyrs into heroes.

One of the central poems in the collection dedicated to Saint Lawrence begins as follows:

Rome, ancient mother of temples,
now given up to Christ,
Lawrence has led your triumph
trampling down barbaric rites.[11]

Lawrence, a deacon in the Church of Rome in the middle of the third century, suffered martyrdom during the persecution under Emperor Valerian, probably in A.D. 258. To this day his church, San Lorenzo fuori le mura, is one of the seven pilgrimage churches in the city of Rome. According to tradition, Lawrence, the most senior deacon, was in charge not only of "holy things," that is, liturgical objects like chalices and candlesticks, but also the church's treasury. The prefect of the city, who had heard that Christian priests offer the sacrifice in "vessels of gold" and "silver cups" illuminated by "golden candlesticks," asked Lawrence to place before him the wealth of the church. To which Lawrence replies,

Our church is rich.
I deny it not.
Much wealth and gold it has
No one in the world has more.

He promises to bring forth all the "precious possessions of Christ," but to tantalize the prefect asks for time to make a list of the church's treasury. A bargain is struck, and Lawrence is excused. For three days Lawrence goes about the city gathering the sick and the poor. The people he collected included a man with two eyeless sockets, a cripple with a broken knee, a one-legged man, a person with one leg shorter than the other, and others with grave infirmities. He writes down their names and lines them up at the entrance to the church. Only then does he seek out the prefect to bring him to the church. When the prefect enters the doors of the church, Lawrence points to the ragged company and says, "There are the church's riches, take them." Enraged at being mocked, the prefect orders Lawrence to be executed but adds, "I shall not let you die in a hurry."

Then follows the famous scene of Lawrence being roasted slowly on a gridiron, at a low temperature to stretch out the agony. With biting irony (given the circumstances) Prudentius gives Lawrence the following speech to the prefect of Rome:

> When slow, consuming heat had seared
> The flesh of Lawrence for a spell,
> He calmly from his gridiron made
> This terse proposal to the judge:
> "Pray turn my body's side,
> It has burned long enough
> Turn it round and taste
> What your god of fire has wrought."

The prefect orders him turned, and Lawrence says, "It is done, eat it up, try whether it is nicer raw or roasted."

Lawrence's martyrdom takes place in the city of Rome, and as Prudentius brings the poem to a close he suggests that the martyrdom of Lawrence represents something new for the ancient city. The martyr becomes the embodiment not simply of religious faith, but also of civic devotion, even of patriotism in the new Christian and Roman *civitas*. In a revealing phrase Prudentius says that by his death Lawrence won the "civic crown" in that city, where the "eternal senate" sits. Playing with the term "eternal," an epithet for Rome, Prudentius subtly reminds his readers that the destiny of the earthly city is to be seen in relation to another kind of eternity, the eternity of God. Yet he does not forget that Lawrence was a citizen of Rome, and it is Rome that now honors the martyrs with a civic crown: "You have two homes, Blessed Lawrence, one for your body here on earth, the other for your soul in heaven."[12] The earthly city still makes a claim on its citizens, but now as a city that worships the one true God.

Prudentius's term for Lawrence is *vir* (hero), the word used at the beginning of Virgil's *Aeneid*, "Arma virumque cano" (I sing of warfare and of a hero). In contrast to the heroes of Rome, the Christian hero "overcame the foe by death,"[13] not by the sword. Yet the martyrs would not have been capable of facing death had they not been schooled in the military virtues, courage, for example. The collection of songs to the martyrs begins with a poem to two soldier martyrs, Emeterius and Chelidonius, who had "abandoned Caesar's ensigns for the standard of the cross." The strength that suited them to "war and fighting" prepared them to "fight for holy things."

Unlike the apologists of the second and third centuries who spoke as members of a small religious sect in the midst of a dominant and sometimes hostile society, Prudentius lived at a time when the Roman Empire was being transformed into a Christian empire and the foundations were being laid for a Christian culture. His assignment was different from theirs. Like the architects who set about designing churches for the growing Christian community and artists who took up the challenge of depicting Christ, the Virgin Mary, and the stories of the Bible with paint and mosaics and stone, Prudentius put language at the service of the new civilization, offering his words as a vehicle for the Word. In the *Crown of Martyrdom* Prudentius shows that the church has a body of stories as fitted to the poetic imagination as the myths and fables of ancient Rome, and he produces for the first time a collection of Christian poetry at once religious and civic and literary to edify the soul, please the mind, and delight the ear.

Spiritual Warfare

Prudentius's most popular and influential work was his long narrative poem *Psychomachia* (Spiritual Warfare). This poem, more than any of his other writings, displays Prudentius's originality, for *Psychomachia* is not a metrical version of the Christian story but a story of Prudentius's own making, at once biblical in inspiration and classical in its allusions. Unlike earlier Christian poets, he did not rewrite the stories of the Bible in classical verse. He wanted to do something new, and what he created was without precedent, a poem about the life of the soul told in the form of an allegory. So great was the popularity of *Psychomachia* that the number of medieval manuscripts of it rivals that of Saint Augustine's major writings. The poem was equally cherished in the vernacular, as manuscripts in Old English attest. Its account of pitched battles between virtues and vices also inspired artists to illustrate manuscripts of his poems with vivid pictures of the central characters contending with each other.

Allegory as a device for interpreting texts was widespread in the ancient world. It had long been applied to the poems of Homer, and when Christians began to interpret the Scriptures, particularly the Old Testament, they adopted some of its techniques. But what one finds in Prudentius's *Psychomachia* is compositional allegory, the imaginative creation of a new narrative to express ideas or attitudes or feelings. Interpretive allegory takes the details of a text, whether fictional or not, and seeks to discover what philosophical or theological or moral principles are symbolized in its words and images. Compositional allegory begins with moral principles or spiritual truths and creates a fictional tale to display them in narrative form. Other writers had created allegories, for example, Ovid in the *Metamorphoses,* Virgil in the *Georgics,* Apuleius in the tale of Cupid and Psyche, but Prudentius was the first to conceive an entire poem as a work of allegory. He would have many imitators, most brilliantly Edmund Spenser in *The Faerie Queene* and John Bunyan in *Pilgrim's Progress.*

Prudentius begins his poem with Abraham, "the first of believers." In the Bible Abraham is, of course, the first example of faith, and Prudentius reminds his readers of the story of the sacrifice of Isaac. In obedience to God's command Abraham set out to offer his only son—the son born to Abraham's wife, Sarah, long after her child-bearing years had passed—as a sacrifice to God. What Prudentius chooses to accent in the story, however, is not faith, but love and the affections. Abraham offered that which was "dear to the heart." The *Psychomachia* is a poem about the inner life, about the struggle within us to set free the "heart that is enslaved," a battle that is waged over who or what should rule our lives. In a phrase that has distinctly Augustinian overtones, Prudentius says that "human nature is divided." *Psychomachia* is a poem about how to rid ourselves of double-mindedness and attain purity of heart.[14]

To set the stage for his story Prudentius chooses an apparently insignificant incident in the life of Abraham, his exploits as a military hero in Genesis 14. Shortly after Abraham had settled in the region of Hebron, he was forced to go to war against an alliance of four kings who had attacked Sodom and Gomorrah, seized what they wished in the city, and took Lot, who lived in Gomorrah, as captive. When Abram (he had not yet been given the name Abraham) hears that Lot had been taken captive, he marshals a force of 318 men to rescue his nephew. He catches up with them in the north of Israel, near Dan, and routs them near Damascus: "Then he brought back all the goods, and also brought back his kinsman Lot with his goods, and the women and the people" (Gen. 14:16).

Prudentius says that the story of the battle to capture Lot is to be interpreted *ad figuram,* that is, as an allegory. The story in which Abraham "inspired by love of God . . . unsheathes his sword and puts to flight the haughty kings" is a tale of the struggle between the forces of good and evil in the soul. It sets before us a model of how we must fight to keep our heart free of unruly desires. As Abram was able to deliver Lot from his captors, so with the help of Christ the Christian can free himself from the appetites and passions that hold him in bondage. Only when the soul "glows with the torch of Christ" will it triumph over its foes.[15]

Once Prudentius has stated his theme through the story of Abraham, he begins the poem proper. Now, instead of giving the reader an allegorical interpretation of a biblical narrative, he begins to tell a story of his own invention. The protagonist is no longer Abraham but a series of characters invented by Prudentius to represent the virtues and vices. The first person to step on the field of battle is Faith, "her rough dress disordered, her shoulders bare, her hair untrimmed, her arms exposed." She is met by Worship-of-the-Old-Gods, that is, Idolatry. At once Worship-of-the-Old-Gods lunges at Faith with his sword, but Faith adroitly parries and scores a hit. As Worship-of-the-Old-Gods falls to the ground, "the victorious legion drawn from a thousand martyrs by their queen Faith leaps with joy and is inspired to face the foe."[16]

Prudentius's allegory may seem crude, but recalls the time in which he was writing. His readers had long heard tales of the martyrs in which the struggle always ended with the death of the martyr. How satisfying to hear a poem that ends with the death of Worship-of-the-Old-Gods lying in defeat and Faith victorious. Vindication is always sweet, and Prudentius no doubt voiced long-submerged feelings. But there is more here than spite. Underneath Prudentius's allegory runs a prominent biblical metaphor, Saint Paul's depiction of the believer as a "soldier in Christ" (2 Tim. 2:3) and the martial imagery of psalms ("Blessed be the Lord who trains my hands for war," Ps. 144:1). The Christian contends not against external enemies but against the "rulers of this present darkness" or "spiritual hosts of wickedness." To triumph on this field of battle, as Saint Paul said, one must "take the whole armor of God" (Eph. 6:12–13).

In the *Psychomachia* Prudentius puts spiritual warfare at the center of the Christian life. The great foe is sin, and the message is clear: without struggle against sin there can be no virtue, and without victory over sin, no peace. It is a theme that will resonate across the centuries in Christian poetry. The Red Cross Knight in Spenser's *Faerie Queene* is a descendant of Prudentius's Faith, and the vice he first meets, Error, is reminiscent of Worship-of-the-Old-Gods. Indeed, what John Milton said of the

knights of *The Faerie Queene* could be said of Prudentius's heroes: "I cannot praise a fugitive and cloistered virtue unexercised
and unbreathed, that never sallies out and seeks her adversary,
but slinks out of the race, where that immortal garland is to be
run for, not without dust and heat."[17]

Immediately behind Faith follows Modesty, who is met on the
field of battle by Lust. Modesty, unlike Faith, whose shoulders
were bare, is not defenseless: she wears shining armor. Lust
thrusts a torch of pinewood blazing with pitch and sulphur into
her face, but Modesty strikes Lust's hand with a stone, then
lunges with her sword and pierces her throat. As "clots of putrid
blood" flow from Lust's neck, Modesty realizes she has struck
home and cries out,

> Your end has come,
> Prostrate you lie.
> No longer shall you dare to hurl
> Your deadly flames 'gainst God's servants
> Whose pure hearts
> The torch of Christ alone enflames.[18]

Then come battles between other virtues and vices. After
Worship-of-the-Old-Gods and Lust come Wrath, Pride, Indulgence, Avarice, Discord, which are met in turn by Patience,
Humble-Mind, Soberness, Uprightness, Simplicity, Hope, Reason, Concord. In all, there are seven vices (there are more virtues than vices), though they do not correspond to the familiar
list of seven from medieval literature.

Prudentius struggles to find a way of translating each virtue
into a martial figure. How, for example, can one portray Patience
rushing against a foe or Humble-Mind gloating over the down-

fall of the enemy? Prudentius seems to realize the limitations of his scheme, and in the contest between Indulgence and Soberness he makes Indulgence into a wily foe, a sly and sensuous woman riding in a magnificent chariot throwing violets and rose leaves to the opposing army. Seduced by a "tipsy dancer," the virtues at first lay down their arms at her feet. Masquerading as Frugality to deceive the pious Christian, Avarice craftily exploits her gullible and unsuspecting friends. As the literary critic C. S. Lewis observed, this is one of the few examples in classical literature in which there is any "recognition of the great fact of self-deception."

Prudentius knew that the passions rage with such ferocity that contending with them can be likened to combat on a field of battle. Virgil spoke about "savage wars" between peoples, but Prudentius speaks of "savage wars" that "rage within our bones" as man's "divided nature" roars in rebellion.[19] Though he does not write with the psychological depth of Augustine, he had learned from Saint Paul and his own experience, "I do not do what I want but I do the very thing I hate," for "sin dwells within me" (Rom. 7:15–17).

Psychomachia is a story about everyman, about a struggle that takes place in every human soul visited by grace. But the poem tells another story, far grander and played on a larger stage: the story of the love that sought out human beings. Woven into Prudentius's poem is a narrative in which God, not the human soul, is the actor. This story begins with creation, receives its plot from the fall, finds its direction in the call of Abraham, offers hope in the promises of the prophets and the holy men and women of Israel, and comes to fulfillment in the life of Christ and the sending of the Holy Spirit to gather the church. The poem is not simply an allegory of the moral life, but also a celebration of God in Christ, who triumphed where man was defenseless. After Modesty has triumphed over Lust, she says,

A Virgin brought forth a child,
Now where is your power?
In that virgin mother
Human nature lost its primal stain and
Power from above made flesh new.
A maid unwed gave birth to God, Christ,
Man from his Mother,
God from his Father.
From that day all flesh is divine,
For flesh gave him birth and by this union
Shares in God's nature.
The Word made flesh ceased not to be
What he was before, though joined to flesh.
Not made less by commerce with flesh
His majesty lifts up unhappy men.
What he always was he remains, and
What he was not he begins to be.
Now we are not what we were,
but born to better things.
He gives to me yet remains himself.
By becoming what is ours God is not less,
In giving us what is his he lifts us to heavenly gifts.[20]

The two stories are made explicit here, one the glorious deeds of Christ, and the other, the inner life of the Christian. Notice that in the midst of his account of the Incarnation, Prudentius introduces somewhat unexpectedly the first person pronoun:

"He gives *to me* yet remains himself." By interweaving these two stories Prudentius gave Christian poetry its distinctive shape. At the beginning of the *Psychomachia* Prudentius addressed the reader, inviting him to become part of the narrative. In Prudentius's poetry the reader is not a bystander but a participant. Whoever wishes to make "a pleasing offering to God" must offer that which is "most precious and dear to his heart." He must expel the disorders that well up within his breast and put down the "rebellion" so that his heart can be won for Christ. Like Milton's *Paradise Lost, Psychomachia* is not, "a vehicle for sublime ideas"; the poem coaxes readers to attend to themselves and by embracing Christ change their lives. Only the heart that is pure can welcome Christ and have the privilege of "serving as host to the Holy Trinity."[21]

Jerome, the most learned Christian to write in Latin in the fourth century, said that in his leisure he found himself turning to Cicero and to Plautus the comic playwright for pleasure. The language of the Bible was plain and inelegant, and it troubled him that he found more satisfaction in reading the great Latin writers of Roman antiquity than the books of the Bible. Once, when feverish, he dreamed he had been brought before a judge in a courtroom. When asked who he was, Jerome replied, "I am a Christian." But the judge said, "You are lying, you are a disciple of Cicero, not of Christ. For 'where your treasure is there will your heart be also.' " The judge ordered him flogged, and Jerome pleaded for mercy. From that day Jerome claimed, improbably, that he read the Holy Scriptures with the fervor and zeal he had once given to literature.[22]

Unlike Jerome, Prudentius did not reject the Muses. He saw no reason Christians should shun literature. With his "swift iambs" and "quick-revolving trochees," he made it possible for Christians to find pleasure as well as edification in poetry. For him, poetry was neither simply instrumental, a felicitous vehicle for teaching, nor simply aesthetic, the singing of verses empty of content. In all memorable verse form and content are complementary, and Prudentius took as much care with the presentation of theological ideas and the narration of biblical stories as he did with vocabulary and meter. Nor did he neglect the form of the whole. No poet since Horace had produced anything like the cycle of poems in *The Daily Round* and *Peristephanon*. Prudentius wanted Christian poetry to find a place not only in the church's worship but in the world's literature. He achieved a richness of form unknown to earlier Christian writers and a freshness of spirit long absent from Latin poetry. His oeuvre is at once deeply Christian and indisputably literary, and it set the Christian intellectual tradition on a course that would find place for poets as different as Dante Alighieri, William Langland, Edmund Spenser, John Milton, Gerard Manley Hopkins, T. S. Eliot, and Geoffrey Hill.

Chapter 10

Making This Thing Other

We already and first of all discern him making this thing other.

DAVID JONES

ONE OF THE practices most despised by ancient critics of Christianity was devotion to the dead, particularly veneration of the bones of martyrs and saints. A zealous foe of the church, Julian, Roman emperor from 361 to 363, complained that Christians had "filled the whole world with tombs and memorials to the dead," even though nowhere in the Scriptures is it said one should "haunt tombs or show them reverence."[1] By the end of the fourth century the cities of the Roman world were sprinkled with shrines housing relics, that is, the bones of holy men and women, and pious Christians devoutly made their way to these sacred places to pray.

As early as the second century Christians had begun to honor

the dead by gathering at their tombs for worship and intercession. At the tomb of Saint Peter in Rome a niche was carved in
the wall to hold a plaque with the inscription, "Peter is here." At
these shrines one would find an altar and benches where the
faithful could sit gazing at a stone coffin containing the precious
body of the saint. The bones not only reminded visitors to the
tomb that someone was buried there, but also conveyed palpably
the presence of the holy person. "When the faithful look at the
relics," wrote Gregory of Nyssa of the tomb of Saint Theodore,
"it is as though with the eyes, the mouth, the ears, indeed all the
senses they embrace the living body itself still blooming with
life. With tears of reverence and tender feeling they address
prayers of intercession to the martyr as though he were actually
present there before them."[2]

Gregory of Nyssa was one of the most philosophical thinkers
in Christian history, a Christian Platonist, who believed that
what was "truly real" was to be found not in material things but
in a spiritual realm accessible to the mind alone. Yet in this
sermon he says that to touch and kiss the bones of this holy man
was a gift beyond imagining. Even the dirt holding the bones is
dear. When he looked into the tomb he felt he could address the
saint face to face.

Gregory's was not an uncommon experience. In New York
harbor on Ellis Island there is a museum where millions of
immigrants first stepped off ships from abroad to enter their new
country. Housed in the original building that greeted the immigrants, the museum has the feel of a shrine. Visitors to the
museum are able to stand in the very place where families of
anxious parents and bewildered children huddled together as
they straggled down from the ships on to firm land after weeks at

sea. The place does more than recall the immigrants, it allows one to see with one's own eyes and touch with one's fingers the actual things that bear the imprint of their presence: the tall desks at which clerks recorded their names, a pile of suitcases and boxes secured with knots reflecting the different countries of origin. The Ellis Island Immigrant Museum has a strange, mysterious power. Memory, never simply a mental act, is bound to places and sights and smells.

In a provocative passage in one of his most philosophical works, Gregory of Nyssa, somewhat to the reader's surprise, criticizes his opponent Eunomius for ignoring Christian practices and relying solely on theological ideas. It is foolish and idle, says Gregory, to think that Christian faith consists only in teachings. It also has to do with making the sign of the cross when one speaks the "venerable names," Father, Son, and Holy Spirit, with the "mystery of regeneration" (immersion in water at Baptism), and the "mystic oblation" (the offering of consecrated bread and wine in the Eucharist). If one slights these "sacramental tokens" and thinks that Christianity consists solely in "doctrinal precision," the "Christian mystery" becomes a pious fable.[3]

We saw in the previous chapter how an early Christian poet created a resonant language to sing the praises of God and celebrate the glorious deeds of Christ. Christian thinkers also attended to other kinds of things, the bones of saints and martyrs, the dirt and stones of holy places, the oil of chrism, water, bread and wine, and, not least, pictures painted on wood and mosaics fixed on a wall. Pictorial art, like poetry, began early in the church's history. Because of the Incarnation Christianity posits an intimate relation between material things and the living God.

Paintings Surpass Words

The eyes are more learned than the ears, and in the early church the most pervasive metaphor to speak of knowing God was seeing. "No one has ever seen God; the only Son, who is in the bosom of the Father, he has made him known" (John 1:18). We come to know God by looking at a human face, the face of Jesus Christ. Commenting on the story of the man born blind in the gospels, Cyril of Alexandria wrote, when the blind man asked, "Who is he, Lord, that I may believe in him?" Jesus did not say, "Seek the nature of God by analogical reasoning," but "You have seen him: the one who speaks with you is he (John 9:36–37)." He pointed to the "reality of his body," which could be seen with the eyes.[4] Of course, seeing meant more than seeing with the eyes (Jesus was speaking to a blind man), but Christianity's unique claim is that spiritual knowledge begins with things that can be seen with the eyes and touched with the hands: "That which was from the beginning, which we have heard, which we have seen with our eyes, which we have looked upon and touched with our hands, concerning the word of life . . . that which we have seen and heard we proclaim also to you" (1 John 1:3). The events narrated in the Scriptures, Abraham's sacrifice of Isaac, the deliverance of the Israelites from Egypt, Moses standing before the burning bush, David dancing before the Ark of the Covenant, Jesus' baptism in the Jordan river, his agony in the Garden of Gethsemane, his death and Resurrection could all be seen. Hence they could be depicted in paintings. On the walls of the catacombs Christians painted pictures of persons and events recorded in the Scriptures, for example, Moses striking the rock at Kadesh, Daniel in the lion's den, the miracle of the loaves and fishes, the raising of Lazarus.

The earliest preserved Christian art is limited to burial places such as the catacombs, to objects like lamps and bowls used in the home, and to rings for the finger. During the first three centuries Christians were able to build only a few places of worship. But in the fourth century, supported by the largesse of Constantine, the first Christian emperor, Christian communities in cities across the Roman Empire began to construct church buildings in earnest. These they decorated with paintings and mosaics of Christ, the Virgin Mary, the saints, and stories from the Bible. With few exceptions Christian leaders welcomed paintings in the churches, and bishops praised the work of these artists. In a homily preached in the middle of the fourth century on Saint Barlaam, a martyr during the time of Emperor Diocletian at the beginning of the fourth century, Basil of Caesarea commended artists (he calls them "brilliant painters"): "Fill out with your art the faint image of this leader. Illuminate with the flowers of your wisdom the crowned martyr whom I have only portrayed indistinctly. Let my words be surpassed by your drawing of the heroic deeds of the martyr. . . . and I will see this athlete of the faith presented more brilliantly in your painting."[5]

As this passage illustrates, one of the purposes of paintings in churches was didactic. A painting gave the faithful an image to carry in the mind and served as a book for those who could not read. Over time, however, it became customary not only to look at the pictures, but also to touch them, kiss them, light candles in front of them, even address prayers to them. John Chrysostom, it was said, had a painting of Saint Paul, and when he read Paul's epistles "he looked intently at it as though he were looking at the living person himself" and directing his thoughts at Paul and "speak[ing] with him through the image."[6] These icons (the Greek term for an image or portrait) came to be treated with the same reverence one would show the actual person. Like the bones of the saints, they were not simply reminders: they made the holy person present. The paintings themselves became objects of veneration.

As Christian devotion to icons became more fervent, it seemed, at least to some, that veneration of icons bordered on idolatry. In practice the faithful could have difficulty distinguishing the picture, a thing of wood and paint, from the person depicted in the picture, Christ or the Virgin Mary. In the early eighth century Emperor Leo III in Constantinople, supported by a group within the church, mounted an offensive against the veneration of images. Called iconoclasts from the Greek term for "breaking images," they argued that the law of Moses forbad the making of graven images: "You shall not make for yourself a graven image, or any likeness of anything that is in heaven above, or that is in the earth beneath, or that is in the water under the earth; you shall not bow down to them or serve them" (Exod. 20:4–5). They also claimed that the most authentic representation of Christ was to be found in the Eucharist and that the true image of a holy man or woman was not an icon but a virtuous life, the living image displayed in tales and sayings. Hearing in this view is more important than seeing.

As has often been the case in the church's history, the challenge of a divergent point of view became the occasion to clarify what was believed. In this case, the controversy over the veneration of images prompted a monk living in the Holy Land, John of Damascus, to defend the veneration of icons in three thoughtful treatises that set forth what was at issue in the controversy over images and the reverence Christians gave to other sensible objects and things.

Christian Monk in a Muslim World

John of Damascus was born during the last half of the seventh century in the generation after the fall of Jerusalem to the Muslims in 638. By the time of his birth the Christian lands of the eastern Mediterranean, Syria, Palestine, and Egypt, had been conquered by the advancing armies of the new religion, and the city of Damascus had become the political and administrative center of the Muslim caliphate. John's grandfather and father both held high positions at the court of the caliph residing in Damascus. As a child John learned Arabic, the language of the conquerors, as well as Greek, the language of the Christian community, and he seems also to have studied the Qur'an. He was the first Christian thinker to discuss Muhammad in his writings and to cite passages from the Qur'an.

Like his father and grandfather, John began his career in service to the caliph. But early on he was drawn to the religious life, and he soon left Damascus to become a monk at the famous monastery of Mar Saba, located in the Judean desert six miles east of Bethlehem high up on a bluff overlooking the Wadi Kidron. Under Muslim rule it became an intellectual center and one of the first places in which Christians began to translate Greek books into Arabic. Today it remains a working monastery. There, like others before and after him, John prayed and worked and studied the Scriptures and the writings of the fathers. But being a man of unusual gifts, he also began to write theological and philosophical treatises.

The establishment of Islam in lands that formerly had been ruled by Christians brought far-reaching changes to the Middle East. With a will driven by zeal the new rulers gradually transformed the society, language, political institutions and

laws, calendar, and in time the religious practices of many of
the inhabitants. Faced with a world in which Christianity was
in retreat, John set for himself the daunting task of handing
on to later generations the heritage of the Christian past. His
best-known work, the *Fount of Knowledge,* is a compendium of
Christian teaching drawn from the writings of early thinkers,
and in another work, the *Sacra Parallela,* he compiled a collection of scriptural and patristic texts on the moral and ascetic
life.

Although John lived within Muslim society in Palestine he
was drawn into the debate over the veneration of icons in distant
Constantinople, the capital of the Byzantine Empire. In John's
view the prohibition of icons challenged the fundamental Christian belief in the Incarnation, that the God who is beyond time
and space was made known through a human being, Jesus of
Nazareth, who was born of a woman and lived in a particular
place and time in history. Because God had taken on human flesh
it was possible to paint an image of God: "When he who is
bodiless and without form, immeasurable in the boundlessness
of his own nature, existing in the form of God, empties himself
and takes the form of a servant in substance and in stature and is
found in a body of flesh, then you may draw his image and show
it to anyone willing to gaze upon it."[7] How is this done? "Depict
his wonderful condescension, his birth from the Virgin, his Baptism in the Jordan, his Transfiguration on Tabor, his sufferings
which have freed us from passion, his death, his miracles. . . .
Show his saving cross, the tomb, the resurrection, the ascension
into the heavens."[8] If Christ could not be painted as a human
being, John argued, how could one claim that God had become
incarnate? More was at stake in the iconoclastic controversy than

the legitimacy of pictorial representations of Christ, the Virgin Mary, and the saints.

In ancient Israel it was forbidden to make an image of God. According to the law of Moses, the making of images was idolatrous. John, of course, agrees, and he calls attention to several texts in the Pentateuch that express the prohibition in other ways. God had said to Moses, "You cannot see my form" (Exod. 33:20). Similarly, when Moses explained to the Israelites what had happened on Mount Horeb, that is, Mount Sinai, he told them to take heed, for "you saw no form on the day the Lord spoke to you at Horeb out of the midst of the fire" (Deut. 4:15). Therefore, Moses continues, do not make an image for yourself "in the form of any figure whether male or female." John contrasts the ancient prohibitions with the language of the New Testament. In 2 Corinthians Saint Paul said, "With unveiled face we behold the glory of God" (3:18), and Paul calls Christ the "image" of God. In former times one could not "see God," hence images could lead only to idolatry, but now that God has appeared in the form of a human person, images are essential to a mature Christian piety.[9]

God has "been *seen* on earth." Again and again John speaks of what has been seen, and at one point he calls sight the "noblest sense." Only by seeing are we brought into intimate relation to God: "I have seen God in human form, and my soul has been saved. I look at the the image of God, as Jacob did, but in a wholly different way." Jacob saw only with "spiritual sight" what was to come in the future. Because he saw God "without matter," his vision was limited. Now we are able to see God "visible in human flesh," and, says John, the image of God has been "burned into my soul."[10]

The veneration of icons is the church's most palpable way of proclaiming that God appeared in human flesh in the person of Jesus Christ. What is more, Christ's assumption of human flesh was not a temporary expedient, like putting on a coat in winter that is set aside in spring. Christ's flesh remains his own even after his return to the Father, and the identity of the Logos is forever bound up with this human flesh, with matter. That finally is why it is possible long after Christ's sojourn on earth to depict the divine Logos by painting an image of Christ. "I boldly draw an image of the invisible God not as invisible," John writes, "but as having become visible for our sakes by sharing in flesh and blood." What is depicted in the image of Christ is neither simply the human Jesus nor the invisible God, but the image of God become flesh.

At one level an icon of Christ is a picture of Christ as he was seen by those who knew him during his lifetime. But Christ is not a historical figure from the past; he is the resurrected and living Lord exalted at the right hand of the Father in communion with the Holy Spirit. When John says that one can make an icon of Christ he means, of course, that one can paint a picture of Christ as one would paint a picture of any person; but he also means that in looking at the face of Christ one sees something that cannot be seen with the eyes, the one who exists in the form of God. At the second Council of Nicaea in 787, at which the church's teaching on icons was given its definitive form, the bishops insisted that an icon of Christ was more than a picture of the historical Jesus. In looking at an icon of Christ, they said, one does not simply see the man Christ but "the *Logos* become flesh." And when one looks at an icon of the Nativity, the icon presents to us the "*God* become man for our salvation." Hence

Icon of Christ Pantocrator, first half of sixth century. Monastery of
St. Catherine at Mt. Sinai.

Icon of Ascension, sixth century. Monastery of St. Catherine at Mt. Sinai.

the icon invites the confession, "He who is without flesh, became flesh. . . . The uncreated one was made. The impalpable one was touched." An icon of the Nativity does more than remind the viewer of an event that took place in the past, the birth of Jesus of Nazareth: it is an icon of the *Incarnation,* of the mystery of God taking on human flesh. In Cyril of Alexandria's phrase, Christ's flesh is the "flesh of the invisible God."[11]

Although the iconoclastic controversy was not a debate about the legitimacy of art in general but of sacred art—indeed, it was the first debate in the church's history about the nature of religious art—in his defense of icons John praises the work of the artist. In a lyrical passage early in the first essay, he cites God's charge to Bezalel, a craftsman assigned the task of making the decorations for the ancient tabernacle: "The Lord said to Moses, 'See I have called by name Bezalel the son of Uri, son of Hur, of the tribe of Judah: and I have filled him with the Spirit of God, with ability and intelligence, with knowledge and all craftsmanship, to devise artistic designs, to work in gold, silver, and bronze, in cutting stones for setting and in carving wood, for work in every craft." (Exod. 31:1–2) To which John comments, "Look how matter is honored which you [the iconoclasts] despise." And then with deep irony, he adds, "What is more insignificant than colored goatskins? Are not blue and purple and scarlet merely colors? Behold the handiwork of men becoming the likeness of the cherubim."[12]

"Look how matter is honored." Matter, the stuff of this earth from which all things are made, is intrinsically good. As God created each thing in the account in Genesis he looked at what he had created and saw that "it was good." In his dispute with the Manichees, Augustine had defended the goodness of matter on the basis of these words. John of Damascus, however, wants to say more. His point is that matter has within itself the capacity to become a resting place for God, to become something other while remaining what it is. In Christ, John writes, the Creator of matter "worked out my salvation through matter." For this reason, "I treat all matter with reverence and respect, because it is filled with divine grace and power."[13] Matter, what can be seen with the eyes and touched with the fingers, has the potential to become an icon, an image of God and of the things of God. When God ordered the ark to be constructed of wood and gilded on the inside and outside (and Aaron's staff and the golden urn containing the manna to be placed in it), matter became "carriers of memory." As the Israelites looked at the image they were reminded of what had happened in the past and of what was promised for the future. John has read the Scriptures carefully and discerned a distinctive feature of biblical religion, namely, that things can become the vehicle of God's presence among us. When David decided to bring the ark of God from the house of Abinadab it was carried on a new cart. According to 2 Samuel, as the ark moved toward the city "David and all the house of Israel were making merry *before the Lord* with all their might, with songs, and lyres and harps and tambourines and castanets and cymbals" (2 Sam. 6:5). In dancing before the ark David was dancing before the Lord.

It is not always appreciated that John's treatises in defense of icons deal with things other than pictorial representations. To be sure, icons of Christ, of the Blessed Virgin, and of the saints are at the heart of his argument, but he also discusses the holy cross on which Christ died, the rock of Golgotha, the stone at Christ's tomb, even the nails, the lance, the robe. And he mentions other things that appear in the Bible as part of the great story of salvation, the burning bush, the ark of the covenant, the twelve stones. In John's view these too are images or icons. God has always employed visible things in dealing with human beings, and through the Incarnation the ways of old are confirmed and exalted. In a felicitous phrase John says that all these material things, stones, bushes, chests, were "piercing heralds" that brought to mind God's works and led the faithful "to remember the mighty works of old and to worship God."[14]

Receptacles of Divine Power

At the very end of Willa Cather's *Lucy Gayheart* Harry Gordon returns to the place where many years earlier Lucy, a thirteen-year-old girl, had skipped across wet cement leaving three slight footprints in the sidewalk. Later as a young woman she died in a skating accident on a frozen river, but her footprints remained "delicately and clearly stamped in the greywhite composition. The travel of the years had not made them fainter." Harry had loved Lucy and would often return to this stretch of sidewalk at the edge of the town for "nothing else seemed to bring her back so vividly into the living world for a moment. Sometimes, when he paused there, he caught for a flash the very feel of her; an urge at his elbow, breath on his cheek, a sudden lightness and fresh-ness like a shower of spring raindrops."

Other things reminded Harry of Lucy, but it was the foot-prints in the cement that seemed to bring back her person most vividly. The footprints were not a mental image: they had re-ceived the imprint of her youthful body, her feet had actually touched the wet cement. Unlike a metal highway sign that tells us what is to come and is useful only for what it signifies, these footprints were palpably and irrevocably part of Lucy. In themselves they were precious.

In discussing things other than pictorial images, John gives special attention to holy places. Like the footprints in cement that brought Lucy back to Harry, such things have an iconic character. Through them the faithful were brought into tangible relation with the mysteries of the faith.

The tomb of Christ, the cave in Bethlehem, the mount from which Christ ascended, the wood of the cross on which he hung —all these things physically touched the body of Christ and retain the marks of his presence. Just as perfume leaves an odor in the jar after it has been poured out, so God has left traces of his sojourn among us in specific places in Palestine. Even after the jar has been emptied one is able to savor the lingering fragrance of the perfume that is now gone, and through the traces of Christ left on earth we can touch the life that once dwelled among us. The holy places, wrote Gregory of Nyssa, had "received the footprints of Life itself," and for this reason they are to be cherished and venerated. It is often forgotten that events take place in space as well as in time, and the events on which Christian faith is based happened not only at a particular time in history, but also at specific places. Where something happened is as significant as when it happened. There is no better way to fix an event or person in the mind than to visit the actual place where the event occurred or where the person lived. In a mysterious way tangible things have the capacity to stir the inner eye, as though there exists a kind of mystic harmony between things of the spirit and objects of sense. When pilgrims to the Holy Land returned home, they carried blessings, as they were called —water from the Jordan River, flasks of oil from a church built at the site of a holy place, even dust from the Holy Land in a small box—to keep their memories alive and to sanctify their homes.

Among the many things that impressed pilgrims to the Holy Land was that the liturgy could be celebrated at the actual spot where the saving events had taken place, at the tombstone where Christ was buried, on the Mount of Olives from which he ascended into heaven. Egeria, a fourth-century pilgrim, wrote, "What I admire and value most is that all the hymns and antiphons and readings there, and all the prayers the bishops say, are always related to the day that is being observed and to the *place* in which they are used." Preachers in Jerusalem reminded the faithful that the events celebrated in the Liturgy had taken place on the very spot where they gathered to worship. Here Christ was crucified and here the Spirit was poured out on the church, they said. Jerome, who lived in Bethlehem, said, here Christ was wrapped in swaddling clothes. An Arabic Christian writer several generations after John said, "Christ has given us . . . traces of himself and holy places in this world as an inheritance and a pledge of the kingdom of heaven."[15]

The scenes of sacred history work on the mind of the faithful in uncommon ways and draw the pilgrim into a deeper participation in the saving events. No doubt living in the Judean desert only a few miles from Bethlehem and Jerusalem and visiting the holy places often deepened John's understanding of the sacredness of space. More than any other writer in his time he saw that the historical character of Christianity is as much bound to place as it is to time. In his words, the "places in which God had accomplished our salvation" were no less an image of Christ than pictures. By means of such icons "things which have taken place in the past are remembered." He specifically mentions Nazareth, the cave at Bethlehem, the mountain of Golgotha, the tomb, which he called "the fountain of our Resurrection," the stone that sealed the sepulcher, Mount Zion, the Mount of Olives, the pool of Bethsaida, the garden of Gethsemane, and "all other similar places." John calls these places as well as things like the holy cross "receptacles of divine power." By this phrase he means they were not simply historical sites that mark the site where something noteworthy happened long ago, but tangible evidences of God's continuing presence on earth. In the same way the Arabic Christian writer cited above said that through these places Christ has given "blessing, sanctification, access to him, pardon for sins . . . spiritual joy . . . and witnesses that confirm what is written in the book of the Gospel."[16]

A piece of cloth, like a footprint in the sidewalk, is a lifeless thing, no more valuable than the stuff of which it is made, but if it is a shirt or a blouse of someone I love it becomes something other than a piece of cloth. "I have often seen lovers gazing at the garments of their beloved," writes John, "embracing the garments with their eyes and their lips as if the garment were the beloved one."[17] In the same way the faithful kissed the wood of the cross that held the precious body of Christ, knelt in adoration at the rock on which he was crucified, and bent down to kiss the stone on which his body was laid. The way to God passes through things that can be seen and touched.

In the third century Origen had argued that it was only when men and women came to know God in human flesh that they learned to serve the one God and turn away from the worship of idols. In the eighth century John said, the "mind which is determined to ignore corporeal things will find itself weakened and frustrated." Only by turning to what can be seen do we learn to see the God who cannot be seen.[18]

If No Image, No Incarnation

Although holy places and holy things came into play in John's defense of the veneration of icons, pictorial images remained at the center of the debate. Pictorial images, however, can be of many kinds. One can, for example, paint the baptism of Christ or the Crucifixion, but it is also possible to depict Christ in the figure of a lamb. Both are pictures, but their relation to what is pictured is different. The one depicts Christ or an event in the life of Christ, and the other uses a biblical symbol to represent an aspect of Christ's person or work, that Christ, like a lamb, was sacrificed for the sins of the world. Although the symbol of the lamb could be found in churches, a generation before the dispute over icons the church had ruled against depicting Christ as a lamb.

The official position was set down in a decree of a synod in Constantinople in 692, and in the course of the iconoclastic controversy the *iconodules,* or defenders of icons, drew on its arguments to support the veneration of icons. Here is what the synod said:

> Some of the sacred icons depict a lamb, to which John the Baptizer is pointing. . . . Even though we honor the ancient types and foreshadowing as authentic symbols and anticipations of the truth . . . we nonetheless prefer the grace itself and the truth itself. . . . In order to bring this reality before the eyes of everyone in an image, we decree that from now on the *human likeness of Christ our God,* the

lamb who takes away the sins of the world, should be painted on icons, in place of the ancient lamb. In this way we will grasp the depth of humility of the Word of God, and will be prompted to remember his life in the flesh, his suffering, his salvific death, and the salvation that has come to the world.[19]

The decree aimed to highlight the reality of the Incarnation, that the ancient symbols had taken historical form in the person of Jesus Christ. The key phrase is "human likeness of Christ our God." By depicting the actual person of Christ or an event in the life of Christ, the icon brings the person himself before the beholder in accord with the "narrative of the Gospel,"[20] as it was put in the decree of the Council of Nicaea in 787. Only the icon can portray events. When we look at an icon of Christ, we come face to face with the living person, and by showing reverence to the icon we venerate Christ himself.

This close identification between icon and person is implicit in the writings of Saint John of Damascus, but it fell to the next generation of Christian thinkers to explain it more fully and with greater theological precision. The commanding figure was Theodore of Studium (d. 826), abbot of a monastery near Constantinople at the beginning of the ninth century. Theodore was a spiritual guide and teacher as well as a gifted administrator and legislator. He was also a penetrating thinker, and his essays in defense of the veneration of icons are a discerning companion to John's treatises.

The iconoclasts had argued that a genuine image must be of the same essence as its original, just as Christ is of the same essence as the Father.[21] An icon, however, is made of wood and paint and has no intrinsic relation to the Christ it portrays. Hence the iconoclasts argued that the only true image of Christ is the Eucharist because in the Eucharist the bread and wine that have been blessed become the body and blood of Christ. "We hold," they said, "that Christ may be represented but only according to the holy words we have received from God himself. For he said, 'Do this in remembrance of me,' implying that he cannot be represented otherwise than by being remembered. Only this image is true and this act of depiction sacred."[22] Unlike the consecrated bread and wine of the Eucharist, a picture is not the same substance as Christ. Hence it cannot be a genuine image of Christ.

Theodore grants that the icon of Christ by its very nature is something other than the Christ who is depicted in the icon. Indeed, he accentuates the difference and makes it the basis for his refutation of the views of the iconoclasts: "No one could ever be so foolish as to suppose that shadow and truth, nature and art, original and copy, cause and effect are the same in essence; or to say that each is in the other, or either one is in the other. But that is what one would have to say if he supposed that Christ and his image are the same in essence."[23] Christ is one thing, and his image is something else. In other words, the icon has a distinct character, and if one insists that the image correspond wholly to the Christ it portrays, as in the Eucharist, it would no longer be an image but the thing itself.

Yet the icon is called Christ and receives its identity from the relation it has to Christ. Theodore offers two intriguing biblical examples to support his point. In 2 Kings 23 it is reported that King Josiah pointed to the tomb of the "man of God" who had prophesied and said, "What is that monument that I see over there?" The men of the city said, "It is the man of God who came from Judah." Theodore observes that they did not say, "That is the *tomb* of the man of God," but "It is the man of God." In other words, they identified the stone of the tomb with the person who was lying in the tomb. Another more telling example comes from the book of Exodus. God said to Moses, "Make for me two cherubim of gold," not make for me two "images of cherubim."[24] Theodore concludes that it is not unreasonable to identify the image with the person depicted on the image even though the image is made of wood or stone or gold. The image directs attention not to itself but to the original, the prototype, and is capable of presenting the person of Christ before the believer.

But how does the icon do this? Theodore draws on ideas that had been developed in the debate over the person of Christ after the Council of Chalcedon in 451. At Chalcedon the church had affirmed that Christ "was known in two natures, without confusion, without change, without division, without separation." The decree taught that Christ was both divine and human and that the two natures were bound in an intimate and indivisible unity. For that reason, it was not possible to speak of Christ's divine nature without referring to his human nature, or to refer to the man Christ without seeing him as God incarnate. If the two natures cannot be separated, a portrait of Christ depicts not simply his human nature, but the God who has become man. Because the Son of God took on human flesh "the human nature of Christ is not simply associated with the person of the Logos. . . . Christ's human nature has its existence in the person of the Logos."[25] There is no man Jesus other than God incarnate.

Theodore was convinced that the iconoclasts thought much

too abstractly about Christ. Their language suggested that the divine Logos had assumed humanity in general, "flesh without distinguishing features." But something that is general can be grasped only by the intellect, not by the senses: "If Christ assumed our nature in general . . . he can be contemplated only by the mind and touched by thought." A symbol can depict an idea or concept or abstract quality, but an icon displays the reality itself, in this case the person of Christ. The original is present in the icon because of its likeness to the person.[26]

So close was the identification between the image and what the image depicts that Theodore comes to the apparently paradoxical conclusion that unless there is an image of Christ there is no Christ. This is a deepening of John's argument. One would have expected him to say, as John had argued, that unless there had been the Incarnation there could be no image of Christ. But he turns the matter around and says, "There would not be a prototype [that is, no Christ] if there were no image." The prototype has a necessary relation to the image, for each has its being in the other: "If Christ cannot exist unless his image exists in potentiality, and if the image subsists in the prototype before it is produced artistically, then anyone who does not acknowledge that His image is also venerated in Him destroys the veneration of Christ."[27]

Like a shadow inseparably related to the body that casts it, the image is indivisible from the original. Even when the form that casts the shadow is not seen, it exists in potentiality. When a seal leaves its imprint in the wax, the wax bears an exact replication of what was on the seal, but in a different kind of material. Though the one may be of metal or ivory and the other of wax, the original can be known from the impression. As Christ bore the imprint of God and was the "very stamp of his nature" (Heb. 1:3), so the wood and paint of the icon bear the imprint of the person of Christ.

The most profound and telling point in the debate occurs at the beginning of Theodore's second treatise against those who attack icons. His opponent had cited the commandment, "You shall venerate the Lord your God, and him alone shall you worship." We are commanded, he said, to venerate the Lord, not an image of God. My good fellow, Theodore replies, this debate is not about theology. Theology (*theologia*), as Theodore uses the term here, refers to *theo-logos*, words and ideas used to express the nature of the ineffable God. All such talk, Theodore opines, is speculative. We cannot know God's nature as it exists in itself. If one attempts to speak about God's nature in itself there can be no talk of an image or likeness. It is blasphemous to think that a painting could express what is inexpressible or contain what is not bound to space. No, my friend, Theodore says, we are talking about the "divine economy," about God become flesh. Because God has taken our nature and lived among us it is possible to draw an image that portrays Christ who is God incarnate, the original from which the image is drawn. The God who created everything "became matter, that is, flesh," hence his image is palpable, visible, sensible. Yet the iconoclasts say that Christ is known sufficiently by "mental contemplation" through the Holy Spirit. But, asserts Theodore, "If merely mental contemplation had been sufficient, it would have been enough for him to come to us in a merely mental way." Because he came as a human being with a body, the icon is "the most visible testimony of God's saving plan.[28]

Making This Thing Other

David Jones, the Welsh poet, begins his poem *Anathemata* with the words, "We already and first of all discern him making this thing other."[29] The reference is to the prayer of consecration in the Mass by which the bread and wine become the body and blood of Christ. But the sentence has a double meaning because "making this thing other" also refers to the transformation of ordinary things, stone, wood, metal, into works of art. The words "first of all" suggest that the making of things into something else, that is, into objects of beauty, is a distinctively human work that is as old as humankind.

Both the iconoclasts and the iconodules believed that matter could become something other. But they differed on how. For the iconoclasts the prime example of matter becoming holy was the bread and wine of the Eucharist. Through the blessing of the priest over the gifts "that which is made by human hands becomes that which is not made by human hands."[30] Icons, however, were common things and had not been blessed and sanctified by a prayer of consecration.

The *iconodules* argued that the icon did not need a prayer of consecration to become something other. In Theodore's words, "The very form of it is sufficient to receive sanctification." The wood and paint become something other while remaining wood and paint. It is the image painted on the wood, the person depicted by the icon, that make it precious. When the image fades or is effaced, it is no longer an icon, no longer a holy object, and can be thrown into the fire. But as long as it bears the image of the person the icon is holy. Though the material elements of the icon are wood and paint, "because of the image of the person depicted, the icon is called Christ or image of Christ; Christ because of the identity in name, image of Christ because of the relationship of the image to Christ."[31] Hence it was proper to kiss it and kneel before it, just as one would kiss and venerate Christ himself.

For some the physicality of the icon made it an unsuitable vehicle to foster a spiritual relation to God. The God of the Scriptures was a spiritual being not bound by space, wholly everywhere at the same time. If Christianity promised to turn men and women away from the worship of things to worship God in spirit and in truth, why did the church promote devotion to objects of wood and paint and gold? The defenders of icons responded that if one does not venerate the Christ who is depicted in the image, one "also abandons the spiritual veneration of Christ." Just as one cannot look at the sun with the naked eye, one cannot see the living God with the mind alone. It is the point made by Origen against Celsus at the very beginning of this book and repeated again and again by early Christian thinkers. One must first kneel and turn one's face to the ground to see the beams reflected from the earth. Hence Theodore concludes that nothing is more capable of raising the mind to spiritual things than an image.[32]

The term Theodore uses for lifting up the mind is *anagogy*, a word that was often used to refer to the spiritual sense of the Scriptures. Over time the term came to be used to designate future hopes and hence to carry eschatological overtones. Theodore seems to understand icons in this sense because he says that in looking at the image one is able to anticipate seeing God face to face, "with one's own eyes."[33] Because the icon is an image of the living Christ, it looks forward as well as back, anticipating the vision of God. The Christ who is depicted on the icon lives and will one day return in glory and in judgment. The icon, a thing of wood and paint, unites memory and hope with presence in a single object of devotion, bringing together the historical events of the gospels, the Christ who will come in glory at the end of the ages, and Christ who is alive and present.

Christianity is an affair of things. At the center of Christian worship is a material, palpable thing, the consecrated bread and wine, through water one is joined to the church, and through things, the Holy Cross, the rock of Calvary, the sacred tomb, God accomplished the salvation of the world. When a bishop at the Council of Nicaea in 787 said that icons were "of equal power with the Gospel and the Holy Cross," he was referring not to the message of the Gospel or the idea of the Cross, but to the *book* of the Gospel and the *wood* of the Holy Cross. Icons, like the consecrated bread and wine, the wood of the cross, the book of the gospels, are witnesses to God's sojourn among us as a human being. Without the icon, without the image of the person of Christ, the Incarnation would become an "illusion."[34]

We tire easily of abstractions and crave visible signs. The icon was a tangible pledge that things could become other than they are. This was no less true of human beings. For if wood and paint could depict the living God, then creatures of flesh and blood could aspire to likeness with God. "By surrendering his godhead to our flesh," writes John of Damascus, "God has deified our flesh." There is no greater evidence of the transfiguration of human flesh than the lives of the saints. Just as the icon of Christ bids us fall on our knees to worship the one who created matter, so the icons of the saints inspire us to "follow their example and by imitating their virtue to give glory to God."[35]

Chapter 11

Likeness to God

Beloved, we are God's children now; it does not yet appear what we
shall be, but we know that when he appears we shall be like him,
for we shall see him as he is. And everyone who thus hopes in him
purifies himself as he is pure.

1 JOHN 3:2—3

IN A SCENE in *The Brothers Karamazov* shortly before Father
Zossima's death, the elder gathers his fellow monks and those
dear to him in his cell for a final conversation. He recalls that as a
child he owned a book with beautiful pictures entitled *A Hundred
and Four Stories from the Old and New Testaments*. From this book
he learned to read, and as an old man he kept it on a shelf close to
his bed. Father Zossima remembered the many tales of good and
holy men and women, of Job and Esther and Jonah, the parables
of Jesus, the conversion of Saul, and the lives of the saints Alexei
and Mary of Egypt, stories that planted a mysterious seed in his
heart. Some of these sacred tales, like the story of Job, he could
not read "without tears." Like bright sparks in the darkness, these

stories of God's holy people shone brightly in his memory. In them, says Father Zossima, he "beheld God's glory." "What is Christ's word," he asks, "without an example?"

Without examples, without imitation, there can be no human life or civilization, no art or culture, no virtue or holiness. The elementary activities of fashioning a clay pot or constructing a cabinet, of learning to speak or sculpting a statue have their beginnings in imitation. This truth is as old as humankind, but in the West it was the Greeks who helped us understand its place in the moral life, and in the Roman period it is nowhere displayed with greater art than in Plutarch's *Lives*. "Virtuous deeds," he wrote, "implant in those who search them out a zeal and yearning that leads to imitation. . . . The good creates a stir of activity towards itself and implants at once in the spectator an impulse toward action."[1]

By the time Christianity made its appearance in the Roman Empire, the practice of writing lives of virtuous men was well established. Only in the third century, however, did Christians begin to write lives of their holy men and women. There were, of course, heroic tales in the Scriptures, apocryphal acts recounted the wonders of the apostles, and martyrs' acts celebrated the courage of these witnesses to Christ in their final hours. Yet the writing of edifying lives did not begin until later. The supreme model was Jesus, whose life was recorded in the gospels. "I have given you an example," he said, "that you also should do as I have done" (John 13:15). Even Saint Paul, whose adventures would have been fit subjects for an edifying life (he was whipped with lashes, beaten three times with rods, stoned once, shipwrecked three times), invited imitation only because he followed the example of Christ. "Be imitators of me," he wrote, "as I am of Christ" (1 Cor. 11:1). Others followed in his train. Ignatius of Antioch in the early second century exhorted the Philadelphians "to imitate Jesus Christ as he imitated the Father."[2]

In the middle of the third century, Pontus, a disciple of Cyprian of Carthage, the most illustrious bishop in the African church before Augustine, composed what may be considered the first life of a Christian saint. His *Passion and Life of Cyprian,* written shortly after Cyprian's death as a martyr (ca. A.D. 259), was the work of a man who had served as deacon under Cyprian and knew him well. A more conventional disciple would have told Cyprian's triumph in the style of other acts of the martyrs, but Pontus consciously breaks with convention. Cyprian, he says, "had much to teach *independently* of his martyrdom; what he did while he was alive should not be hidden from the world." By writing the *Life* Pontus wished to hold up not only his valor at the end, but the "noble pattern" that was displayed in the deeds and accomplishments of Cyprian's life. His entire life was worthy of preservation in "eternal memory."[3]

Pontus anticipated a seminal development in Christian history, the writing of lives as a way of teaching virtue. In the next century Athanasius of Alexandria would write a *Life of Antony,* the first Christian monk, that would set the pattern for later lives. Christians, of course, taught by precept ("You know what precepts we gave you through the Lord Jesus," said Paul), but, like Plutarch, they knew that only deeds can stir the soul to action.[4] Even a very partial listing of some of the many lives that appeared during the next three hundred years testifies to the vitality and breadth of this new genre of Christian literature: *Life of Pachomius,* Palladius's store of lives in his *Lausiac History, Life of John Chrysostom,* Gerontius's *Life of Melania* (the first full life of a woman ascetic), Theodoret of Cyrus's *Religious History* (lives of monks of Syria), Gregory the Great's life of Benedict, Cyril of Scythopolis's lives of the Palestinian monks, Sulpicius Severus's *Life of Martin of Tours,* a soldier, the life of Daniel the Stylite and of John the Almsgiver, and on and on and on. They are many and varied. Some dwell on the eccentric and grotesque, telling of men who sat for years on pillars or dwelled in huts too narrow to stretch out in; others read like romances or adventure stories; still others depict fierce inner struggles and describe unexceptional and unheralded acts of mercy and alms-giving and love.

With few exceptions these lives hold up imitation as the path to virtue. In the *Life of Antony* Athanasius wrote that when people hear of Antony's deeds they will want "to imitate him." Imitation was, however, not simply a matter of mimicking the virtuous deeds of another person. Deeds were not isolated acts of mercy or justice disconnected from a person but signs of character, and moral instruction had to do with the formation of character. In a letter placed at the beginning of his *Lausiac History,* Palladius said, "Words and syllables do not constitute teaching. . . . Teaching consists of virtuous acts of conduct. . . . This is how Jesus taught. . . . His aim was the formation of character." As Plutarch had recognized earlier, deeds need not mean great and noble displays of bravery of strength. "A slight thing, like a phrase or a jest," he wrote, often reveal more of a person's character than "battles where thousands fall."[5]

With their rustic heroes and homespun language the ancient lives are deceptively simple. In his lives of the holy men and women of Syria, Theodoret of Cyrus recounts the visit of a monk, Avitos, to Marcianos, another man of the desert. When

Avitos arrived Marcianos invited him to share dinner with him: "Come, my dear friend, let us have fellowship together at the table." But Avitos declined, saying, "I don't think I have ever eaten before evening. I often pass two or three days in succession without taking anything." To which Marcianos, who was younger, replied (not without irony), "On my account change your custom today for my body is weak and I am not able to wait until evening." Still Avitos refused, and Marcianos became disconsolate because he had disappointed his visitor: "I am disheartened and my soul is stung because you have expended much effort to come and look at a true ascetic." Finally Avitos relented, and Marcianos said, "My dear friend. We both share the same existence and embrace the same way of life. We prefer work to rest, fasting to nourishment, and it is only in the evening that we eat, but we know that love is a much more precious possession than fasting. For the one is the work of divine law, the other of our own power. And it is proper to consider the divine law more precious than our own."[6]

The story is uncomplicated and the narration artful but the message subtle. Marcianos knew how "to distinguish the different parts of virtue," says Theodoret. There was more to the lives than charming stories or pithy sayings. Like all skilled storytellers, the ancient hagiographers knew they must entertain as they instructed, yet they display an astute understanding of human nature.

Medical Art for the Soul

In the Roman world the closest analogy to the moral philosopher was the physician, one who, in the words of Cicero, practiced "a medical art for the soul." Ethics was centered on the moral agent, and the virtuous life was learned in a one-to-one relation with a tutor. Seneca wrote letters to Lucilius to guide his formation in virtue, and in a sermon (or moral lecture) on wealth, Clement of Alexandria exhorted his hearers to seek out a man of God as director and entrust themselves to him as to one who "sees to your cure." To be sure, in early Christian literature there are treatises (or sections of treatises) that deal with such moral issues as lying, sexuality, marriage, and public amusements, and here and there one will find discussions of topics such as suicide, war, abortion, and homosexual acts. But the vast bulk of writings on ethics, whether Christian or pagan, has as its theme the formation of individual lives.[7]

In a little work written in appreciation of Origen his disciple, Gregory the Wonderworker left an engaging account of what it meant to have Origen as teacher. Gregory says he had come to Palestine, where Origen was living, to have "fellowship with this man." He was attracted by Origen's great learning and fame as an interpreter of Scripture, but his essay accents Origen's spiritual and moral qualities. From the time Gregory came to study with him Origen urged him to "adopt a philosophical life." He said that "only those who practice a life genuinely befitting reasonable creatures and seek to live virtuously, who seek to know first who they are, and to strive for those things that are truly good and to shun those which are truly evil . . . are lovers of philosophy."[8]

The term for philosophy in the early centuries of the Roman Empire was *life, bios* in Greek, a word that is best translated in English as "way of life." Philosophy was not simply a way of thinking about life; it was a way of instilling attitudes and training people to live a certain way. Musonius Rufus, a second-century philosopher, said the task of philosophy is "to find out by discussion what is fitting and proper and then to carry it out in action." When Justin Martyr embraced the Christian philosophy instead of the philosophy of Plato and Pythagoras, he said he had found a life that was "sure and fulfilling." Clement of Alexandria, who wrote the first treatise on Christian ethics, entitled *The Tutor,* said that its purpose was to "heal the passions": "The role of the tutor is to improve the soul, not to educate nor give information but to train someone in the virtuous life."[9] In another treatise Clement set forth the theological and philosophical grounds for the Christian life, yet his goal always remained the same, to form the soul in virtue.

In an original and insightful book entitled *Seelenfuehrung* (Directing the Soul), Paul Rabbow, a German scholar, made the imaginative suggestion that the best place to learn the techniques used by Roman moral philosophers (and Christians like Clement) to train their disciples in virtue was found in the exercises of Ignatius Loyola, the sixteenth-century founder of the Society of Jesus. Rabbow observed that the ancient texts embodied a system of "spiritual direction" in the form of moral exercises, cultivation of good habits, self-examination, meditation on edifying sayings, contemplation of noble examples, all under the watchful eye of a master. The philosopher Galen said that twice a day he pondered sayings attributed to Pythagoras, reading them over and reciting them aloud. His aim was not to understand certain metaphysical or moral truths but to practice self-control, for example, in matters of food, desire, drink, and the emotions. Philosophy demanded that its adherents engage in an "inner battle between the old and the new life."[10] In short, the moral life required conversion of the affections as well as of one's behavior.

At first, Gregory resisted Origen's efforts to change him. Though Origen's words "struck like an arrow" Gregory held back from practicing philosophy. He was not ready to undergo the discipline imposed by Origen. Instead, he preferred to spend his time "in argument and intellectual debate." Origen, however, expected more of him than cleverness and verbal agility. His aim was to "move the soul," and he challenged his disciples to open their hearts and allow their wills to be molded by the good. If someone claimed to have studied ethics and had not been changed, he had studied something else. In Gregory's apt phrase, Origen "taught us to *practice* justice and prudence."

Although learning precepts was part of the instruction (there is extant a set of precepts put together by a Christian philosopher from this period),[11] what counted for more was the example of the master and the bonds of friendship formed with the disciple. This kind of relation, however, was rarely achieved in more casual human intercourse. Friendship, says Gregory, "is piercing and penetrating, an affable and affectionate disposition displayed in the teacher's words and his association with us." Through Origen's friendship with him, Gregory learned to love Christ, the Word, but he also began to love Origen, "the friend and interpreter of the Word." Only when "smitten by this love" was he persuaded to give up "those objects which stood in the way and to practice the philosophical life."

Gregory compares his new relation with Origen to the friendship between David and Jonathan, one of the most affecting stories of love in the Scriptures. As the soul of Jonathan was attached to David, so was Gregory joined to Origen. Gregory does not say the obvious, that as a disciple he admired and cherished his teacher; rather he says that it was Origen's love for him, the teacher's love for the student, that drove the relation: "This David of ours holds us, binding us to him now, and from the time we met him; even if we wish, we are not able to detach ourselves from his bonds." The master had first to know and love his disciples before he could cultivate their souls and, like a "skilled husbandman," bring forth fruit from an "uncultivated field." To correct, reprove, exhort, and encourage his students, the master had to know their habits, attitudes, and desires. Origen's love for his disciples was part of the process of formation.

"The most important thing of all," writes Gregory, is the "divine virtues" that form character and still the unruly passions of the soul. Gregory specifically mentions the four cardinal virtues, prudence, justice, courage, and temperance, to which he adds religious devotion, "the mother of the virtues." The goal is to be "like God and to remain in him." The section on the virtues is the longest in the work, and there more than in any other part of it Gregory is not satisfied with general comments. He discusses the virtues in detail, and at the end he sums up Origen's teaching: "This remarkable man, friend, and herald of the virtues . . . has, by his own virtue, made us love the beauty of justice, whose golden face he truly showed us." Origen, who was himself an "example of a wise man," taught us "by his own conduct." In an effort to help us "gain control over our inclinations," he instructed us, says Gregory, "more by what he did than by what he said."[12]

Virtuous deeds are the form of the moral life, yet deeds in themselves were not sufficient. To be moral, an act had to be done for the right reason. Hence instruction also attended to the inner life. This task Origen carried out by "digging deeply and examining what was most inward, asking questions, setting forth ideas, listening to the responses" of his students. When he found anything "unfruitful and without profit in us," writes Gregory, he set about clearing the soil, turning it over, watering it, and using all his "skill and concern" that we might bring forth pleasant fruit. Without self-knowledge, "attentiveness to one's soul," in Gregory's phrase, virtue would languish. In one of his own writings Origen explained why the disposition of the agent is essential to the virtuous life. It is true, he says, that "if someone is just he pursues justice." But it does not follow that "if someone pursues justice, he is just." For one must "pursue justice justly." Origen explains that the adverb is essential, for it is possible to pursue justice unjustly. Some persons do things that are good, giving to the poor, for example, but only to be praised. They act out of vanity, not because they have the "disposition of justice."[13] Virtue required a conversion of the affections.

In the end, however, Gregory acknowledged that even the mighty Origen was unable by his skill to produce virtue in his students. Though he labored industriously he was hindered, says Gregory, by our thick and sluggish nature. Virtue is the work of God: "The virtues are very great and lofty, and can only be attained by someone in whom God has breathed his power."[14]

Imitation, the virtues, interior disposition, character, likeness to God—here was the soil in which early Christian ethics took root. Christian thinkers found the classical moral tradition congenial, and the philosophical framework adumbrated in Gregory's essay, at least in its general outlines, remained remarkably intact in Christian writers. Yet changes there were, and one place to observe how Christians adapted and altered what they had received from the classical moral tradition can be seen in the interpretation of the Sermon on the Mount.

The Beatitudes

Jesus said, "Be ye therefore perfect, even as your Father which is in heaven is perfect" (Matt. 5:48). In some form this exhortation is echoed throughout the New Testament in the writings of Saint Paul (2 Cor. 7:1), in the Epistle to the Hebrews (12:14), and in 1 Peter: "As he who called you is holy, be holy yourselves in all your conduct; since it is written, 'You shall be holy, for I am holy'" (1 Peter 1:13). Whether the term is *perfection* or *holiness*, the New Testament presents Christian faith as life oriented toward an end, toward a goal, what in the language of ancient moral philosophy was called the final good, the *summum bonum*.

In the phrase "be ye perfect" the term for "perfect" derives from the Greek word for *goal, telos,* from which comes the word *teleology.* That human actions are to be understood in relation to ends is an inheritance from the Greeks. In his *Nicomachean Ethics* Aristotle observed that every activity or undertaking is directed at some good, and that good we desire for its own sake, for which all other things are done, is the "supreme good." Echoing Aristotle, Cicero, the Roman statesmen, gave one of his treatises on ethics the title "On Ends" (*De finibus*). In it he argued that human actions are praiseworthy only if they are directed toward worthy ends, the highest of which is the supreme good, that goal which is not itself a means to something else.[15]

When Christianity came on the scene there was already in place a well-developed system of moral formation in the Greco-

Roman world. Its aim was to lead people toward a happy life. By happiness the ancients meant something quite different from what we understand today. For us the term *happiness* has come to mean "feeling good" or enjoying certain pleasures, a transient state that arrives and departs as circumstances change or fortune intervenes. For the ancients, happiness was a possession of the soul, something that one acquired and that, once acquired, could not easily be taken away. Happiness designated the supreme aim of human life, in the language of ancient philosophy, living in accord with nature, in harmony with our deepest aspirations as human beings. Moral philosophy was promissory, it dealt with what could be. For this reason ethics in antiquity was a matter less of what one ought to do according to universal notions of right and wrong than of what kind of person one can become by living a certain way. Hence it had to do with deeds practiced over the course of a lifetime and the disposition of the soul. The bumper sticker "Do random acts of kindness" would have seemed risible to the ancients.

The church fathers noted that the beatitudes begin with the term *happy*, a key term in ancient philosophy. Modern English translations of the beatitudes usually translate the word as "blessed," as in "Blessed are the pure in heart for they shall see God." But the beatitude is better translated as "*Happy* are the pure in heart for they shall see God." To Christian thinkers schooled in ancient moral philosophy it appeared that, according to Jesus, happiness was the goal of human life, a serendipitous congruence of the Bible and the wisdom of the Greeks and Romans. On this interpretation the beatitudes depicted the character of a person who was happy, and in some writers the string of beatitudes were seen as steps leading to that goal. At the beginning of his *Homilies on the Beatitudes* Gregory of Nyssa said his first task is to explain the meaning of the term *happy*. "Happiness, in my view," he writes, echoing Aristotle, "is possession of all things considered good." He also noticed that the first word of the first psalm is "happy": "Happy is the man who walks not in the counsel of the wicked." Gregory writes, "Just as the art of the physician looks to health, and the aim of farming is to provide for life, so also the practice of virtue has as its aim that the one who lives virtuously will become happy."[16]

In describing the moral life in terms of its goal, that is, teleologically, Gregory shows himself very much the Greek philosopher. But Christian ethics was also formed by a distinctively theological understanding derived from Scriptures. The saying from the Sermon on the Mount, "Be ye therefore perfect, even as your Father which is in heaven is perfect" (Matt. 5:48), presents the moral life as oriented not to the "supreme good" but to God. God is the highest good, "the source of our bliss . . . and the goal of our striving," as Augustine said, and it is only in communion with God that human lives are brought to fulfillment.[17] Jesus' words, let it be remembered, are drawn from the book of Leviticus, where the language is explicitly religious, even cultic: "You shall be holy; for I the Lord your God am holy" (Lev. 19:2).

The Bible as understood by early Christian thinkers not only spoke about the goal of the moral life, by its account of the creation of human beings in God's image, it also showed, as we have seen, that the end was anticipated in the beginning. The only *telos* that can bring genuine happiness is life with God, or, more precisely, a *"return* to fellowship with God." In a revealing passage in the *City of God* Augustine says, "By our election of him as our goal—or rather our *re-election* (for we had lost him by our neglect), we direct our course towards him with love." We turned away from the God who made us to follow our own way. As a consequence, evil has been "mixed in our nature," said Gregory, and we are "prone to sin." Though human beings were made in the image of God, sin had defaced the image, and human nature "has been transformed and made ugly . . . and joined to the evil family of the father of sin." Because of the inescapable fact of sin, indeed, its rootedness in human life, ethics could never be a matter of perfecting the good that is within us. The "return to God" must begin in "repentance," in turning away from sin.[18]

For Christians the moral life and the religious life were complementary. Although thinking about the moral life moved within a conceptual framework inherited from Greek and Latin moralists, Christian thinkers redefined the goal by making fellowship with the living God the end, revised the beginning by introducing the biblical teaching that we are made in the image of God, and complicated the middle with talk of the intractability and inevitability of sin. Without an understanding of the ancient moralists Aristotle, Seneca, Cicero, and Epictetus, one cannot enter the world of early Christian ethics, yet as soon as one takes in hand the essays of Clement or Tertullian or Ambrose or reads the sermons of Gregory of Nyssa or Augustine, it is clear that something new is afoot.

Divine Poverty

For the Greeks the goal of the moral life was "likeness to God," and Christian thinkers welcomed the language of likeness to God or "divinization." In the opening paragraphs of *The Tutor* Clement says that the goal toward which the instructor, Christ, leads his pupils is "likeness to God." The notion of likeness to God was an inheritance from the Greeks, but it was also found in the Bible, most notably in the oft-cited passage in 1 John, "We know that when he appears we shall be *like* him, for we shall see him as he is" (1 John 3:2). As we saw in chapter 3, when the Platonic notion of likeness to God was filtered through the language of the Bible it acquired overtones that were alien to Greek notions, and in time the content of the phrase was transformed. For the God of the Bible, of whom Jesus said, "Be ye perfect as your father in heaven is perfect," had been revealed in the person of Christ. Hence, when Clement explained "likeness to God" he found himself speaking about "imitation of Christ."[19]

For Clement's contemporaries "likeness to God" meant practicing the virtues. Christian writers agreed. Yet they were uncomfortable speaking about the virtues without invoking Christ and the Holy Spirit as the guide to perfection.[20] The model given to imitate was drawn not from notions of divine perfection but from the perfect life of a human being, Jesus Christ, God in human flesh. Gregory of Nyssa wondered aloud whether it made sense to urge human beings to be like God. Though he believed that the "end of the virtuous life is to become like God," nevertheless he asks, Can human beings be like God, who "alone has immortality and who dwells in unapproachable light"? (1 Tim. 6:15–16). If the perfection of God can never be ours, likeness to God, it would seem, is beyond our reach.

Some things about God can, however, be imitated. The one divine attribute Gregory singles out is the poverty mentioned by Jesus in the beatitude "Blessed are the poor in Spirit, for theirs is the kingdom of heaven." This poverty is found in "voluntary humility," he says. Saint Paul directs our attention to God, "who being rich, for us became poor that we through his poverty might become rich" (2 Cor. 8:9). Even though everything else associated with the divine nature is beyond our capability, says Gregory, humility is within our grasp, indeed, it is the mark of true virtue. Only through humility can we free ourselves from the distinctively human sins of pride and arrogance. Therefore, says Gregory, we "imitate God" by becoming humble.[21]

Gregory reminds his hearers of the well-known passage in Philipians 2 about Christ's humiliation: "Let this mind be in you, which was also in Christ Jesus; who being in the form of God, thought it not robbery to be equal with God, but emptied himself, taking the form of a servant." What greater poverty, writes Gregory, than for the divine Son to take on human flesh and, sharing our nature, become a servant. The good comes to us through space and time. The goal remains likeness to God, but God has become visible in the person of Jesus Christ. Let his example, he invites his congregation, "be the measure of your humility."[22]

But Gregory goes further. Christ was not only the model, but also the goal. He observed that *justice* (or *righteousness*), the term used in the fourth beatitude, "those who hunger and thirst for justice," and in the eighth, "persecuted for the sake of justice," is used of Christ elsewhere in the Bible. In 1 Corinthians, Paul says that Christ Jesus is "our wisdom, our justice and sanctification and redemption" (1 Cor. 1:30). In the beatitudes, then, *justice* does not simply mean "give to each according to his worth," what is called distributive justice, but a higher form of justice, "the justice of God which is truly to be desired," Christ, who is "justice itself."[23]

Gregory was puzzled by the wording of the eighth beatitude, "Blessed are those who are persecuted for the sake of justice, for theirs is the kingdom of heaven" (Matt. 5:10). How could persecution be a good? Happiness, according to Aristotle, requires "the gifts of fortune." Gregory answers that this is why the beatitude reads not simply, "Happy are those who are persecuted for the sake of justice," but adds the phrase "for theirs is the kingdom of heaven." If one is to be happy, one must possess the good. There must be an end beyond being persecuted (which itself is not a good). Hence Gregory asks, "What is it that we will obtain? What is the prize? What is the crown? It seems to me that for which we hope is nothing other than the Lord himself. For He himself is the judge of those who contend, and the crown of those who win. He is the one who distributes the inheritance, he himself is the good inheritance. He is the good portion and the giver of the portion, he is the one who makes rich and is himself the riches. He shows you the treasure and is himself your treasure. . . . According to his promise those who have been persecuted *for his sake* shall be *happy,* for theirs is the kingdom of heaven." Happiness is possessing Christ. The beatitudes are not simply moral maxims, but invitations by Christ to his disciples "to ascend with him" that they might enjoy "fellowship with the God of all creation."[24]

Virtue can never be simply a matter of spiritual athleticism. It is possessed in Christ and sealed by the Holy Spirit. Christian life is trinitarian, oriented toward God the supreme good, formed by the life of Christ, and moved toward the good by the indwelling of the Holy Spirit. Again Gregory goes right to the heart of the matter. In his little essay on the Holy Spirit he says that only the Spirit has the power to bestow the good, by which he means moral good. For whatever is good comes from God through the Son and is perfected by the Holy Spirit. How can one "cleave to

God," he asks, unless the Holy Spirit works in us? And let it not be forgotten that the virtues were practiced in a community nurtured by the sacraments. In baptism, says Ambrose, the Spirit is poured out, the "spirit of wisdom and understanding, the spirit of counsel and strength, the spirit of knowledge and devotion, the spirit of holy fear" (Isa. 11:2–3). These virtues, says Ambrose, are no less important than the cardinal virtues, for nothing contributes more to a holy life than devotion to God, knowledge of God, and fear of God.[25]

Cardinal Virtues and Some

In the ancient world the chief virtues, what came to be called the cardinal virtues, were four: prudence, justice, temperance, and fortitude. Long before the beginning of Christianity these virtues had achieved a prominent place in moral discourse. As early as Clement of Alexandria, Christian writers began to appropriate the cardinal virtues as a vehicle for presenting the distinctive marks of the moral life. As we have seen, Christian writers, however, claimed that the cardinal virtues were not the exclusive property of the Greeks or Romans, for they were also found in the Bible. The Wisdom of Solomon mentions them explicitly: "And if any one loves righteousness, her labors are virtues; for she teaches self-control [temperance] and prudence, justice and courage [fortitude]; nothing in life is more profitable for men than these" (Wisdom 8:7). Clement cites this text to accent the priority of the cardinal virtues and, with some playfulness, suggests that the Greeks learned them from the Hebrews.[26]

The cardinal virtues quickly acquired a privileged status within Christian tradition. In the fourth century when Ambrose bishop of Milan wrote a general treatise on ethics, he not only took the title from Cicero's essay, *De Officiis,* but also organized his book, as had Cicero, around the cardinal virtues. Yet as soon as one moves beyond the introductory paragraphs and looks at Ambrose's discussion of specific virtues as well as at the examples he used to illustrate them, Cicero is displaced by the Scriptures.

Cicero had written that prudence (or wisdom) consisted in "knowledge of the truth." Lacking a desire to know the truth, he said, one could not be virtuous. Ambrose agreed, and in his discussion of prudence he follows Cicero closely, even citing his definition. Ambrose, however, says that the prime example of prudence is Abraham because he "believed in God." Prudence or wisdom is identified with knowing God and hence with faith. If one does not know God and trust him one cannot be wise, that is, possess the virtue of prudence. It is the fool who says "there is no God." A wise person would never make such a statement, for "the fear of the Lord is the beginning of wisdom."

Although Ambrose uses the philosophical term *prudence* (*prudentia*), he prefers the word that is more frequent in the Bible, *wisdom* (*sapientia*). In the Scriptures wisdom is not a human achievement, but a gift from God and is granted only to those who know and worship God. Nothing, says Ambrose, is more important for human beings than to "revere God." Those who are wise, according to the Wisdom of Solomon, "obtain friendship with God." The wise man or woman lives in an intimate relation with God, and no one possessed greater wisdom than Jacob, who wrestled with God, for "he had seen God face to face" (Gen. 32:30).[27]

Similarly, in dealing with justice, Ambrose gives the virtue a distinctively theological cast. Like prudence, justice begins in reverence and devotion. Justice, he writes, is "first directed toward God." Only when God is given his due is it possible to deal justly with others, that is, to love them. Ambrose subtly shifts the emphasis toward the biblical teaching of love of neighbor. For Cicero justice had a retributive side and was measured by the way one had been treated. Hence it was wrong to harm another person "unless one is provoked by wrong." Ambrose disputes this view and supports his argument with a whimsical interpretation of a passage from the gospels. According to the Gospel of Luke, when Jesus sent messengers ahead of him to enter a Samaritan village, "the people would not receive him." In response the disciples James and John said to Jesus, "Do you want us to bid fire come down from heaven and consume them." Jesus, however, rebuked them and without a further word took the disciples to another city. Ambrose takes Jesus' action to mean that Christ came to bring grace, not harm.[28]

As these examples indicate, Ambrose realized that Christians could not appropriate the classical tradition without significant modification. Yet he saw the wisdom in the writings of the Roman moralists and sought to adapt their thinking to Christian use. In his effort to reconcile the classical tradition with Christianity, Ambrose is not always successful. The language of the Scriptures, for example, faith and love, sometimes pull him in another direction, and biblical saints fit uncomfortably in the classical categories. Ambrose is less a philosopher interested in critical analysis than a teacher with an eye on what works. Perhaps for this very reason his treatise had enormous influence on later Christian tradition. It is quite remarkable that a prominent bishop, writing more than three hundred years after the beginning of Christianity, would adopt the work of the great Roman statesman to present a comprehensive approach to ethics. By drawing on the scheme of the cardinal virtues, Ambrose was able to pour biblical language and biblical themes into a well-tested system of moral instruction. Not the least of his accomplishments was to secure a place within Christian tradition for the virtues as the framework for teaching ethics.

As indispensable as the cardinal virtues were for presenting the moral life, however, when measured by the Bible the list of four seemed partial and incomplete. If one looks at the several catalogues of the gifts of the Spirit in the Scriptures, one way the Bible speaks about the virtues, the list one comes up with is quite different from the classical catalogue. "The fruit of the Spirit," writes Paul in Galatians, "is love, joy, peace, patience, kindness, goodness, faithfulness, gentleness, self-control"(Gal. 5:16). "Self-control" could perhaps be read as "temperance"; with some stretch "faithfulness" could be rendered as "fortitude"; and perhaps "kindness" could be understood as "justice." But Paul's catalogue in Galatians, as well as other lists in the Scriptures (Isaiah 11:2, for example), cannot easily be reduced to the cardinal virtues. Accordingly, the catalogue of virtues was expanded and not only by the addition of the "theological virtues," faith, hope, and charity.

I was reminded of this extension one morning a few years ago as I was praying in the cathedral of Christ Church in Oxford, England. During the singing of the morning office I noticed several large medallions set in the stone floor at the front of the apse. From where I was sitting I could see that one was *prudentia*, then I noticed *temperantia* and *fortitudo*. I knew there had to be a fourth, *justitia*, and after the service I went to the front of the church. To my surprise I noticed there were five, not four, medallions. The fourth was indeed *justitia* but the fifth was *misericordia,* mercy. Whoever designed the cathedral understood that the four cardinal virtues did not say everything Christians believed about the moral life.

Tertullian of Carthage, a contemporary of Clement of Alexandria, wrote an essay on patience. Unlike Clement, who had written a general work on the moral life, Tertullian's approach is piecemeal. He wrote treatises on, among other things, idolatry, on the spectacles in the ancient amphitheaters loved by the Romans, on modesty, on marriage. But the work that never fails to charm and edify is his little meditation *On Patience.* It is the first treatise in the history of the church on a specific virtue, and the choice is significant. Not only is patience explicitly mentioned in the Scriptures, for example, in the passage from Galatians cited above, but it was not considered a virtue by the ancients. Cicero and Seneca had written admiringly of the virtue of endurance, by which they meant perseverance in adversity, but said nothing about patience as Tertullian understood it.

Tertullian had in mind what the King James translation of the Bible called "long suffering," an attribute of God, as in the phrase, "slow to anger": "The Lord is slow to anger, and abounding in steadfast love, forgiving iniquity and transgression" (Num. 14:18). The first epistle of Peter says that "God's patience [that is, long suffering] waited in the day of Noah" (1 Pet. 3:20), and out of mercy God refrained from punishing those who had done wrong. Tertullian's claim is that patience is not confined to God. In the wisdom books, for example, this divine quality becomes a virtue attributed to human beings: "He who is slow to anger has great understanding" (Prov. 14:29).

The chief example of patience, however, is "God himself," and Tertullian begins his treatise with a discussion of divine patience. God scatters light across the world to the just and the unjust, he allows the earth to yield fruit to the worthy and unworthy, he bears the sins and wrongdoing of men, he restrains his wrath as evil men go about their life oblivious to God. The most visible sign of God's patience, however, is the Incarnation. For God allowed himself to be conceived in the womb of a woman and waited patiently for the months to pass before the birth of Christ. When God is born as a human being he patiently underwent the various stages of childhood and adolescence leading to maturity. And when Christ reached adulthood he did not rush to be recognized and even allowed himself to be baptized by his own servant. The supreme example of patience was Christ's passion, says Tertullian, an observation that was echoed centuries later by Augustine in a sermon on the Lord's Passion. "The passion of our Lord," he wrote, "is a lesson in patience." All this shows, says Tertullian, that "it is God's nature to be patient." Conversely, impatience becomes the primal sin, and the chief example of impatience is the devil. "Who," says Tertullian, ever committed adultery "without the impatience of lust?"[29]

For Tertullian the singular mark of patience is not endurance or fortitude but hope. To be impatient, says Tertullian, is to live without hope. Patience is grounded in the Resurrection. It is life oriented toward a future that is God's doing, and its sign is longing, not so much to be released from the ills of the present, but in anticipation of the good to come. Hence patience becomes the key to the other virtues, including love, which can never be learned, he says, "without the exercise of patience." In a beautiful passage toward the end of his treatise, in his inimitable aphoristic prose, Tertullian sums up the work of patience:

> Patience outfits faith, guides peace, assists love, equips humility, waits for penitence, seals confession, keeps the flesh in check, preserves the spirit, bridles the tongue, restrains the hands, tramples temptation underfoot, removes what causes us to stumble, brings martyrdom to perfection; it lightens the care of the poor, teaches moderation to the rich, lifts the burdens of the sick, delights the believer, welcomes the unbeliever, commends the servant to his master and his master to God, adorns women and gives grace to men; patience is loved in children, praised in youth, admired in the elderly. It is beautiful in either sex and at every age of life. . . . Her countenance is tranquil and peaceful, her brow serene. . . . Patience sits on the throne of the most gentle and peaceful Spirit. . . . For where God is there is his progeny, patience. When God's Spirit descends patience is always at his side.[30]

On Patience is a work of spiritual discernment wholly out of character of the author. Tertullian himself was not a patient man, yet he showcased a dimension of the moral life that could easily have been shoved to the periphery. His prescience is evident in the generations after him. The two other major writers of Christian North Africa, Cyprian in the third century and Augustine in the fifth, also wrote books on the virtue of patience. By introducing his readers to a virtue that was modeled on the biblical portrayal of God's relation to the world and to human beings, Tertullian redefined what it means to be "like God."

Cardinal Virtues as Forms of Love

The most thoroughgoing reinterpretation of the virtues took place in Saint Augustine. Like Ambrose, Augustine assumed that the cardinal virtues—he called them "four virtues that are useful for life"—were the framework in which to present the form of the moral life. But as he sought to imprint them with the contours of the church's faith they underwent a transformation. For Augustine the starting point of the Christian life (as well as its end) was the love of God. He understood the words of Jesus "You shall love the Lord your God" as a command ("Love the Lord your God") and as a goal (only in loving God will we find happiness). This is why Saint Paul said, "All things work together for *good* to them who love God" (Rom. 8:29).[31]

Like other Christian thinkers, Augustine believed that happiness was found in likeness to God, and, like Gregory of Nyssa, he knew that likeness to God did not mean becoming divine but cleaving to God and living in fellowship with God. As we draw near to God we are filled with his life and light and holiness. Augustine, however, was forced to think more systematically about the wellsprings of Christian life because of the challenge of Pelagius, and his writings give close attention to how human beings are able to turn toward God and hold fast to the good. He is also more conscious than others of the persistence of inner conflict within the life of the Christian: "Whoever thinks that in this mortal life a person may so disperse the mists of bodily and carnal imaginings as to possess the unclouded light of changeless truth, and to cleave to it with the unswerving constancy of a spirit wholly estranged from the common ways of life—such a person understands neither what he seeks, nor who he is who seeks it."[32] For this reason the commandments, the Sermon on the Mount, and free will are insufficient to make one virtuous. A person must love the good and delight in it and be bound to God by the tethers of affection.

Augustine wrote essays on moral topics, but it was in the debate with Pelagius, and to a lesser extent with the Manichees, that his thinking on the Christian life took form. For Pelagius the practice of virtue rested on free choice, the capacity of human beings to choose right or wrong. When the will is instructed by the commandments and the teaching of Jesus (free will and the commandments were gifts from God and hence works of grace), human beings could live virtuously. If Jesus taught that human beings should be perfect, he argued, then perfection was within our grasp. In fact, some of the saints in the Old Testament had lived a perfect life, for example, Job, whom the Scriptures call a "blameless and upright man" (Job 1:8).

Augustine, of course, wrote a small library of books against Pelagius and his followers, but his central argument is captured in a trenchant paragraph in his treatise *On the Spirit and the Letter*. Against Pelagius he argued that something more is needed than free will and the commandments. We must be changed from within, and that takes place only when we are endowed with the Holy Spirit. For the distinctive work of the Holy Spirit is to engender love for God. When the heart is fired "to cleave to the creator," a person is able to do good and hold fast to it. "There can be no devotion and no good unless it be delighted in and loved," he wrote. The two biblical texts that frame Augustine's discussion are Psalm 73:28, "For me it is good to cleave to God," and a passage from Romans: "God's love has been poured into our hearts through the Holy Spirit which has been given to us" (Rom. 5:5). In contrast to most other exegetes, ancient as well as modern, Augustine consistently takes Romans 5 to refer to the love we have for God, not to God's love for us. Though idiosyncratic, his interpretation is plausible. In 5:5 Paul employs a moral vocabulary to illustrate the consequences of faith: "suffering that produces endurance, and endurance that produces character, and character that produces hope." Saint Paul's wording, "Love has been poured into our hearts," suggests that love is something we have received and becomes our own. Again and again Augustine returns to this passage from Romans, and his point is always the same: the love that turns us toward God and draws us close to God is the gift of the Holy Spirit: "Through love we become conformed to God and this conforming, this fashioning . . . is the work of the Holy Spirit."[33]

For Augustine, love, poured into our hearts by the Holy Spirit, is the soul's movement, the will's energy, the wind that fills the sails of virtue and leads us to embrace the good. Virtue, he writes, "is nothing else than perfect love of God" and can be brought to perfection only in love. If so, he reasons, the virtues can be understood as forms of love. Temperance can be understood as love "giving itself fully to that which is loved," fortitude is "love bearing all things for the sake of that which one loves," justice "is serving only the loved object," and prudence is "love wisely distinguishing what hinders and what helps it." Admittedly the definitions are somewhat artificial, and because Augustine makes the virtues forms of love, one wonders whether he has emptied them of their distinctive character, in effect, displacing them by a single virtue, love.[34]

Thomas Aquinas gently chided Augustine for collapsing the cardinal virtues into forms of love and tried to put the best construction on his words. According to Saint Thomas, what Augustine meant was not that each virtue is "love simply," but that it depends in some way on love.[35] Thomas's reservations are well founded, and he makes up what is lacking in Augustine by presenting in detail the distinctive marks of each virtue. As a moral theologian, he wished to recover aspects of the classical tradition that had been forgotten. Augustine, however, lived at a time when this tradition was still intact, and he sought to orient it to the language of the Bible and the God of the Bible. The classical tradition was oriented toward ends, in particular the goal of happiness, and the virtues offered a way to speak concretely about the form of the moral life. But the Triune God was not an end in the conventional sense. Likeness to God was not a goal that could be reached in this life, and, as we shall see in the final chapter, the God who was sought continued to be sought even when he was found. God is not an inert, passive destination. By sending Christ, God had come near and displayed human life in a new way and by sending the Holy Spirit had drawn human beings toward himself. God was the goal but also the way. Though the ancient vessel was useful (Augustine's word), it could not contain the rich and fragrant wine of the Gospel.

Jesus had said, "You shall love the Lord your God with all your heart and with all your soul and with all your might." For early Christians the moral life was the religious life, a life oriented to God in love. Virtue was about the ordering of one's love, and the first and greatest love, the love that animates all other loves, is the love of God. Only in seeking God, in following God, in holding on to God is virtue possible. Saint Bernard wrote, "Virtue is that by which one seeks continuously and eagerly for one's Maker and when one finds him, adheres to him with all one's might." The virtues work through love, for the sake of love, and receive their grace and strength from love. Seek not this good or that good, says Augustine, but the "good of every good" and cleave to it in love.[36] When love is fixed on God virtue becomes radiant.

Chapter 12

The Knowledge of Sensuous Intelligence

Abiding provenance I would have said
the question stands
even in adoration
clause upon clause
with or without assent
reason and desire on the same loop—
I imagine singing I imagine
getting it right—the knowledge
of sensuous intelligence
entering into the work—
spontaneous happiness as it was once
given our sleeping nature to awake by
and know
innocence of first inscription

GEOFFREY HILL

IN THE GREEK version of the Song of Songs read in the early church, the bride says to her beloved, "I am wounded by your love" (Song of Sol. 2:5). Gregory of Nyssa took this to mean that the "arrows" of the bridegroom had "penetrated the depths of her heart." The sublime arrow that enters our "inmost being," he wrote, is Christ, the "chosen arrow" of the prophet Isaiah

(49:2). When the soul is wounded by the piercing shafts of Christ's love, it is set ablaze and, in his happy phrase, offers a "reciprocating love." Saint Theresa of Avila, the great Spanish mystic, would echo this sentiment centuries later: "Love calls for love in return."[1]

Nothing is more characteristic of the Christian intellectual tradition than its fondness for the language of the heart. In the famous passage at the beginning of Augustine's *Confessions*, it is the heart that is restless until it rests in God, and much later in the same book he says it is love that carried him to God: "By God's gift we are set on fire and carried upwards; we grow red hot and ascend. We climb 'the ascents in our heart'" (Ps. 83:6). In a memorable passage in the *City of God* Augustine says that the "flame on the altar of the heart" is the "burning fire of love." We "direct our course toward [God] with love."[2]

In the first chapter of this book I quoted Origen's response to Celsus's taunt, "What was the purpose of God's descent to human beings?" Origen answered that God had entered our world in the person of Christ to "implant in us the happiness that comes . . . from knowing him." Origen's two locutions, "happiness" and "knowing God," can serve to draw together the many themes that have been in play in this book. For the knowledge that brings happiness is ours only in love. Unlike knowledge from a distance, for example, observing an object in the world, the knowledge of God, says Origen, is "fellowship with God through Christ."[3] The church fathers were very sure of their footing on this point, as Gregory of Nyssa shows in his explanation of the term *see* in the beatitude, "Blessed are the pure in heart for they shall *see* God." In the usage of the Scriptures, says Gregory, see means the same as have. When the psalmist says,

"May you *see* the good things of Jerusalem," he does not mean that one will look at the good things of Jerusalem, but that one will possess them. Therefore the one "who *sees* God *possesses* . . . all there is of the things that are good." Jesus did not teach, "It is blessed to know something *about* God"; he said that blessedness "is possessing God within oneself," to be known by God, not only to know God.[4] Happiness is found not in receiving something from God but in enjoying the presence of God, what the psalmists call the "face of God." Love is the one human endowment that moves us to seek the face of God.

At one point in the *Paradiso* Dante asks Beatrice why God willed "precisely this pathway for our redemption," namely, the Incarnation. Beatrice begins her response by reminding Dante that what she is about to explain to him "is buried from the eyes of everyone whose intellect has not matured within the flame of love."[5] Unless we invest ourselves in the object of our love, we remain voyeurs and spectators, curiosity seekers, incapable of receiving because we are unwilling to give. With God irony is blasphemy. Only when we turn our deepest self to God can we enter the mystery of God's life and penetrate the truth of things. If love is absent, our minds remain childish and immature, trying out one thing then another, unable to hold fast to the truth. Human beings, said Dante, are those creatures who "have intelligence *and* love."[6] In this final chapter the subject must be love.

Agape and Eros

Although the language of love permeates the Scriptures, in the early centuries of the church's history it was not apparent how it was to be appropriated and understood. In Greek (and also in Latin) there were several words for love. One term, often simply transliterated into English as *agape,* signified charity, care for others, whereas another, *eros,* designated erotic love, and a third, *philia,* referred to friendship. But the boundaries between the several terms were fluid, and the sense was fixed more by context than by the words themselves. In his *Commentary on the Song of Songs* Origen observed that the Scriptures prefer the term *agape* to *eros* when speaking of love so that "no moral lapse would come about in its readers." Yet the appearance of the term *agape* instead of *eros* is sometimes anachronistic. In Genesis it is said that Isaac "took Rebecca, and she became his wife and he was charitable toward her [loved her with agape]." What is meant, of course, is not charity but erotic love. Likewise, when the Bible says of Rachel, "But Rachel was beautiful in form and fair in countenance and Jacob was charitable toward her" (Gen. 29:17), the writer is speaking of eros. According to Origen, the Scriptures avoid the word *eros* to avoid offending sensitive readers.

There are, however, some instances in which the term *desire* or *erotic love* is used with respect to spiritual matters. In Proverbs it is said of Wisdom, "Love her passionately [that is, love her with *eros*], and she will preserve you; embrace her, and she will exalt you" (Prov. 4:6). And in the book of the *Wisdom of Solomon,* it is written, "I have become a passionate lover of her [Wisdom's] beauty" (Wisdom 8:2). Origen opines that even though *agape* is more frequent in the Bible, the Scriptures allow both terms, and in some cases when it uses *agape* it means *eros.*[7] Clearly he is trying to find a way to domesticate the term *eros* for Christian use. Even at this early stage in Christian history one of its most acute thinkers sensed that in relation to God something more than agape was called for.

Early Christian thinking, as we have seen on various occasions in this book, was often in direct conversation with philosophical ideas current in Roman society. In some cases, Christians were sharp critics of traditional views, as, for example, how God was known; in other cases, for example, the cardinal virtues, they welcomed the wisdom of the past, adapting and modifying it as they saw fit. In discussing the term *love*, Origen gives the impression he is engaged in an exercise in biblical lexicography, but the issue was philosophical and theological, not philological. His interpretation of biblical language was in fact addressing an ancient philosophical debate about the role of the passions in the moral life.

According to the Stoics, the life of virtue required detachment from the passions, those unruly motions like fear, anger, jealousy, and passionate love that drive human behavior against reason toward unwanted ends. The sage strives to be totally self-sufficient, free of the disordered impulses that deflect one from pursuing what is good and noble. Tranquility of soul is the mark of wisdom. Consequently, if one is to live virtuously the passions were not to be moderated or channeled, but rather rooted out or, in the language of the Stoics, extirpated. Modern scholarship has shown that the Stoic account of the passions is more subtle than the views often attributed to them. Yet in antiquity the lines were drawn clearly, and Christians found that they had to choose whether to side with the Stoics or take up intellectual arms against them.[8]

Some Christian thinkers were attracted to the views of the Stoics and thought that Jesus was the exemplar of a life freed of the passions, what the ancients called *apatheia*, indifference to the passions. Clement of Alexandria said that by his mastery over pain and suffering Jesus showed he was beyond passion, and his disciples, by following the Lord's teaching and example, had learned to live in an "unwavering disposition of self-discipline." Like Christ, they were able not only to overcome anger, fear, and desire, but also to learn to be indifferent even to such emotions as zeal and joy. "Apatheia is the fruit of eliminating desire completely." Other writers adopted a position similar to Clement. One of the most influential was the monastic writer Evagrius Ponticus. In his view the chief impediment to spiritual growth was thoughts, those distracting images that crowd the mind and lure it away from contemplating God. For Evagrius such thoughts were associated with the passions, chiefly desire and anger. Only when these refractory impulses are tamed can one achieve the goal of apatheia. Apatheia is the sign of a "healthy soul," a soul cleansed of turbulent emotions.[9]

Yet even when Christian thinkers defended apatheia as the goal of life, they could not avoid the language of love. In the passage from Clement cited above, after he presents the apostles in the guise of Stoic sages, he adds, almost parenthetically, that nothing can separate the mature Christian from "love toward God." For the true Christian "always loves God and is turned toward him." How, one might ask, can love be a matter of indifference? Here as in other places in his writings Clement's philosophical instincts pull him in one direction, while the language and logic of the Scriptures point him in another. Even for Evagrius love is the "offspring of apatheia." The Stoic notion of apatheia rests uneasily alongside the biblical injunction to love God with all one's heart and is hard to reconcile with passages in the Bible that urge the believer to desire wisdom or thirst for God, not to mention the frequent references to such affections as joy, gratitude, sorrow, compassion, zeal, fear, even anger. As

Jonathan Edwards, the eighteenth-century American theologian, wrote in his book on the religious affections, "The holy Scriptures do everywhere place religion very much in the affections; such as fear, hope, love, hatred, desire, joy, sorrow, gratitude, compassion, and zeal."[10]

Without Anger There Is No Virtue

By the third century some Christian thinkers, on the basis of the Scriptures, already had begun to question the conventional Stoic presentation of the moral life. The first was a little-known Latin writer by the name of Lactantius, sometimes called the Christian Cicero because he wrote graceful Latin prose. Lactantius lived at the end of the third century and was the author of several works, one of which was a wide-ranging defense of Christianity to the cultured elite of the Roman world. He does not have the depth of Origen or Augustine, yet on certain matters his instincts are uncommonly perceptive, and he notices things that escape others. He was the first thinker in Western culture to defend freedom of religion on religious grounds. Religion must be voluntary, he wrote, for "nothing requires freedom of the will as religion."[11] He also wrote a fascinating book entitled *On the Wrath [or Anger] of God* that argued against the philosophical assumption of the impassibility of God. According to the Bible, he said, God was moved by love *and* wrath.

Lactantius thought that the Stoic rejection of the passions rendered moral life otiose. The Stoics call "mercy [*misericordia*], desire, and fear diseases of the soul."[12] But in the beatitudes Jesus urges his followers to be merciful: "Blessed are the merciful for they shall receive mercy [*misericordia*]" (Matt. 5:7). Although Lactantius begins his discussion with a citation from the Scriptures, as the argument unfolds it is clear he is drawing on a philosophical critique of human action. The key failing of the Stoic doctrine was that it could not give an adequate account of what moved the soul to act.

As Lactantius knew well, the term *moved* came from Aristotle and had a venerable pedigree in ancient moral philosophy. In discussing the movements of the soul in his treatise *The Movement of Animal Beings,* Aristotle had argued that all movement can be reduced to thought and desire. Without a conception of what is to be done, we do not know what we are to do, but without desire, without an inner movement that draws us to that we have envisioned, there will be no action. "The proximate reason for *movement,*" writes Aristotle, "is desire." Drawing on this explanation of human action, Lactantius argued that the Stoics "deprive human beings of all the affections by whose impulse the soul is *moved,* namely, desire, delight, fear, grief." These affections have been implanted in us by God for a reason, and without them it is impossible to live virtuously. Even anger, when properly used, can contribute to virtue. In a surprising phrase, Lactantius drives home the point: "Without anger there can be no virtue."[13]

Lactantius's criticism of the Stoics, though inspired by the Holy Scriptures, moves along a path worn smooth by Greek and Roman philosophers. In the fourth century, however, Gregory of Nyssa took up the topic afresh and related it to a deeper issue, how human beings know God and cleave to God. His discussion of the passions, though an exercise in moral psychology, is driven by a theological agenda. In Gregory's view, the passions prepare the way for love of God.

Love Never Ends

In antiquity the passions were understood to derive from two fundamental human impulses, desire and fear. Desire is the yearning to possess something we do not have, and fear is aversion to what we do not want. To these two passions were added joy, the possession of what we desire, and grief, having to undergo what we fear. Just as there are four cardinal virtues, prudence, justice, courage and temperance, so there are four cardinal passions, desire, fear, joy, and grief. It should be observed that the passions refer not primarily to bodily drives, for example, hunger or thirst or lust, but have to do with the soul, and in that sense are intellectual, just as, for example, emotions such as envy and jealousy are attitudes, not bodily urges.

Gregory asks whether the two fundamental passions, desire and fear, are intrinsic to the soul. Are they part of human nature, that is, given at creation? or did they come about because of sin? Gregory believes that human beings were not created with passions—in his phrase, they are not "consubstantial with human nature"—but he is clearly uncomfortable with that answer. Somewhat implausibly he brings forth Moses as an example of a holy man of God who overcame the passions (ignoring Exodus 32:19, in which Moses' anger "burned hot" against the worship of the golden calf), but his more telling examples are biblical figures who used the passions in god-pleasing ways. The first is Phineas, who is said to have pleased God when his anger was inflamed against the Israelite who married a Midianite woman (Num. 25:11), and Daniel who, in the Greek Bible, is called a "man of desires" (Dan. 9:23, 10:11,19). Further, the Scriptures say that fear is the beginning of wisdom (Prov. 9:10) and grief leads to salvation (2 Cor. 7:10). Accordingly, the affections are not in themselves good or evil, but "impulses of the soul" that can serve good or evil ends. When they move saints to "choose good" they are to be praised; when they drive others to evil they are called passions. Everything depends on the ends toward which they are directed.[14]

Gregory knew that the term *desire* often carried negative overtones in the Scriptures. For example, Saint Paul writes, "Those who belong to Christ Jesus have crucified the flesh with its passions and desires" (Gal. 5:24). Yet Gregory cannot dispense with the term because it is akin to love. At one point he says flatly, "We are led to God by desire, drawn to him as if pulled by a rope." When the soul glimpses the beauty of God, it yearns to see more. Gregory's writings are filled with a seemingly inexhaustible fund of images to depict the longing for God: a lover asking for yet another kiss, a person tasting a sweetness that can be satisfied only by another taste, the dizziness one experiences standing at the edge of a precipice as one peers into a vast space. Even Moses, who had spoken with God face to face (Deut. 34:10), was not satisfied: "He sought God as if he had never seen him. In the same way, all of those in whom the desire of God is deeply imbedded, never cease yearning for more. Every delight in God becomes kindling for a still more ardent desire."[15]

For Gregory this ceaseless yearning has its source in God's infinite beauty and splendor in whose presence one never grows weary: "Every desire for the beautiful that draws us on in this ascent is intensified as the soul progresses toward it. This is what it means to see God: never to have this desire satisfied. . . . No limit can be set to our progress toward God, first because no limits can be put upon the beautiful, and second, because as our desire increases it never finds satisfaction."[16] Because God is not bound by space or time, the desire for God is unlike desire for things in this world. When, for example, we have yearned for food or drink and receive what we have longed for, our desire ceases. Often our enjoyment falls short of our expectations, and in the very moment of satisfaction, we begin to desire something else. But our yearning to see God will be satisfied only by knowing God more fully and more intimately. The more we know, the more we desire to know.

Desire or eros, then, draws us to God. But Gregory realizes, as he admits in his treatise *The Soul and Resurrection*, that if desire alone moves us, his argument would be working at cross purposes. He had insisted that the passions had come about as a consequence of the fall. Desire is acquisitive and self-centered, driven more by our needs and pleasures than by the object we seek. Hence Gregory says that as one comes into the presence of God desire gives way to love, and what was formerly sought by desire is now possessed in love. As the soul conforms more closely to God, all of its former habits give way to the "interior disposition" of love by which it becomes attached to the beautiful. This is why, writes Gregory, Saint Paul said, "Love never ends." One hopes for that which is not present, and faith has to do with the "assurance of things hoped for." When the promise arrives, however, "the operation of love remains." Love has primacy among the virtues and is first among the commandments.[17]

Only love is continuously fashioning itself according to the beloved. "If love is taken from us how will we remain united to God?" he asks. Desire is a restless activity, a yearning for something one craves but does not possess. Love, even though it is passionate, has within it an element of repose, of satisfaction, of joy that comes from delight in the presence of the beloved. Desire feeds on absence, love lives off presence. With love come delight, peace, happiness, and, yes, wonder. In one of his more vivid images Gregory compares the contemplation of God to a person looking at a spring that bubbles up from the earth:

> As you came near the spring you would marvel, seeing
> that the water was endless, as it constantly gushed up and
> poured forth. Yet you could never say that you had seen
> all the water. How could you see what was still hidden in
> the bosom of the earth? Hence no matter how long you
> might stay at the spring, you would always be beginning
> to see the water. . . . It is the same with one who fixes his
> gaze on the infinite beauty of God. It is constantly being
> discovered anew, and it is always seen as something new
> and strange in comparison with what the mind has already
> understood. And as God continues to reveal himself, man
> continues to wonder; and he never exhausts his desire to
> see more, since what he is waiting for is always more mag-
> nificent, more divine, than all that he has already seen.[18]

God is ever new, and it is only love that allows us to dwell within the house of God's abundant life. The knowledge of God is not a sudden glimpse of a strange, unfamiliar reality, but a deep, abiding joy that continually changes the lover. "Through the movement and activity of love," writes Gregory, "the soul clings to [the good] and mingles with it, fashioning itself to that which is being continually grasped and discovered anew." By love we dwell in God and God dwells in us, and as we come to know God by loving him, we discover that what we thought we knew we do not know, and what we did not know, we now know. In words of Saint Paul Gregory was fond of citing, "If any man imagines that he knows something, he does not yet know as he ought to know. But if one loves God, one is known by him" (1 Cor. 8:2).[19]

Love and Gladness in the Life to Come

Almost every topic that provoked discussion in the early church (and many that did not) appears somewhere in Augustine's *City of God*. In it Augustine also takes up the subject of the passions in Christian life, and his reasoning moves along lines sketched out by Lactantius a century earlier and Gregory in the generation before him. In fact, the topic presented itself to him in the same terms it did to Lactantius. What, in light of the Scriptures, is a Christian thinker to make of the Stoic rejection of the passions? Like Lactantius, Augustine realized that the philosophers were divided on the topic; he first sets forth the views of the Platonists and Aristotelians that the passions can be regulated by reason, and then the view of the Stoics that the passions have no place in the life of a sage. Yet Augustine believes that the differences between the schools have more to do with definitions than with the subject matter itself, for both "champion the mind and reason against the tyranny of the passions." He cites an apt passage from Virgil to drive home his point: "His mind unmoved, the tears roll down in vain."[20]

The chief target of Augustine's criticism, however, is the Stoic philosophers, and the starting point for his critique is the language of the Scriptures. Like Lactantius, he singles out the word *compassion* and chides the Stoics for condemning this passion as an emotion of the weak. Compassion, replies Augustine, is surely proper if it is directed to a good end. Why should one not be disturbed when someone is in danger and come quickly to the person's aid? The question is not whether one is angry or sad or fearful, but why. Everything turns on the object. For this reason Christians, "citizens of the Holy City of God," believe that the passions, "fear and desire, pain and gladness," have an honorable place in Christian life. If their "love is right," then the "passions are right in them."[21]

Augustine gives some apt examples from the Scriptures. It is right to fear eternal punishment and to desire eternal life, to fear sin and desire to persevere in faith. Jesus said, "Because wickedness will abound, the love of many will grow cold" (Matt. 24:12), and the Scriptures make clear that one should "feel gladness" in doing good works, for it is written, "God loves a *cheerful* giver" (2 Cor. 9:8). He mentions Paul as someone who rejoices with those who rejoice, was troubled by fears within, desired to depart and be with Christ. He longs to see the Christians in Rome, is jealous for the faithful at Corinth, and experiences "pain in his heart" and grief. Augustine's point is clear. It is not possible to live a mature Christian life without the affections. Even the saints are moved to action by feelings and attitudes and emotions. Hence he concludes that the "emotions and feelings that spring from love of the good and from holy charity" are not, as the Stoics claim, "morbid or disordered passions" but virtues. Even the Lord displayed human emotions when it was called for.[22] The movements of the soul are the springs of activity that move the will to the good.

Certain of the passions, for example, fear and grief, are necessary only in this life. If not disciplined by reason, like the legs of a young colt they bolt out of control. With respect to these passions, apatheia, detachment from the passions, does have a place in the life to come, but only with respect to them. One would hardly claim, says Augustine, that the goal is to be "free of any emotion whatsoever." "Only a man utterly cut off from truth would say that *love* and *gladness* will have no place" in the life to come. For only in love can we enjoy the presence of God. Augustine ends very much at the same place Gregory did. "Let us come," he says, "not with our feet but with our affections; let us come not by moving from one place to another, but by loving. . . . When someone is transported by the heart he changes his affection by the movement of the heart."[23]

The Blessed Passion of Love

In matters of the spirit Maximus the Confessor writes with the certainty only experience can give. His language is more scholastic than Augustine's, but like Augustine he speaks about what he knows. And what he knew was that God could be known only in love. Here Maximus's thought flows deep, and he speaks about the affections with the authority of a spiritual master. In Christian thinking the affections are an affair of first things. One of Maximus's most bracing books, *Quaestiones ad Thalassium,* is a penetrating and original exposition of difficult texts from the Bible. At the very beginning, in the first question, Maximus poses a question that had troubled earlier writers: Are the passions evil or do they become evil through use?

Like Gregory, Maximus believed that the passions were not part of the original creation of human beings, but he also knew that such an answer was so incomplete as to be misleading. For without the movement of the affections there could be no virtuous life, and without love to hold us to God we would have no enduring relation to God. Hence he answers the question in this way: "In the devout person the passions become good when they prudently turn away from earthly things and put themselves at the service of possessing heavenly things." "Desire," says Maximus, "brings about an insatiable spiritual movement that drives us toward divine things," that is, to God, and delight becomes "the quiet joy that comes from the activity of the mind firmly attached to the divine gifts." Maximus's language is unconventional, but his point is original. Knowledge "without passion" does not bind the mind to God. Love gives "reality to faith" and "makes hope present."[24]

Maximus also mentions the two negative passions, fear and grief, but the thick oxygen that courses through his discussion is the positive passions, desire that draws us toward God and delight in God. For the movement *away* from evil is always a movement *toward* God, and the goal of human life is to enjoy the presence of God. Not having passions, human beings would be unable "to hold fast to virtue and knowledge" and would have an inconstant and irresolute attachment to the One who alone is to be enjoyed. As biblical warrant for his view he cites 2 Corinthians 10.5: "We destroy arguments and every proud obstacle to the knowledge of God, and take every thought captive to obey Christ." Maximus understands Paul's "thought" to refer to the unruly passions, hence what Paul is saying is that the passions "become good" when properly used, that is, when they are subject to Christ. "In no other way," he writes, "except through the passions that are implanted in us can we have a spiritual relation to God."[25]

Although Maximus defends the right use of the passions, he also holds to the term *apatheia*, impassibility. For him *apatheia* means not Stoic detachment, but spiritual freedom, the gift of love by which we give ourselves in total devotion to God. Apatheia is a "firm and steadfast disposition" by which one "comes to rest" in that which is "ultimately desirable." The alternative to apatheia is not being unmoved but being moved by self-love, the "mother of the passions," which distorts our desires and turns them into vices. Apatheia, like ascesis, is not a negative goal, giving up something, but a turning toward something, a loosening of the bonds that enslave us to disordered loves, the freedom to attach ourselves to God in love. In love, he says, the mind "transfers its whole longing to God." Indeed Maximus identifies apatheia with love. In prayer, he says, one can reach the "full measure of apatheia and love."[26]

Like Origen and Gregory and Augustine—indeed, like all of the thinkers considered in this book—Maximus knew that the knowledge of God was participatory, a knowledge that changes the knower: "Blessed are the pure in heart for they shall see God." Only those who have been cleansed, purified, and transformed can know God. Maximus puts it this way: "Knowledge of divine things *without passion* does not persuade the mind to disdain material things completely, but is like a mere thought of a thing known by the senses. . . . For this reason there is a need for the blessed *passion of holy love* that binds the mind to spiritual realities [that is, God] and persuades it to prefer the immaterial to the material and intelligible and divine things to those of sense."[27]

In the third century Origen had explained that in the Scriptures the term *knowledge* was used in a very particular way. Commenting on John 8:19, "You know neither me nor my Father. If you knew me, you would know my Father also," he says,

"One should take note that the Scripture says that those who are united to something or participate in something are said to *know* that to which they are united or in which they participate. Before such union and fellowship, even if they understand the reasons given for something, they do not know it." As illustration he mentions the union between Adam and Eve, which the Bible described as "Adam knew his wife Eve," and 1 Corinthians 6:16–17, union with a prostitute. These passages show, he says, that *knowing* means "being joined to" or "united with."[28] Then Origen adds, if we do not take *know* to mean "being united with," how do we explain the words of Paul, "But now having known God, or rather to be known by God" (Gal. 4:9)?

When knowledge is understood as participation and fellowship, love is its natural, indeed necessary, accompaniment. Love is self-giving, passionate, unitive, erotic, and Maximus interprets the biblical agape with eros: "For in the mind of one who is continually in converse with God desire increases beyond measure into divine eros and even one's entire irascible element [anger] is transformed into divine agape. For by continual participation in the divine illumination the mind becomes altogether filled with light. It makes the passible element one with itself and turns it . . . into burning love [eros] that is without end and agape that never ceases, passing over completely from earthly to heavenly things."[29]

Here, as always, Maximus is scrupulous in his choice of terms. He self-consciously and deliberately fills the biblical term *agape* with echoes that are heard in *eros* while at the same time holding steadfastly to the biblical word. It is a shrewd move, one he may have learned from Pseudo-Dionysius the Areopagite, the enigmatic thinker who lived a century earlier. In a deliberately playful passage, Pseudo-Dionysius explains how the language of love works in the Scripture. "Do not think," he says, "that in giving status to the term *eros* I am running counter to Scripture." What, for example, does one make out of this passage from Proverbs about Wisdom (which for Dionysius was Christ): "Desire her and she shall hold you; exalt her and she will extol you" (Prov. 4.6). The careful reader of the Bible will discover that in places the biblical writers used the term *agape* when they mean desire or erotic love, implying that this is the case in other passages. Dionysius's example comes from the Septuagint version of the first chapter of 2 Samuel (1:26), David's lament of the death of his friend Jonathan. David cries out, "Your love for me was greater than love for women." Whereas one would expect to find the term *eros*, or friendship, the Scriptures use *agape*, which leads Dionysius to say, "To those who listen carefully to divine things the term *agape* is used by the sacred writers in divine revelation with the exact same meaning as the term *eros*."[30]

Maximus loved paradoxical phrases and oxymorons such as "ever-moving repose," "stationary movement," "temperate madness," "sober inebriation," "moving rest," and "blessed passion of love." He was searching for a vocabulary to say what the psalmist meant with "seek the face of the Lord always," that the soul that loves God is at rest in God yet at the same time in restless movement toward God. "All things created according to time," he writes, "become perfect when they cease their natural growth. But everything that the knowledge of God effects . . . when it reaches perfection, moves to further growth." The end becomes a beginning, for God unceasingly does good things "as though he had never begun them."[31]

One comes away from reading Maximus, as one does from

reading Augustine, with the sense that the old vessels cannot contain the new wine. He moved in a world that would have been recognized by Augustine. In his *Homilies on First John*, Augustine had described the Christian life as a "holy desire": "That which you desire you do not yet see; but by desiring you become capable of being filled by that which you will see when it comes. For just as in filling a leather bag . . . one stretches the skin . . . and by stretching it becomes capable of holding more; so God by deferring that for which we long, stretches our desire; as desire increases it stretches the mind, and by stretching, makes it more capable of being filled." Maximus may have been exposed to Augustine's writings when he lived in Carthage. The most profound modern interpreter of Maximus's thought, Hans Urs von Balthasar, believed, however, that Maximus was much too original to be dependent on Augustine. "Maximus speaks less as one who has learned something from someone else," von Balthasar writes, "than as one who is in full control of what is distinctively his own."[32] Von Balthasar is surely correct. Yet it is perhaps more to the point to observe that both Maximus and Augustine had taken the words of Jesus to heart: "You shall love the Lord your God with all your heart, and with all your soul, and with all your mind; and your neighbor as yourself" (Matt 22:40).

In a famous passage in the *Confessions* Augustine recalled that Cicero's *Hortensius* had "changed my feelings." The book did not give him a new perspective on wisdom or change his opinions, but moved him to love wisdom itself, to "hold fast to it," to "embrace it," and take it to himself. Suddenly everything else seemed vain and empty, for Wisdom lit a fire in his heart. Elsewhere in the *Confessions* Augustine, addressing God, says that his desire was "not to be more certain *about* you, but to be more stable *in* you." The goal of human life is not to know something about God, but to know God and be known by God, to delight in the face of God. The psalmist had written, "My heart has said to thee, I have sought thy face, O Lord, will I seek," and Augustine comments, "This is magnificent. Nothing could be spoken more sublimely. For those who truly love will understand. What does the psalmist seek? 'To gaze upon the Lord's loveliness all the days of his life.' His fear is that he should be deprived of what he loves. And what is that? What does he love? Thy face.' "[33]

The Christian intellectual tradition is an exercise in thinking about the God who is known and seeking the One who is loved. Lacking concepts in the mind and words on the tongue, we cannot speak about what we know, but if we do not love the God to whom these words lead, we do not understand. "Knowledge becomes love," says Gregory, "because that which is known is by nature beautiful." Christian thinking, like all thinking, requires questioning, reflection, interpretation, argument. But reason has short wings. Without love it is tethered to the earth. "Reason and desire," wrote the poet Geoffrey Hill, "on the same loop—I imagine singing I imagine getting it right—the knowledge of sensuous intelligence entering into the work."[34]

Epilogue

"AMOR IPSE NOTITIA EST" (Love is itself a form of knowledge), wrote Gregory the Great at the end of the sixth century.[1] Along with Ambrose, Jerome, and Augustine, Gregory is one of the four Latin doctors, that is, teachers, of the early church. By another calculus he is the first medieval Christian teacher. Sitting astride two worlds, he looks back toward Greek and Latin antiquity and to the church of the Roman Empire and forward to the great flowering of Christian civilization in the high Middle Ages. Revered more as a doer than a thinker, in conventional accounts of early Christian thought his role is not a large one. He lived at a time when the institutions of society had collapsed and as bishop of Rome new tasks were thrust upon him. Vast territories in southern Italy and Sicily had come under the control of the pope, and some of his letters deal, improbably, with such unlikely matters as the price of wheat in Sicily and the selling of cattle and farm implements. The great theological battles of the early church were past, and Gregory's writings are pastoral, administrative, homiletical, and devotional. Yet his union of life and thought, of contemplation and action, gives him an honored place among the church fathers. For Gregory, as for all the figures who have made an appearance in the pages of this book, thinking about the things of God, like grammar, was not an end in itself; its aim was the love of God and holiness of life. He did not construct a world of ideas for others to admire but one to live in.

Gregory's most beloved and enduring work, the *Moralia on Job,* is a huge, capacious opus in thirty-five books, a leisurely stroll chapter by chapter across every verse of the book of Job. Many of the great themes of early Christian thought appear in the *Moralia,* derived wondrously and mysteriously (at least to modern readers) from the arcane words of Job and his loquacious friends. It is a masterful undertaking, a wise, humane book, at once a compendium of the church's teaching on God, Christ, human beings, and grace and a matchless guide to the spiritual life. Gregory's *Moralia* would be unimaginable without the Bible. His language is suffused with the words of the Scripture, and its metaphors, stories, and heroes pressed themselves on his imagination and gave texture and concreteness to his thinking. His most mature work, the *Moralia* is an audacious yet disciplined meditation on the church's Bible. In the year 600 Gregory is still trying to sort out biblical passages on "seeing God" and to explain how Saint Paul can say that "no one has ever seen or can see" God (1 Tim. 6:16) and the book of Genesis report that Jacob saw God "face to face" (Gen. 32:30).[2]

These biblical texts and others posed a daunting challenge to Christian thinkers. It was not possible, in the fashion of contemporary biblical scholarship, to account for the differences by appeals to historical context or to the contrasting spiritual worlds of the biblical authors. The issue was not that of locating ideas on a historical grid or situating religious beliefs on a topographical chart, but of discerning what it meant to "see God" and learning to seek God more zealously. Interpretation was directed not at the text as such, but at the *res,* the reality borne by the text. The enterprise was theological and spiritual and demanded an intellectual account grounded in authentic religious experience. As Christian bishops and theologians expounded the Scriptures the vision of God became one of the great themes of Christian thought and the hearts of the faithful were taught to seek God's face always. "The vision of God is our mind's true refreshment,"[3] wrote Gregory.

The unique vocation of early Christian thought was to provide a unified interpretation of the Scriptures, one that was comprehensive, centered on the triune God, and definitive. This task required more than what is considered interpretation today. For the Bible of the early church was a living voice, not only a document from ancient history. The church fathers were no less aware than we that the books of the Bible came from disparate authors and different historical periods. Yet the Scriptures they sought to understand was a single book, and all its tributaries and rivulets flowed into the great river of God's revelation, the creation of the world, the history of Israel, the life of Christ and the beginning of the church, the final vision of the heavenly city.

Already at the end of the second century in the debate with the Gnostics, Irenaeus showed by a careful exposition of specific passages from the Old Testament, from the epistles of Saint Paul, and from the gospels that the Bible was a book about the one God, creator of heaven and earth, witnessed to by the law and prophets, made known in Christ, and proclaimed in the rule of faith at baptism. Exegesis was theological, and theology was exegetical.

The interpretation of the Scriptures was, however, not primarily a defensive undertaking. It was an effort to understand the Bible as the book of the church in accordance with the church's faith as confessed in the creed. Content, not method, drove interpretation. In the New Testament passages from the psalms and from the prophets were filled with the new reality of Christ. In the first chapter of Hebrews, Psalm 2, "Thou art my Son, today I have begotten thee," became a psalm about Christ the Son of God. At the end of the second century Tertullian drew out the implications of the term *word* in Psalm 45:1, "My heart poured forth a good word," and in John 1, to reject a strictly monarchian view of God, and to express the nature of the relation between the Son and the Father. Basil of Caesarea set forth the outlines of a theology of creation on the basis of the words "in the beginning" in Genesis 1. This kind of exegesis did more than explain words and titles; it was a way of thinking, what one might even call *the* Christian way of reasoning, as the church's first thinkers thought through the deepest theological, philosophical, and moral issues with the pages of the Holy Scriptures before them. Whether the subject was the nature of God, the person of Christ, the beginning of the world, or the Christian life, how the topic was approached, formulated, and debated turned in large measure on the interpretation of specific words and texts from the Scriptures.

Even when the church fathers took up a classical philosophical problem it was treated as a question of the interpretation of the Bible. In the essay on free will in his treatise *First Principles* Origen first states the issues in language drawn from the philosophical tradition, that is, whether moral acts are within our power. But then he reformulates the question by citing a series of biblical texts that introduce a gracious God into the discussion. He quotes the words of Moses in Deuteronomy, "See I have set before you this day life and the way of death. Choose the good and walk in it" (Deut 30:15), and other passages that imply we are free to choose right or wrong. Then he observes that certain passages in the Old and the New Testaments suggest an opposite conclusion. He mentions the story of Pharaoh and God's statement recorded in Exodus, "I will harden Pharaoh's heart" (Exod. 4:21) and the words of Paul, it is "not of him that wills nor of him that runs but of God that has mercy" (Romans 9:16). Only after he has systematically considered these and other biblical texts does Origen bring them all together to offer his understanding of human action under the influence of God's grace. For the philosophers freedom of choice was a moral problem, whereas under the influence of the Scriptures it became a theological as well as a moral issue.

Set against the vast horizon of classical thought, Aristotle's treatises on logic and ethics, Plato's dialogues on epistemology and the state, and the urbane political writings of Cicero, the biblicism of early Christian thought seems embarrassingly parochial, a severe narrowing of vision. Discussion always begins with the Scriptures and hence with very particular things, terms,

persons, and events. It was assumed that theological and philosophical matters were to be adjudicated on the basis of the Scriptures. The Bible displaces all other books, and its language, its
men and women, its history trump all others. To Celsus, a Greek
philosopher, Origen argued that the gospel had a proof proper to
itself, one that is "more divine than a Greek proof based on
dialectical argument." Christ, a human being who lived in a
corner of the world, is the truth.

The particularity and apparent parochialism of Christian
thinking did not escape Greek and Roman critics. Julian the
Apostate, Roman emperor in the fourth century, and a keen
adversary of Christianity, contemptuously entitled his book on
the Christians *Against the Galilaeans*. Raised a Christian, Julian
knew the title would be a reproach to Christians who claimed that
Jesus was the incarnate Son of God, creator of the universe. The
term "Galilaeans" not only exposed the barbarian origins of
Christianity, but also ridiculed the claim that God was revealed
only in Judea and among the Jews. The God worshipped by Jews
and Christians, he pointedly observed, is a tribal god, a regional
deity who presides over a tiny part of the world, not the god of all.
Why should this god be preferred to the gods of the Greeks?
Measured against Greek wisdom in the arts, philosophy, and
science, the teachings of the Christians are manifestly inferior.

Although Julian exploits the contrast between Athens and
Jerusalem for the purpose of exalting the wisdom of Greece and
belittling the religion of Christianity (as many others have done
since), there is truth to what he says. Christians did claim that the
God of all was revealed in a particular place and in a specific
person. But it was precisely this particularity that gave Christian
thinking its pluck and confidence. The way to truth passes

through the concrete and the personal. The church fathers resolutely followed out the implications of what they had come to know in Christ and in the Scriptures. This they did not because of any loss of nerve or shortening of horizon, but because converse with the living God made known in Judea trained their minds to look at the world and human beings afresh. The very rootedness of biblical revelation drew Christian thinkers more deeply into the truth of things. If the God in whom we live and move and have our being has been known in human flesh, God's face is evident in the things of this world. Turning toward the center was not a retreat from reason, but rather made their thinking bolder and more adventuresome. The first task, then, was to attend to the precious gift that had been received.

The intensity of the light that beamed from Christ, however, did not blind Christians to the wisdom that radiated from Athens. Christians do not speak of the period prior to Christianity the way Muslims speak of the period prior to Islam, as *al-Jahiliyyaha*, "the time of ignorance." Darkness there was, but not deep darkness. Before the rise of Christianity there was in place a well-formed tradition of moral philosophy, and Christian teachers found the cardinal virtues a fitting framework for instructing the faithful in the Christian life. They saw a convergence between the ancient philosophical goal of happiness and the words of Jesus in the beatitudes, "Happy are the meek for they shall inherit the earth," and Psalm 1, "Happy the man who walks not in the counsel of the ungodly." To be sure, they gradually filled the cardinal virtues with a more biblical content and expanded the list of virtues, but the teleological structure of classical ethics remained intact and was handed on in Christian dress to the medieval world.

In like manner, the early apologists drew on Greek ideas of God to explain and interpret God's otherness and ineffability. They introduced nonbiblical terms, for example, *immutability* and *unoriginate,* to express the biblical view that God is without beginning and eternal. When Saint Augustine read the books of the Neoplatonists, they helped him think his way through to a spiritual understanding of God. Unable to conceive of God except in substantive categories, that is, as something like that which the eye could perceive, he imagined a thin, ethereal substance that was diffused throughout the world. It was taken as self-evident that if something does not occupy space it is nonexistent. By studying the writings of the Neoplatonists he found the conceptual tools to think of God as spiritual, always and everywhere at the same time, "Deus totus ubique simul," as the axiom went.

Most of the major writers in the early church had been trained in the rhetorical schools of the later Roman Empire. They were skilled public speakers and accomplished stylists who could draw on a rich literary tradition. Gregory Nazianzus, the dear friend of Basil of Caesarea, was so wedded to the rhetorical conventions of his day that he wrote only in accepted literary genres, letters, orations, and poems. When the emperor Julian challenged Christians by prohibiting them from teaching in the schools ("Let them go teach Matthew and Luke in the church," said Julian), Gregory reminded him that the Greek language was not the property of the pagans. The intellectual accomplishments of the early church would be much less compelling had Christian bishops not been trained in classical rhetoric and known how to to use words effectively, to persuade and to inspire, and, not incidentally, to give pleasure to their readers.

Many factors were at work in the formation of the early Christian intellectual tradition. In ways large and small the church fathers drew on the philosophical, moral, and literary traditions of the ancient world, but the Bible created a new milieu and unloosed their tongues by offering a fresh and versatile vocabulary to express the things they believed. To be sure, the relation between biblical text and res, the matter under discussion, was always complex and often subtle (as the debates about the meaning of key scriptural texts make evident), and interpretation required thinking about biblical words like *wisdom* and *word* and passages like "made in the image and likeness of God" on several levels. Terms such as *Father* when applied to God and *Son* to Christ had to be understood in a very abstract sense emptied of their material and bodily implications. In some writings, for example, Gregory of Nyssa's *Against Eunomius*, arguments move on a very sophisticated theological and philosophical plane. Yet the distinctive feature of early Christian thinking was the interplay between biblical text, the spiritual reality discerned in the text, and theological reasoning. The res was understood by means of the text, and the res in turn interpreted the text.

Of course not everything of significance in the church's life makes an appearance in the early church. For many Christian thinkers today, natural law, particularly as developed by Thomas Aquinas, is an essential tool for contemporary Christian intellectual life. Yet it plays but a small role in the church fathers. There are passages in the Scriptures in which natural law is assumed, Romans 2, for example, and Saint Thomas uses the phrase "eternal law" from Augustine to introduce his discussion of natural law. There are occasions when the church fathers draw on natural law, most famously in Augustine's treatise *On the Good of Marriage*. The first good, that is, purpose, of marriage is procreation, an argument from natural law that is also found in the writings of Greek and Roman philosophers. Yet Augustine does not present the matter in that way. Instead he cites Genesis 1:28, "Increase and multiply and fill the earth." Natural law is a minor tributary in Christian antiquity.

The intellectual tradition that began in the early church was enriched by the philosophical breadth and exactitude of medieval thought. Each period in Christian history makes it own unique contribution to Christian life. The church fathers, however, set in place a foundation that has proven to be irreplaceable. Their writings are more than a stage in the development of Christian thought or an interesting chapter in the history of the interpretation of the Bible. Like an inexhaustible spring, faithful and true, they irrigate the Christian imagination with the life-giving water flowing from the biblical and spiritual sources of the faith. They are still our teachers today.

Notes

REFERENCES

I have cited most works by English titles, e.g., *The Trinity* rather than the customary Latin, e.g., *De Trinitate*. When a writing appears in different editions and in several English versions I cite only the name of the work with book and chapter or section, e.g., *The Trinity* 2.5.10. If, however, the citation comes from a particular edition and the page number is necessary to find the reference (e.g., the works of Gregory of Nyssa), I cite the edition and page number. When there is more than one source cited in a paragraph I have given only one reference at the end of the paragraph and listed the sources in the order in which they appear.

ABBREVIATIONS

ACW	*Ancient Christian Writers*
ANF	*Ante-Nicene Fathers*
CC	*Corpus Christianorum*
CSCO	*Corpus Scriptorum Christianorum Orientalium*
ECF	*Early Church Fathers*
FOC	*Fathers of the Church*
GNO	*Gregorii Nysseni Opera*
LCC	*Library of Christian Classics*
NPNF	*The Nicene and Post-Nicene Fathers*
PG	*Patrologia Graeca*
PL	*Patrologia Latina*
PO	*Patrologia Orientalis*
SC	*Sources Chrétiennes*
WSA	*Works of Saint Augustine for the 21st Century*

INTRODUCTION

1 Matt. 5:48; 1 Peter 3:15; Augustine, *Predestination of the Saints* 5 (*PL* 44:962–63).
2 Hans Urs von Balthasar, "The Fathers, the Scholastics, and Ourselves," *Communio* 24 (1997): 371.
3 *City of God* 19.1.
4 *Paradiso* 7.59–60.

CHAPTER 1 *Founded on the Cross of Christ*

1 *Against Celsus* 1.14.
2 *Epistle* 10.96.
3 Eusebius, *Ecclesiastical History* 4.11.8.
4 *Dialogue with Trypho* 2.
5 *Dialogue with Trypho* 7.
6 *Dialogue with Trypho* 8.
7 *Dialogue with Trypho* 8; Augustine, *Confessions* 13.9.10.
8 Plato, *Timaeus* 28c; *Against Celsus* 7.42; 7.36.
9 Alcinous (Albinus), *Didaskalikos* 10 (ed. John Whittaker, *Alcinoos. Enseignement des doctrines de Platon* [Paris, 1990], p. 23, ln. 31–33; p. 24, ln. 27–p. 26, ln. 2).
10 *Against Celsus* 4.2; "For the Time Being," in W. H. Auden, *Collected Poems* (New York, 1969), 138; *Against Celsus* 4.5.
11 M. J. Routh, *Reliquiae Sacrae* (Oxford, 1846), 1:379; *Against Celsus* 7.42.
12 *Against Celsus* 7.42.
13 *Apology* 13–16; Athenagoras of Athens, *Embassy* 10; *Against Celsus* 3.40.
14 *Against Celsus* 1.2.
15 *Against Celsus* 3.4; 1.13; Clement, *Stromateis* 1.2.19–20.
16 Ignatius, *Epistle to the Philadelphians* 9.2; Maximus, *Ambigua* (*PG* 91,1057d); Justin *1 Apology* 5.
17 *Homily on Jeremiah* 9.1; *Commentary on John* 1.27.
18 *Embassy* 5.3; see also Augustine, *The Trinity* 2.1.
19 *Against Celsus* 3.14.
20 *Against Celsus* 5.43; 5.42; 4.31.
21 *Against Celsus* 4.32.
22 *Against Celsus* 7.42; 3.47; Irenaeus, *Against Heresies* 4.6.4.
23 *Homily on Luke* 3.1; also Irenaeus: "Man cannot see God on his own. If God wills to be seen he will be seen by those to whom he wills to be seen, when he wills, and in what way he wills" (*Against Heresies* 4.20.5).

24 *Against Celsus* 7.43.

25 Athenagoras, *Embassy* 10.3; Origen, *Commentary on the Song of Songs,* Prologue 2:17 (*SC* 375:102).

26 *Homily on Luke* 3.4.

27 *Homily on Ezechiel* 1.2.20; *Against Heresies* 4.20.5; *Commentary on John* 19.24–25; *Against Celsus* 4.6.

28 *Against Celsus* 6.57; *Against Celsus* 7.33.

29 Etienne Gilson, *The Spirit of Mediaeval Philosophy* (New York, 1940), 5; *Against Celsus* 8.75. "The coming of Christ to this earth . . . was the *central* event of the universe" (John Lukacs, *At the End of an Age* [New Haven, 2002], p. 223).

30 Augustine, *City of God* 19.18; John of Damascus, *On the Divine Images* 1.11.

31 *Sermon* 82.6 (*PL* 54:426).

CHAPTER 2   *An Awesome and Unbloody Sacrifice*

1 The *Quicunque vult,* sometimes known as the Athanasian Creed. Text and translation in J. N. D. Kelly, *The Athanasian Creed* (New York, 1964), 17; Augustine, *On the Spirit and the Letter,* 36.66.

2 *Against Heresies* 4.18.4–5.

3 *Embassy* 11.2.

4 *1 Apology 61,* 65–67.

5 *1 Apology* 65.

6 In Greek, "makes Eucharist."

7 Ignatius, *Smyrnaeans* 7.1; *La Liturgie de Saint Jacques,* ed. Dom B.-Ch. Mercier (*PO* 26.2; no. 126; Turnhout: 1074), 206.

8 *Exposition of Psalm 21* 2.1; Bernard Botte, *Hippolyte de Rome: La Tradition apostolique* (*SC* 11:48–52).

9 *La Liturgie de Saint Jacques,* 200–02.

10 *Mishnah Pesachim* 10.5; the term in Latin is *repraesento,* "manifest" or "realize anew." See Tertullian, *Adversus Marcionem* 1.14; *Treatise on the Passover* 3; *La Liturgie de Saint Jacques,* 204.

11 John Chrysostom, Hom. in Heb. 17.3 on Heb. 9:24–26.

12 *Sermon 63* (*PL* 54:356).

13 *Apology* 1.61.

14 *Baptism* 4; Cyril of Jerusalem, *Catechetical Lectures* 13.9.

15 *Journey of Egeria* 45.1–4.

16 Augustine, *Confessions* 8.2.5.

17 *Baptism* 3.4; *Baptism* 4.1.

18 *Baptism* 4.4; *Baptism* 9.4.

19 *Ephesians* 18.2; *On the Baptism of Christ* (*PG* 46:592d–593a); *Homily on Epiphany 33* (*PO* 43:565).

20 *Sermon* 339.4.

21 *Life of Augustine* 31.4.

22 *Sermon* 26.2.

23 *GNO* 9:277–80.

24 *Expositions of Psalm 36, Sermon* 3.4; *Exposition of Psalm 90, Sermon* 2.1; *Apostolic Constitutions* 8.12.43–44.

25 *Homily* 41.4 on 1 Cor. 15:35 (*PG* 61, 361a-b).

26 *Mystagogical Catecheses* 5.6; Georg Wobbermin, *Altchristliche liturgische Stuecke aus der Kirche Aegyptens* (Texte und Untersuchungen 17 [Leipzig, 1898], p. 5, trans. in Deiss, 114–15.

27 *Dialogue* 4.60; *Homily on Luke* 23:8.

CHAPTER 3 *The Face of God for Now*

1 *Hymns on Paradise* 5.3 (*CSCO* 174:16); translation by Sebastian Brock, *St. Ephrem the Syrian: Hymns on Paradise* (New York, 1990), 103.

2 *Stromateis* 1.1.11.

3 *Exhortation* 1.1–2.

4 *Exhortation* 1.2.2–3.

5 *Exhortation* 1.4.4; 1.6.1; 1.10.3; 8.77.1.

6 *Stromateis* 6.11.95,4; *Stromateis* 6.11.96, 4. Clement is citing Wisdom 8:7.

7 The passage is in *Stromateis* 2.22.131–36; Plato, *Laws* V, 715e–716a; Alcinous, *Didaskalikos* 28 (ed. John Whittaker, *Alcinoos: Enseignement des doctrines de Platon* [Paris, 1990], 57). The phrase "likeness to God" comes from Plato's *Theaetetus* 176a.

8 Clement of Alexandria, *Exhortation* 9.87.1–3; 1.10.2; Cassiodorus, *Exposition of the Psalms*, preface 3 (*CC* 97:11).

9 *Commentary on Isaiah* 29:11–12 (*PG* 70, 655a); Augustine said that in all the things spoken in the Scripture there is "one discoure" (unus sermo) and out of the many mouths comes "one word" (unum verbum) (*Exposition of Psalm* 103.4.1).

10 *Against Heresies* 3.3.3.

11 *Against Heresies* 5.36.1.

12 *Metamorphoses* 15.875–78.

13 *Against Heresies* 3.18.7; Rom. 5:12–18; *Against Heresies* 4.34.1.

14 Augustine, *On True Religion* 6.13; Hilary, *Treatise on the Mysteries (SC* 19:122); Irenaeus, *Proof of the Apostolic Preaching* 6 (*PO* 12, 5, no. 61:664; also Joseph P. Smith, S.J., *St. Irenaeus: Proof of the Apostolic Preaching* (New York, 1952), 51.

15 *Against Heresies* 3.18.1; 3.18.7; 4.38.1–2; Irenaeus, *Proof of the Apostolic Preaching* 12.

16 Irenaeus, *Against Heresies* 5.36.1–3.

17 Irenaeus, *Against Heresies* 3.1.1; 3.2.1; 3.9.3; Athanasius calls the interpretation that holds the whole together the "churchly sense" (*Orations against the Arians* 1.44); Augustine, like Irenaeus, uses "rule of faith" (*Christian Doctrine* 3.2.2).

18 *On the Sacraments,* prologue 2 (*PL* 176, 183).

19 *Confessions* 12.1.1.

20 Augustine, *Literal Commentary on Genesis* 1.1; Chrysostom, *Homily on Genesis* 31.8.

21 *Confessions* 9.5.13.

22 Origen, *Homily on Exodus* 5.1; Augustine, *Against Faustus the Manichee* 12.29.

23 Henri de Lubac, *Medieval Exegesis* (Grand Rapids, 1998), 1:237; Augustine, *The Teacher* 10.33 and *The Trinity* 10.1.2.

24 *Morals of the Catholic Church* 1.26; *The Spirit and the Letter* 22.37.

25 *The Spirit and the Letter* 3.5.

26 Paul Ricoeur, *Thinking Biblically* (Chicago, 1998), 280; for example, Augustine, *Exposition* 2.2 of Psalm 18; *Exposition* 2.1 of Psalm 21.

27 Gregory of Nyssa, *Homily on the Song of Songs* 9 (*GNO* 6:292,7–294,2).

28 Bonaventure calls the water and blood that flowed from Christ's side "living water" and relates it to the Eucharist: "The blood and water which poured out when Christ was pierced were the price of our salvation. Flowing from the secret abyss of our Lord's heart as from a fountain, this stream gave the sacraments of the church the power to confer the life of grace, while for those already living in Christ it became a spring of *living water* welling up to eternal life." (Opusculum 3. *Lignum Vitae. De Mysterio passionis* 8.30 [*Doctoris Seraphici S. Bonaventurae . . . Opera Omnia* 8:79]); Augustine, *Sermon* 22.7.

29 *Enneads* 6.5.12

30 *Epistle* 63.78.

31 *Dialogues* 2.3.5–6, ed. Vogue (*SC* 260:142–44).

32 *Moralia in Job* 28.19–20.

33 *Homily* 1.7.8 on Ezekiel.

CHAPTER 4   *Seek His Face Always*

1 *Dialogue with Heraclides* 1 (J. Scherer, ed., *Entretien d'Origène avec Héraclide et les évêques ses collègues sur le Père, le Fils et l'âme* [Publication de la Société Fouad I de Papyrologie; Textes et Documents 9; Cairo: Institut Français d'Archéologie orientale, 1949], p. 120).

2 *Dialogue with Heraclides* 1–2 (Scherer, pp. 120–24).

3 *Dialogue with Heraclides* 2 (Scherer, p. 124).

4 Shepherd of Hermas, *Commands* 1.1; Pliny, *Epistle* 10.96; besides the baptismal formula in Matthew 28:19, see 2 Cor. 13:14 and 1 Peter 1:2; Leonard Hodgson, *The Doctrine of the Trinity* (New York, 1944) 103.

5 *Incomprehensibility of God* 1.7 (*SC* 28:132).

6 *The Trinity* 1.5.

7 *Sermon* 355.2.

8 *The Trinity* 12.24; 1.18.

9 *The Trinity* 1.18; 11.44.

10 *The Trinity* 4.14.

11 *The Trinity* 2.35.

12 *The Trinity* 2.25; 2.1; 8.14–17; *The Trinity* 2.1; 1.17.

13 *The Trinity* 1.12

14 Ibid.

15 *The Trinity* 7.12.

16 *The Trinity* 7.12; 6.19; 7.8.

17 *The Trinity* 7.12.

18 *Commentary on John* 20.1; Wolfhart Pannenberg, *Systematic Theology* (Grand Rapids, Mich., 1988), 1:300.

19 *First Principles* 1.2.1.

20 *First Principles* 1.2.2.

21 Cited by Origen in *Against Celsus* 8.2.

22 *Against Praxeas* 3; *Against Celsus* 4.14.

23 *Commentary on John* 1.151; *Commentary on John* 1.292; *Commentary on John* 10.246 and 1.291.

24 *Against Praxeas* 7 and 11.

25 Tertullian's Latin version used the term *sermo* in the prologue to the Gospel of John, not *verbum; sermo* is also used in Ps. 45:1.

26 *Against Praxeas* 5.

27 Ibid.

28 *Baptism* 19.2.

29 *Oration* 31.26.

30 Hippolytus, *Apostolic Tradition* 4 & 9; Gregory Nazianzus, *Oration* 31.26.

31 Gregory Nazianzus, *Oration* 31.1,5–6; 31.29; Gregory of Nyssa, *Three Gods* (*GNO* 3:1, 47,21–48,2).

32 *Epistle to Serapion* 19–20; also 2 Cor. 1:21–22: "But it is *God* who establishes us with you in *Christ* and has anointed us, by putting his seal on us and giving us his *Spirit* in our hearts as a first installment" (Basil, *On the Holy Spirit* 10.24).

33 *The Trinity* 2.5.10; *Sermon* 270.1.

34 Basil, *The Holy Spirit* 40. John of Damascus cites 1 Cor. 2:11 at the beginning of his *Orthodox Faith*. No one, he writes, knows the Father except the Son (Matt. 11:27) and the Holy Spirit "who knows the things of God as the spirit of man knows the things that are in him." (*Orthodox Faith* 1.1).

35 *Against Eunomius* 1.159 (*GNO* 1:75).

36 *The Trinity* 1.3.5; *The Trinity* 9.1.1; *The Trinity* 15.28.51

37 *The Trinity* 1.3.5.

38 *The Trinity* 9.1.

39 *The Trinity* 9.1; *The Trinity* 1.1.3; *The Trinity* 8.4.6.

40 *The Trinity* 9.1.1.

41 *The Trinity* 15.28.51.

CHAPTER 5 *Not My Will But Thine*

1 *Against Celsus* 5.61.

2 Some ancient manuscripts add the following words after Luke 22:42: "And there appeared to him an angel from heaven, strengthening him. And being in an *agony* he prayed more earnestly; and his sweat became like great drops of blood falling down upon the ground."

3 Cyril of Alexandria, *Epistle* 17.11.

4 Text and translation of the decree of Chalcedon in T. Herbert Bindley, *The Oecumenical Documents of the Faith* (London, 1925), 229–34, 292–98.

5 Athanasius, *On the Incarnation* 54.

6 *Lehrbuch der Dogmengeschichte* (Tuebingen, 1931), 2:349–50.

7 *Commentary on John* 13:31–32 (ed. Pusey 2:376–79).

8 *Commentary on John* 12:23 (ed. Pusey 2:311).

9 *Commentary on John* 13:36 (ed. Pusey 2:52); 16:33 (ed. Pusey 2:656–57).

10 *Oration* 30.12.

11 J. D. Mansi, *Sacrorum Conciliorum Nova et Amplissima Collectio* 11:533d-e.

12 *Opusculum* 4 (*PG* 91:60b).

13 *Opusculum* 6 (*PG* 91:65b–68a).

14 *Opusculum* 7 (*PG* 91:77a).

15 *Opusculum* 7 (*PG* 91:80c-d).

16 Maximus distinguishes between the "gnomic" will and the natural will. Because human beings are fallen creatures they are not always aware of the good and must consider what course of action to follow. Maximus calls this kind of willing gnomic, that is, willing with deliberation. Christ, however, has no gnomic will, only a natural will. Because he was wholly oriented toward the good, he did not have to deliberate about what to do. According to Maximus, our gnomic will brought sin into the world and led to our separation from God. *Opusculum* 3 (*PG* 91:56b); *Opusculum* 7 (*PG* 91:80d).

17 *Opusculum* 6 (*PG* 91:68b-d).

18 *PG* 91:1097c; *PG* 91:1057d.

19 *Epistle* 14 (*PG* 91:540b).

20 H. Denzinger, *Enchiridion Symbolorum. Definitionum et Declarationum de Rebus Fidei et Morum* (Rome, 1963), # 500.

21 *PG* 90:120c.

CHAPTER 6   *The End Given in the Beginning*

1 Cited by Augustine, *Confessions* 7.12.18; Augustine, *Nature of the Good* 1–2.

2 Philip Rousseau, *Basil of Caesarea* (Berkeley, 1994), 3.

3 Gregory of Nyssa, *Apologetic Explanation of the Hexaemeron* (*PG* 44:66a); Gregory Nazianzus, *Oration* 43.67.

4 *Hexaemeron* 1.1; *Homily on Psalm* 45.7 (*PG* 29:428a); *Hexaemeron* 1.1. Basil takes "Midian" in the book of Exodus to refer to Ethiopia.

5 *Hexaemeron* 1.4.

6 *Hexaemeron* 1.2.

7 Plato, *Timaeus* 30a; Basil, *Hexaemeron* 2.2; 1.7; 1.2.

8 *Hexaemeron* 5.1; Augustine, *Literal Commentary on Genesis* 6.14.25 and 6.15.26; Basil, *Homily on Psalm* 114 (*PG* 29:489c).

9 *Hexaemeron* 3.2; 2.6; on the role of the Son in creation, see also Basil, *On the Holy Spirit* 16.38 and epistle 8.11.

10 Philo, *Making of the World* 3.13; Gregory, *Apologetic Exposition of the Hexaemeron* (*PG* 44:72b; 69a). In English Bibles the verse from Daniel can be found in the book of *Susanna* in the Apocrypha at v. 42.

11 *PG* 44:69c; *Greater Catechism* 5 (*GNO* 3,4:18,9–10).

12 Introductory letter to his brother Peter; *PG* 44:128b.

13 *Making of Man* 8 (145c). See Aristotle, *De Anima* 2.3; 414a.

14 Introductory letter to Peter (*PG* 44:128a-b).

15 *Making of Man* 2 (*PG* 44:132d–133a).

16 *Making of Man* 2 & 1 (*PG* 44:133b; 132c).

17 Also "enjoying the good things that exist" (Wisdom 2:6); Gregory,
     Making of Man 3 (*PG* 44:133b); *Homily 8 on Ecclesiastes* (*GNO* 5:
     441,12–15); Augustine, *Confessions* 1.1. Gregory says, "To see God is life
     to the soul" (*On the Early Death of Infants* [*PG* 46:173c]); Maximus says
     that we "yearn for our own proper beginning" (*PG* 90:1084b).

18 *Making of Man* 3 (*PG* 44:133d–136a).

19 *Against Celsus* 6.63; Gregory, *Making of Man* 16 (*PG* 44:180a). The ex-
     pression microcosm first occurs in Democritus, a pre-Socratic philoso-
     pher (Fragment 34 in H. Diels, *Die Fragmente der Vorsokratiker* [Berlin,
     1922], 2:72). *Homilies on the Song of Songs* 2 (*GNO* 6:68).

20 *Psalm Inscriptions* 1.3 (*GNO* 5: 32, 18–19); *The Beatitudes* 6 (*GNO* 7.2: 143).

21 *Making of Man* 9 (149b–152a); *Making of Man* 10 (152b–153c).

22 *Making of Man* 11 (*PG* 44:153d–156b); also Basil: "We are more likely
     to understand the heavens than to understand ourselves" (*Hexaemeron*
     10.2); Augustine, *Confessions* 10.5.7.

23 *Greater Catechism* 5 (*GNO* 3.4:19,20; 20, 4); *Homilies on Ecclesiastes* 4
     (*GNO* 5:335,5–8;336,4–5).

24 *Making of Man* 4 (*PG* 44:136b-c); 16 (*PG* 44:184b); *On Infants' Early
     Deaths* (*PG* 46:173c).

25 *Making of Man* 16 (*PG* 44:183c-d); *The Triduum* (*GNO* 9:280,1–2).

26 *Making of Man* 5 (*PG* 44:137).

27 *Homily on the Song of Songs* 15 (*GNO* 6:458).

28 *Making of Man* 16 (*PG* 44:181a-b); *Homily 1 on Ecclesiastes* (*GNO* 5:283, 18).

29 *Against Eunomius* 2.10 (*GNO* 2:293); *Lord's Prayer* 4 (*GNO* 7,2:47,17–
     18); *Life of Moses* (*GNO* 7,2:42, 20); *On the Sixth Psalm* (*PG* 44:609d).

30 *Greater Catechism* 8 (*GNO* 3,4:30,9–11); *Soul and Resurrection* (*PG*
     46:148c); *Lord's Prayer* 5 (*GNO* 7,2:64, 18–19; 65, 2–4;66,10–15); *Beati-
     tudes* 6 (*GNO* 7,2:145,10–13).

31 *Lord's Prayer* 5 (*GNO* 7,2:63); *Beatitudes* 1 (*GNO* 7,2:81,3–4); Basil, *As-
     cetic Discourse* 1.1 (*PG* 31:869d); *Lord's Prayer* 4 (*GNO* 7,2; 45,23); Au-
     gustine, *The Trinity* 14.4.6.

32 Didymus the Blind, *On Genesis* (*SC* 233:146–50).

33 *Making of Man* 29 (*PG* 44:233d); *Ambiguum* 7 (*PG* 91:1101b).

34 *Homily on the Forty Martyrs (GNO* 10,1:166,10–12); *Homily on St. The-odore (GNO* 10,1:63,25–26); *Care to be Taken for the Dead* 3.5.

35 *Literal Commentary on Genesis* 12.35.68; *Sermon on the Assumption of the Blessed Virgin Mary* 1,2 (Bonaventurae Opera Omnia, vol. 9 [Quar-rachi, 1901]), 690.

CHAPTER 7   *The Reasonableness of Faith*

1 *Against Celsus* 1.9.

2 *Predestination of the Saints* 5 (*PL* 44:962–963); Gregory of Nyssa said that one cannot rightly be called a Christian if someone "has no respect for reason" (*Perfection* [*GNO* 8,1:179, 10]).

3 *First Principles* 2.11.4.

4 *Usefulness of Believing* 1.2.

5 *Confessions* 5.6.

6 *Usefulness of Believing* 1.2.

7 *Usefulness of Believing* 7.13; *Exposition of Psalm* 18.6; see also 62.2; Let-ter of Newman to Henry Wilberforce, August 8, 1868 (*The Letters and Diaries of John Henry Newman* [Oxford, 1973] 24:119).

8 *Usefulness of Believing* 11.25.

9 *Usefulness of Believing* 11.25; *Reconsiderations* 1.14.3 (*PL* 32:607).

10 *Usefulness of Believing* 11.25.

11 *Usefulness of Believing* 12.26.

12 Cited in Cleo McNelly Kearns, *T. S. Eliot and Indic Traditions* (Cam-bridge, 1987), 3; *Usefulness* 6.13.

13 *True Religion* 24.45.

14 Prologue to *Sic et Non.*

15 *Quaestiones quodlibetales* 4, art. 18 (ed. P. Mandonnet, p. 155).

16 *On True Religion* 25.46.

17 *Tractates on 1 John* 1.1.

18 *Commentary on John* 10.298–306.

19 *Commentary on John* 10.298.

20 *Parochial and Plain Sermons* (San Francisco, 1997), 123. The title of the sermon is "Religious Faith Rational."

21 *Against Celsus* 2.63.

22 *Against Celsus* 2.67; 2.69; also *Commentary on Romans* 5.8 (ed. T. Heither, 3:144–46).

23 *Martyrdom of Polycarp* 9.

24 *Tractates on the Gospel of John* 29.6; *Morals of the Catholic Church* 1.17.31.

25 *Tractates on the Gospel of John* 29.6.

26 *Sermon* 144.2.

27 *Benjamin Minor* 13.

CHAPTER 8 *Happy the People Whose God Is the Lord*

1 Peter Brown, *Augustine of Hippo* (Berkeley, 2000), 427–28.

2 *Aeneid* 1.278–79. Augustine cites these lines of Virgil in *Sermon* 105.10.

3 *Sermon* 105.9.

4 Melito of Sardis, *Fragment* 1 (ed. Stuart George Hall, *Melito of Sardis: On Pascha and Fragments* [Oxford, 1979], 62); see particularly book 10 of Eusebius's *Ecclesiastical History*.

5 *City of God* 2.14.1; Augustine, *Letter* 2*.

6 *City of God* 13.16; 20.11.

7 Sheldon Wolin, *Politics and Vision: Continuity and Innovation in Western Political Thought* (Boston, 1960), p. 97.

8 *City of God* 11.1; book 1 preface.

9 *City of God* 2.21.2; 19.12; 19.14.

10 *City of God* 19.2. In a famous passage in the *City of God* Augustine speaks of the "quiet serenity of order" (*tranquillitas ordinis*) (19.13).

11 *City of God* 19.16.

12 *City of God* 19.11.

13 *City of God* 19.11; 22.30; 19.1.

14 *On the Morals of the Catholic Church* 1.30.63.

15 *City of God* 19.5; 19.26; 22.29.

16 *City of God* 19.4; 19.18.

17 *City of God* 19.4.

18 Rom. 8:24 in *City of God* 19.4; *Expositions of Psalm* 62.6.

19 *City of God* 19.6.

20 Rodney Stark, *The Rise of Christianity* (Princeton, 1996), pp. 3–13.

21 *Against Celsus* 8.73.

22 *Letter* 220; 10*.

23 *Letter* 153.6.16

24 *City of God* 19.16.

25 *City of God* 19.17.

26 Ibid.

27 *City of God* 19.22.

28 *City of God* 19.24.

29 *City of God* 19.17; 19.25.

30 *Confessions* 3.9.17.

31 Rowan Williams, "Politics and the Soul: A Reading of the City of God,"
    Milltown Studies 19/20 (1987): 58.

32 The phrase is from the title of the book by Richard John Neuhaus, *The
    Naked Public Square* (Grand Rapids, 1984); *City of God* 22.30.

33 *The Idea of the University*, ed. Ian T. Ker (Oxford, 1976), 428–29.

34 *City of God* 10.7; *Exposition of Psalm* 41.9; *City of God* 19.23

CHAPTER 9 *The Glorious Deeds of Christ*

 1 Sidonius, *Epistle* 1.9.4.

 2 *Crown of Martyrdom* 2.574.

 3 *Confessions* 9.7.15.

 4 *Sermon against Auxentius* 34.

 5 *Ambrogio Inni*, ed. Manlio Simonetti (Biblioteca Patristica; Firenze: Nar-
    dini Editore, 1988), p. 26; translation by John Chandler (1806–76) in
    Twenty-Four Hymns of the Western Church, ed. Howard Henry Blakeney
    (London, 1930), 7.

 6 *Confessions* 9.6.14.

 7 *Aeneid* 8.456.

 8 *Hymn for Every Hour* 7–8.

 9 *Hymn for Every Hour* 82–83.

10 *City of God* 10.21.

11 Text of the poem with English translation in *Prudentius*, ed. H. J.
    Thompson (Loeb Classical Library; Cambridge, 1979), 2:109–43.

12 *Crown of Martyrdom* 2.155.

13 *Crown of Martyrdom* 1.27.

14 *Psychomachia* 14 and 904.

15 *Psychomachia* 57.

16 *Psychomachia* 36–37.

17 John Milton, *Areopagitica* (John Milton, *English Minor Poems. Paradise
    Lost. Samson Agonistes. Areopagitica* [Great Books of the Western World,
    ed. Robert Maynard Hutchins; Encyclopedia Britannica, 1952]), pp. 390–
    91.

18 *Psychomachia* 54–57.

19 *Aeneid* 6.86; *Psychomachia* 902–04.

20 *Psychomachia* 71–86.

21 *Psychomachia*, preface, 6–8; 903–04; the phrase is Stanley Fish's from his book on Milton, *Surprised by Sin* (New York, 1971).

22 *Epistle* 22.30.

CHAPTER 10 *Making This Thing Other*

1 *Against the Galilaeans* 355c.

2 *Holy Theodore* (*GNO* 10.2:63).

3 Gregory of Nyssa, *Against Eunomius* 3.11.58–60 (*GNO* 2:285,17–286, 25).

4 *On the Incarnation* 703e (*SC* 97:268).

5 *Homily* 17 on the Martyr Barlaam (*PG* 31:489a); also Gregory the Great: "What writing supplies to readers painting offers to uneducated viewers; for in painting even the ignorant can see what course they should follow, and in painting the illiterate can read" (Letters, book 11, ep. 13 to Serenus; *PL* 77:1128).

6 *Life of John Chrysostom* by George of Alexandria 192,4 (*Doctrina Patrum de Incarnatione Verbi*, ed. F. Diekamp [Munich, 1907], 330). This passage is cited by John of Damascus in his *Apologies Against Those who Attack the Divine Images* 1.61 (ed. P. Bonifatius Kotter, OSB, *Die Schriften des Johannes von Damaskos* [Berlin, 1975], 3:161). See also Gregory of Nyssa's description of his feelings on looking at an "icon" of the sacrifice of Isaac (*On the Divinity of the Son and Holy Spirit* [*PG* 46:572c]).

7 *Divine Images* 1.8.

8 Ibid.

9 *Divine Images* 1.8; 1.5; 1.16.

10 *Divine Images* 2.5; *Divine Images* 1.17; *Divine Images* 1.22.

11 G. D. Mansi, *Sacrorum Conciliorum Nova et Amplissima Collectio* 13:256c-d; *That Christ Is One* 720c (*SC* 97:322).

12 *Divine Images* 1.16.

13 Ibid.

14 *Divine Images* 2.20; 1.17; 1.18; *Divine Images* 1.18.

15 Egeria, *Itinerarium* 47.5; *Book of Demonstration*, par. 310 (*CSCO* 192,209:193,210).

16 1.13; 3.33–34; *Divine Images* 3.34; *Book of Demonstration*, par. 310.

17 *Divine Images* 3.10.

18 *Against Celsus* 7.42; *Divine Images* 1.11; 22; Commenting on Matt. 11:27, "He who has seen me has seen the Father," Cyril says that "we behold the Son with the eyes of the heart *and* with eyes of flesh" (*Glaphyra in Exodus* 2; *PG* 69:465d).

19 Mansi 13:40e-41a.

20 Mansi 13:377c.

21 Nicephorus, *Antirrheticus* 1.15 (*PG* 100:225).

22 Theodore, *Treatises Against those who oppose Icons* 1.10 (*PG* 99:340). Text of treatise in *PG* 99:327–436); translation by C. P. Roth.

23 *Icons* 1.11 (*PG* 99:341).

24 *Icons* 1.11. Theodore's argument works only on the basis of the Greek text of 2 Kings 23:17, which he was reading. In Hebrew (and in English translations) the term *tomb* appears. Ex. 25:18.

25 *Icons* 3.22 (*PG* 99:400c-d).

26 *Icons* 3.15 (*PG* 99:396); 3.16 (*PG* 99:397).

27 *Icons* 3.4.5 (*PG* 99:429c-d).

28 *Icons* 1.17 (*PG* 99:335d-337a).

29 David Jones, *The Anathemata* (London, 1952), 49.

30 Nicephorus, *Antirrheticus* 2 (*PG* 100:337c).

31 *Icons* 1.11 (*PG* 99:341b-c). Theodore is quoting Dionysius the Areopagite.

32 Ep. 36 (*PG* 99:1220a-b).

33 Ep. 36 (*PG* 99:1220a).

34 *Icons* 3.1.15 (*PG* 99:396d-397a).

35 *Orthodox Faith* 4.16.

CHAPTER 11 *Likeness to God*

1 Plutarch, *Life of Pericles* 1–4.

2 2 Cor. 11:24–27; Ignatius, *Philadelphians* 7.2.

3 Pontus, *Vita et Passio Cypriani*, ed. A. von Harnack, *Texte und Untersuchungen* 39.3 (Leipzig, 1913).

4 1 Thess. 4:2.

5 Athanasius, *Life of Antony*, preface 2–3; Palladius, *Letter to Lausus* 2; Plutarch, *Life of Alexander*, 1.1–2.

6 Theodoret of Cyrus, *Religious History* (History of the Monks of Syria) 3.12.

7 Cicero, *Tusculan Disputations* 3.6; Clement of Alexandria, *Who Is the Rich Man Being Saved?* 41.

8 *Panegyric* 6.75, 78.

9 *Instructor* 1.1.4–1.2.1; 1.6.1.

10 Paul Rabbow, *Seelenfuehrung: Methodik der Exerʒitien in der Antike* (Munich, 1954). Though the book has never been translated, his insight has

been developed in recent times by Pierre Hadot in *Philosophy as a Way of Life* (Blackwell, 1995); Rabbow, *Seelenfuehrung,* 261.

11 *The Sentences of Sextus,* ed. Henry Chadwick. Texts and Studies, no. 5 (Cambridge, 1959).

12 *Panegyric* 9.115; 11.149; 11.147–49; 11.133, 135; 9.123, 126.

13 *Panegyric* 7.93–98; 11.141. Origen, *Commentary on John* 18.102–03. "Pursue justice justly" is the LXX version of Deuteronomy 16:20.

14 *Panegyric* 12.145–46.

15 *Nicomachean Ethics* 1.1; Cicero, *On Ends* 1.42.

16 In *The Sermon on the Mount* 1.3.10 Augustine says that the beatitudes represent seven steps which he identifies with the seven gifts of the Holy Spirit of Isaiah 11:1. The eighth beatitude recapitulates the first with the mention of "kingdom of heaven." Ambrose, commenting on the Lukan version, identifies the four beatitudes with the four cardinal virtues, "steps by which we are able to ascend from lower to higher things." (*Exposition of the Gospel of Luke* 5.60,62); John of Damascus: "Happpiness is acquired by practicing the virtues" (*Barlaam and Joseph,* preface).

17 *City of God* 10.3.2; "Fellowship in the enjoyment of God" (*City of God* 19.17).

18 Augustine, *City of God* 10.3.2; Basil of Caesarea, *On the Holy Spirit* 15.35; Augustine, *City of God* 10.3.2; *Life of Moses* 2.32 (*GNO* 7,1:42, ln. 20); Gregory of Nyssa, *The Beatitudes,* Homily 6 (*GNO* 7,2:144–5); Gregory of Nyssa, *Against Eunomius* 3.10 (*GNO* 1:293); Maximus, ep. 11 (*PG* 91:453b).

19 Clement, *The Tutor* 1.1.4; 1.2.1; the classic text is Plato, *Theaetetus* 176b; "partakers of the divine nature" (2 Peter 1:4); for Clement, see chapter 3.

20 Origen, *On First Principles* 1.3.8.

21 *The Beatitudes* Homily 1 (*GNO* 7,2:82–83).

22 *The Beatitudes* Homily 1 (*GNO* 7,2:84, ln. 28)

23 *The Beatitudes* Homily 4 (*GNO* 7,2:117, ln. 9; 122).

24 *The Beatitudes* Homily 8 (*GNO* 7,2:170; 78, lns 3–9).

25 Gregory of Nyssa, *On the Holy Spirit against the Macedonians* 23 (*PG* 45:1329c); also Origen, *First Principles* 1.3.8; Ambrose, *On the Sacraments* 3.2.8–10.

26 Plato, *Republic* 427e; *Stromateis* 6.11.95.

27 *On Duties* 1.120.

28 *On Duties* 1.127; 1.131.

29 Augustine, *Sermon* 218c; Tertullian, *On Patience* 3.

30 *On Patience* 15.

31 *Expositions of Psalm* 83.11 (*PL* 37:1065); *Morals of the Catholic Church* 8.13.

32 *Morals of the Catholic Church* 12.20; *On the Harmony of the Gospels* 4.10.20.

33 *Morals of the Catholic Church* 13.22.

34 *Morals of the Catholic Church* 1.15.25; *City of God* 10.32; Maximus the Confessor says love is the "most universal of the virtues" for it gathers together all the virtues (*PG* 91:1249b).

35 *Summa Theologiae* 1a 2ae, q. 62, art. 3, obj. 3.

36 Augustine, *City of God* 10.5; 15.22; Bernard of Clairvaux, *On Loving God* 2.2; Augustine, *The Trinity* 8.3.4–5.

CHAPTER 12   *The Knowledge of Sensuous Intelligence*

1 Gregory of Nyssa, *Homilies on Song of Songs* 4 (*GNO* 6:127–28); Homily 13 (*GNO* 6:378, ln. 14); Theresa of Avila, *Opusculum de libro vitae* 22,6–7,14. Bernard of Clairvaux uses the phrase *redamare*, "love in return": "The love of the bridegroom who is love asks only the return of love and faith. Let the one who is loved *love in return*" (*Sermon* 83.5 on the Song of Songs).

2 *Confessions* 13.9.10.

3 *Against Celsus* 4.6. At the first verse of the Song of Songs, "Let him kiss me with the kisses of his mouth," Origen writes that the soul's desire is "union and fellowship with the Word of God and entering into the mysteries of his wisdom and knowledge" (*Commentary on the Song of Songs* 1).

4 *The Beatitudes* 6 (*GNO* 7,2:138, 142).

5 *Paradiso* 7.59–60.

6 *Paradiso* 1.120.

7 Origen, *Commentary on the Song of Songs* (GCS 33:68–70).

8 Seneca, *Epistle* 59.16; 116.1; Cicero, *Tusculan Disputations* 3.13; Martha Nussbaum, *The Therapy of Desire: Theory and Practice in Hellenistic Ethics* (Princeton, 1994), esp. chap. 10.

9 *Stromateis* 6.9.74; *Evil Thoughts* (*De Diversis malignis cogitationibus*) 2 (*PG* 79:1201c); *Praktikos* 56; *Praktikos* 36; *Praktikos* 56 and 78.

10 *Stromateis* 6.9.71; *Praktikos* 81; *The Religious Affections* (Carlisle, Pa., 1984), 31.

11 *Divine Institutes* 5.19.23.

12 *Divine Institutes* 6.14–17. On the Stoic view of *misericordia*, see Seneca, *De Clementia* 2.5

13 Aristotle, *De motu animalium,* ed. Martha Nussbaum (Princeton, 1978); *mot. anim.* 700b18–19, pp. 38–39; *Motu animalium* 701a35; *Divine Institutes* 6.14; *Divine Institutes* 6.15.

14 *PG* 48:57a; *PG* 48:65c.

15 *PG* 46:89a; *Homily on the Song of Songs* 1 (*GNO* 6:32).

16 *Life of Moses* (*GNO* 7,1:116).

17 *PG* 46:93b–97a.

18 *PG* 46:65a; *Homily on the Song of Songs* 9 (*GNO* 6:321).

19 *PG* 46:89a; *Homily* 11 (*GNO* 6:320, 326); *Homily* 12 (*GNO* 6:352).

20 *City of God* 9.4. *Aeneid* 4.449. The "tears" are Dido's, not Aeneas's.

21 Seneca, *De Clementia* 2:5: "Compassion is the vice of a feeble mind"; *City of God* 14.9.1.

22 *City of God* 14.9.3.

23 *City of God* 14.9.4; *Tractate on the Gospel of John* 32.1.

24 Gregory, *Virginity* 12.2.4–11; *Soul and Resurrection* (*PG* 46:49b); *Chapters on Love* 3.66–67; *Epistle* 2 (*PG* 91:396).

25 *Questions to Thalassius* 1 (*CC* 7:48, 38–40).

26 *Ambiguum* 7 (*PG* 91:1069b); *Ambiguum* 7 (*PG* 91:1076b, 1073b); *Chapters on Love* 3.72; *Questions to Thalassius* 1 (*CC* 7:355, 75–81); *Chapters on Love* 4.42; 2.30.

27 *Chapters on Love* 3.66–67.

28 *Commentary on John* 8:19; 19.4.21–25.

29 *Chapters on Love* 2.48.

30 *Divine Names* 4.11–12.

31 *Chapters on Theology* 1.35 (*PG* 90:1096c); trans. G. Berthold, *Maximus Confessor* (New York, 1985), 134–35, slightly revised.

32 *Tractate on the Gospel of John* 4.6 (*PL* 35:2008–09); *Kosmische Liturgie* (Einsiedeln, 1988), 408–09.

33 *Psalm* 26, exposition 2.16.

34 *Soul and Resurrection* (*PG* 46:96c); Geoffrey Hill, "That Man as a Rational Animal Desires the Knowledge which is his Perfection," *Canaan* (New York, 1997).

EPILOGUE

1 *Homily* 27.4 on John 15:12–16.

2 *Moralia* 18.88–92.

3 *Moralia* 31.99.

Suggestions for Reading

Sources in English translation

English translations of many writings of the church fathers can be found in the nineteenth-century editions *Ante-Nicene Fathers* and *A Select Library of Nicene and Post-Nicene Fathers of the Christian Church*, reprinted several times in recent decades. Though the translations are old, they are usually reliable. Many writings can be found in *The Fathers of the Church*, published by Catholic University of America Press, and *Ancient Christian Writers*, published by Paulist Press. *Oxford Early Christian Texts* is a bilingual edition with English translations and facing Greek and Latin texts.

The Early Church Fathers (edited by Carol Harrison) is a new series published by Routledge. Ten volumes have appeared with translations of some works that were formerly unavailable in English.

The Augustinians have begun a complete translation of all of Augustine's works into English. *The Works of Saint Augustine for the 21st Century*, published by New City Press, already includes twenty-five volumes. All of his sermons have been published.

Bindley, T. Herbert, *The Ecumenical Documents of the Faith*. London, 1925. Creed of Nicaea, Definition of the Faith of the Council of Chalcedon, letters of Cyril of Alexandria, Tome of Leo the Great, et al.

Decrees of the Ecumenical Councils. Volume 1: Nicaea I to Lateran V. Edited by Norman B. Tanner S.J. Washington, D.C., 1990.

Encyclopedias and other aids

Atlas of the Early Christian World. Edited by F. van der Meer and Christine Mohrmann. New York, 1958.

Augustine Through the Ages: An Encyclopedia. Edited by Allan D. Fitzgerald, O.S.A. Grand Rapids, 1999. Includes individual articles on each of Augustine's writings, on his life and thought as well as on the influence of his thinking.

Encyclopedia of Early Christianity. 2d ed. 2 vols. Edited by Everett Ferguson. New York, 1997. All aspects of early Christian life, history, and thought.

Encyclopedia of the Early Church. Edited by Angelo di Berardino. Translated by Adrian Walford. New York, 1992. Similar to *Encylopedia of Early Christianity* but written in the main by European scholars.

Oxford Dictionary of the Christian Church. Edited by E. A. Livingstone. New York, 1997. Best one-volume encyclopedia on the whole of Christian history but especially good on the early church.

Oxford Classical Dictionary. 3d ed. Edited by Simon Hornblower and Antony Spawforth. Oxford, 1996. Ancient Greece and Rome.

Late Antiquity: A Guide to the Postclassical World. Edited by G. W. Bowersock, Peter Brown, and Oleg Grabar. Cambridge, U.K., 1999. Encylopedia and essays on the world of "late antiquity," the fourth to eighth centuries, including articles on Islam.

General works on early Christian history and thought

von Balthasar, Hans Urs. *The Glory of the Lord: A Theological Aesthetics*. Volume 1: *Seeing the Form*. San Francisco, 1982.

Brown, Peter. *The World of Late Antiquity*. London, 1971.

Cameron, Averil. *Christianity and the Rhetoric of Empire*. Berkeley, 1991.

von Campenhausen, Hans, *The Fathers of the Greek Church*. New York, 1959.

——. *The Fathers of the Western Church*. New York, 1964.

Fletcher, Richard. *The Barbarian Conversion: From Paganism to Christianity*. New York, 1997.

Hall, Stuart G. *Doctrine and Practice in the Early Church.* London, 1991.

Harnack, Adolph. *History of Dogma.* 3 vols. Translated by Neil Buchanan. New York, 1961.

History of Theology. Volume 1: *The Patristic Period.* Edited by Angelo di Berardino and Basil Studer. Collegeville, 1996.

Kelly, J. N. D. *Early Christian Doctrines.* New York, 1958.

——. *Early Christian Creeds.* New York, 1960. Formation of the Apostles' Creed and the Nicene Creed.

Meyendorff, Jean. *Byzantine Theology: Historical Trends and Doctrinal Themes.* New York, 1974.

Payne, Robert. *The Holy Fire: The Story of the Fathers of the Eastern Church.* Crestwood, N.Y., 1980. Biographical sketches of major Eastern thinkers in the early church, e.g., Origen, Athanasius, Gregory Nazianzus, John Chrysostom, John of Damascus, et al.

Pelikan, Jaroslav. *The Christian Tradition: A History of the Development of Doctrine.* Volume 1: *The Emergence of the Catholic Tradition (100–600).* Chicago, 1971. Volume 2: *The Spirit of Eastern Christendom (600–1700).* Chicago, 1974.

Quasten, Johannes. *Patrology.* 4 volumes. Utrecht,. n.d. Volume 4 edited by Angelo di Berardino with an introduction by Johannes Quasten. Westminster, Md., 1986. Discussion of life and individual writings of the church fathers with bibliography.

Ramsey, Boniface. *Beginning to Read the Fathers.* New York, 1985.

Rousseau, Philip. *The Early Christian Centuries.* London, 2002.

Wilken, Robert L. *Remembering the Christian Past.* Grand Rapids, 1996.

Young, Frances. *From Nicaea to Chalcedon: A Guide to the Literature and Its Background.* London, 1983.

Suggestions for further reading by chapters. Primary sources are listed first. (See Notes for list of abbreviations.)

Chapter 1. *Founded on the Cross of Christ*

Clement of Alexandria. Translated by G. W. Butterworth. Cambridge, 1982.

St. Justin Martyr. The First and Second Apologies. Translated with Introduction and Notes by Leslie William Barnard. *ACW.*

Justin Martyr. *Dialogue with Trypho. ANF*

Origen, *Contra Celsum* (ed. Henry Chadwick). Cambridge, U.K., 1965.

Trigg, Joseph. *Origen. ECF.* Selections from Origen's writings.

Chadwick, Henry. *Early Christian Thought and the Classical Tradition*. Oxford, 1966. Survey of the thinking of the early apologists.

Grant, Robert M. *The Early Christian Doctrine of God*. Charlottesville, 1966.

——. *Greek Apologists of the Second Century*. Philadelphia, 1988.

Hadot, Pierre. *Plotinus, or the Simplicity of Vision*. Chicago, 1993.

Lane Fox, Robin. *Pagans and Christians*. Harmondsworth, 1986.

Norris, Richard A. *God and World in Early Christian Theology*. New York, 1965.

Pannenberg, Wolfhart. "The Appropriation of the Philosophical Concept of God as a Dogmatic Problem of Early Christian Theology." *Basic Questions in Theology* 2:119–83. The early apologists, on the basis of the Scriptures and the revelation in Christ, appropriated the Greek philosophical tradition critically.

Rist, John. *Plotinus: The Road to Reality*. Cambridge, 1967.

Stead, Christopher. *Philosophy in Christian Antiquity*. Cambridge, U.K., 1994. Early Christian thinkers as philosophers.

Wilken, Robert. *The Christians as the Romans Saw Them*. New Haven, 1984. Survey of Greek and Roman thinkers on Christianity.

Chapter 2. *An Awesome and Unbloody Sacrifice*

Brightman, F. E. *Liturgies Eastern and Western*. Oxford, 1985.

Cunningham, Agnes. *Prayer: Personal and Liturgical*. Wilmington, 1985. Prayers from the early church.

Cyril of Jerusalem. Edited by Edward Yarnold, S.J. *ECF*.

Early Sources of the Liturgy. Edited by Lucien Deiss. New York, 1967. Translations of liturgical texts.

On the Apostolic Tradition: Hippolytus. An English version with Introduction and Commentary by Alistair Stewart-Sykes. Crestwood, N.Y., 2001.

Dix, Dom Gregory. *The Shape of the Liturgy*. Glasgow, 1954. Development of classical Christian liturgies.

Finn, Thomas. *From Death to Rebirth: Ritual and Conversion in Antiquity*. New York, 1997. Description and analysis of ancient baptismal rituals.

Harmless, William. *Augustine and the Catechumenate*. Collegeville, Minn., 1995.

History of Theology. Volume 1: *The Patristic Period*. Collegeville, Minn., 1996. In particular chapters 5 and 6 by Basil Studer.

Jungmann, Josef. *The Early Liturgy to the Time of Gregory the Great*. South Bend, 1959.

McDonnell, Kilian. *The Baptism of Jesus in the Jordan*. Collegeville, Minn., 1996. Rich use of Eastern sources.

Peterson, Eric. *The Angels and the Liturgy*. New York, 1964.

Taft, Robert. *The Liturgy of the Hours in East and West*. Collegeville, Minn., 1986.

Chapter 3. *Face of God for Now*

Augustine. *Exposition of the Psalms*. Translated by Maria Boulding, OSB. *WSA*.

———. *On Christian Doctrine*. Translated by D. W. Robertson. New York, 1989.

Irenaeus of Lyons. Translated by Robert M. Grant. *ECF*.

Origen. *Commentary on the Gospel according to John*. Translated by Ronald E. Heine. 2 vols. *FOC*.

Blowers, Paul M., ed. and trans. *The Bible in Greek Christian Antiquity*. South Bend, 1997.

Bright, Pamela, ed. and trans. *Augustine and the Bible*. South Bend, 1999.

Burton-Christie, Douglas. *The Word in the Desert: Scripture and the Quest for Holiness in Early Christian Monasticism*. Oxford, 1993.

Cambridge History of the Bible. Volume 1: *From the Beginnings to Jerome*. Edited by P. R. Ackroyd and C. F. Evans. Cambridge, 1970.

von Campenhausen, Hans Freiherr. *The Formation of the Christian Bible*. Philadelphia, 1972.

de Lubac, Henri. *Medieval Exegesis*. Volumes 1 and 2. Grand Rapids, 1998–2000.

———. *The Sources of Revelation*. New York, 1968. Translation of a chapter from de Lubac's book on Origen and chapters from his *Exégèse Médiévale*.

Gamble, Harry Y. *Books and Readers in the Early Church*. New Haven, 1995. Production and distribution of books in early church.

Grant, Robert M. *The Letter and the Spirit*. London, 1957.

Kugel, James, and Rowan A. Greer. *Early Biblical Interpretation*. Philadelphia, 1986.

Simonetti, Manlio. *Biblical Interpretation in the Early Church: An Historical Introduction to Patristic Exegesis*. Edinburgh, 1994.

Wilken, Robert Louis. "Interpreting Job Allegorically: *The Moralia* of Gregory the Great." *Pro Ecclesia* 10 (2001): 213–30.

———. "In Defense of Allegory." *Modern Theology* 14 (1998): 197–212.

——. "St. Cyril of Alexandria: The Mystery of Christ in the Bible." *Pro Ecclesia* 4 (1995): 454–78.

Young, Frances. *Biblical Exegesis and the Formation of Christian Culture.* Cambridge, 1997.

Chapter 4. *Seek His Face Always*

Athanasius. *Orations against the Arian. NPNF.*

Augustine. *The Trinity.* Translated by Edmund Hill. *WSA.*

——. *Sermon* 52.

Christology of the Later Fathers. Translated by E. R. Hardy and Cyril C. Richardson. Philadelphia, 1954. In particular Gregory of Nazianzus, "The Theological Orations" and Gregory of Nyssa, "An Address on Religious Instruction."

Gregory Nazianzus. *The Theological Orations. LCC.* Also translated by Lionel Wickham and Frederick Williams in Frederick W. Norris, *Faith Gives Fullness to Reasoning.* Leiden, 1991.

Hilary. *The Trinity. FOC.*

The Letters of St. Athanasius concerning the Holy Spirit. Translated by C. R. B. Shapland. New York, 1951.

Origen. *Treatise on the Passover and Dialogue of Origen with Heraclides and His Fellow Bishops on the Father, the Son and the Soul.* Translated by Robert J. Daly, S.J. *ACW.*

——. *On First Principles.* Translated by G. W. Butterworth. New York, 1966.

Ayres, Lewis. "Remember that you are Catholic" (Serm. 52.2): Augustine on the Unity of the Triune God." *Journal of Early Christian Studies* 8 (2000): 39–82.

Barnes, Michel René. "Rereading Augustine's Theology of the Trinity." In *The Trinity: An Interdisciplinary Symposium on the Trinity,* edited by S. T. Davis, D. Kendall, S.J., and Gerald O'Collins, S.J., 145–76. Oxford, 1999.

Cavadini, John. "The Structure and Intention of Augustine's *De Trinitate.*" *Augustinian Studies* 23 (1992): 103–23.

Hanson, R. P. C. *The Search for the Christian Doctrine of God.* Edinburgh, 1988.

Jenson, Robert. *The Triune Identity.* Philadelphia, 1982.

Studer, Basil. *Trinity and Incarnation: The Faith of the Early Church.* Collegeville, Minn., 1993.

Stead, Christopher. *Divine Substance.* Oxford, 1977. Careful and penetrating study of the background and meaning of the term *homoousion,* of one substance, which appears in the Nicene Creed.

Vaggione, Richard Paul. *Eunomius of Cyzicus and the Nicene Revolution.* Oxford, 2000. Thoughtful study of Eunomius (d. 394), the most articulate non-Nicene thinker, with a fresh account of the controversies in the fourth century over the doctrine of the Trinity.

Widdicombe, Peter. *The Fatherhood of God from Origen to Athanasius.* Oxford, 1994.

Williams, Rowan, *Arius: Heresy and Tradition.* London, 1987.

——. "Sapientia and the Trinity: Reflections on *De Trinitate.*" *Augustiniana* (1990): 317–32.

Chapter 5. *Not My Will But Thine*

Augustine. Letter 137.

Cyril of Alexandria. *Select letters.* Edited and Translated by Lionel R. Wickham. Oxford, 1983.

Cyril of Alexandria. Translated by Norman Russell. *ECF.*

Gregory Nazianzus. "Letters on the Apollinarian Controversy" and conciliar documents in *Christology of the Later Fathers.*

Maximus the Confessor. Translated by Andrew Louth. *ECF.*

St. *Cyril of Alexandria On the Unity of Christ.* Translated and with an Introduction by John Anthony McGuckin. Crestwood, N.Y., 1995.

Grillmeier, Alois. *Christ in Christian Tradition.* Volume 1. Atlanta, 1975. Volume 2, with Theresia Hainthaler. London, 1995.

Léthel, François-Marie. *Théologie de l'Agonie du Christ: La liberté humain du fils de Dieu et son importance sotériologique mises en lumière par saint Maxime Confesseur.* Théologie Historique 52. Paris, 1979.

Meyendorff, Jean. *Christ in Eastern Christian Thought.* Crestwood, N.Y., 1975.

Yeago, David. "Jesus of Nazareth and Cosmic Redemption: The Relevance of St. Maximus the Confessor." *Modern Theology* 12 (1996): 163–93.

Chapter 6. *The End Given in the Beginning*

Augustine, *The Care to be Taken for the Dead.* In *Saint Augustine: Treatises on Marriage and Other Subjects,* translated by Roy J. Deferrari. *FOC.*

——. *The Literal Meaning of Genesis. ACW.*

Basil of Caesarea. *Homilies on the Hexaemeron. FOC.*

Gregory of Nyssa. *On the Making of Man. NPNF.*

Balas, David, *Metousia Theou: Man's Participation in God's Perfection*. Rome, 1966.

von Balthasar, Hans Urs. *Presence and Thought: An Essay on the Religious Philosophy of Gregory of Nyssa*. San Francisco, 1995.

Bynum, Caroline Walker. *The Resurrection of the Body in Western Christianity, 200–1336*. New York, 1995.

Callahan, J. F. "Greek Philosophy and the Cappadocian Cosmology." *Dumbarton Oaks Papers* 12 (1958): 29–57.

Gross, Jules. *The Divinisation of the Christian according to the Greek Fathers*. Translated by Paul A. Onica. Anaheim, 2002.

Ladner, Gerhard. "The Philosophical Anthropology of Saint Gregory of Nyssa." *Dumbarton Oaks Papers* 12 (1958): 61–94.

Leys, R. *L'image de Dieu chez saint Grégoire de Nysse*. Brussels, 1951.

May, G. *Creatio ex nihilo*. Edinburgh, 1994.

Nellas, Panayiotis. *Deification in Christ*. Translated by Norman Russell. Crestwood, N.Y., 1987.

Pelikan, Jaroslav. *What Has Athens to do with Jerusalem? Timaeus and Genesis in Counterpoint*. Ann Arbor, 1997.

Young, Robin Darling. "On Gregory of Nyssa's Use of Theology and Science in Constructing Theological Anthropology." *Pro Ecclesia* 2 (1993): 345–63.

Chapter 7. *The Reasonableness of Faith*

Augustine. *On the Usefulness of Belief* and *On True Religion*. Translated by John S. Burleigh, in *Augustine: Earlier Writings*. LCC.

Aubert, Roger, *Le Problème de l'Acte de Foi*. Louvain, 1958.

Dulles, Avery, S.J., *The Assurance of Things Hoped For*. New York, 1994.

Teselle, Eugene. "Faith." In *Augustine Through the Ages: An Encyclopedia*, 347–50. Grand Rapids, 1999.

Chapter 8. *Happy the People Whose God Is the Lord*

Augustine. *Concerning the City of God against the Pagans*. Translated by Henry Bettenson with Introduction by John O'Meara. New York, 1972.

——. *Political Writings*. Edited by E. M. Atkins and R. J. Dodaro. Cambridge, 2001.

Eusebius of Caesarea. *The History of the Church from Christ to Constantine*. Translated by G. A. Williamson. Revised and edited by Andrew Louth. London, 1989.

Brown, Peter. *Augustine of Hippo.* Berkeley, 2000.

Cochrane, Charles Norris. *Christianity and Classical Culture.* New York, 1957.

Cranz, F. E. "The Development of Augustine's Ideas on Society Before the Donatist Controversy." *HTR* 46 (1954): 255–315.

Fortin, Ernest L. *Political Idealism and Christianity in the Thought of St. Augustine.* Villanova, 1972.

Markus, R. A. *Saeculum: History and Society in the Theology of St. Augustine.* Cambridge, 1970.

O'Donovan, Oliver. "Augustine's City of God XIX and Western Political Thought." *Dionysius* 11 (1987): 89–110.

Peterson, Erik. *Monotheismus als politisches Problem. Ein Beitrag zur Geschichte der politischen Theologie im Imperium Romanum.* Munich, 1951.

Van Oort, Johannes. *Jerusalem and Babylon: A Study into Augustine's City of God and the Sources of His Doctrine of the Two Cities.* Leiden, 1991.

Williams, Rowan. "Politics and the Soul: A Reading of the *City of God.*" *Milltown Studies* 19 / 20 (1987): 55–72.

Chapter 9. *The Glorious Deeds of Christ*

Early Christian Latin Poets. Edited and translated by Carolinne White. *ECF,* 2000. Translation of selections from early Christian poets.

Prudentius. 2 volumes. Translated by H. J. Thompson. Loeb Classical Library. Cambridge, 1969, 1979.

Hymns of Prudentius. The Cathemerinon; or, The Daily Round. Translated by David R. Slavitt. Baltimore, 1996.

St. Gregory of Nazianzus. *Poemata Arcana.* Edited by C. Moreschini. Translated by D. A. Sykes. Oxford, 1997.

Curtius, Ernest Robert. *European Literature and the Latin Middle Ages.* Princeton, 1990.

den Boeft, J., and A. Hilhorst. *Early Christian Poetry: A Collection of Essays.* Leiden, 1993.

Fontaine, Jacques. *Naissance de la Poésie dans l'Occident Chrétien.* Études Augustiniennes. Paris, 1981.

Mohrmann, Christine. "La langue et le style de la poésie latine chrétienne." In *Études sur le Latin des Chrétiens* 1 (1961): 179–95.

Raby, F. J. E. *A History of Christian Latin Poetry.* Oxford, 1953.

Chapter 10. *Making This Thing Other*

Byzantine Defenders of Images: Eight Saints' Lives in English Translation. Edited by Alice-Mary Talbot. Washington D.C., 1998.

Egeria's Travels. Translated by John Wilkinson. London, 1971.

John of Damascus. *On the Divine Images.* Translated by David Anderson. Crestwood, N.Y., 1980.

Theodore the Studite. *On the Holy Icons.* Crestwood, N.Y., 1981.

Baggley, John. *Doors of Perception: Icons and Their Spiritual Significance.* Crestwood, N.Y., 1988.

Kitzinger, E. "The Cult of Images in the Age before Iconoclasm." *Dumbarton Oaks Papers* 8 (1954): 83–150.

Ouspensky, Leonid. *Theology of the Icon.* 2 vols. Crestwood, N.Y., 1992.

Pelikan, Jaroslav. *Imago Dei: The Byzantine Apologia for Icons.* Princeton, 1990.

Quenot, Michel. *The Icon: Window on the Kingdom.* Crestwood, N.Y., 1996.

Sahas, Daniel. *Icon and Logos: Sources in Eighth-Century Iconoclasm.* Toronto, 1986.

Schoenborn, Christoph, O.P. *God's Human Face: The Christ-Icon.* San Francisco, 1994.

Chapter 11. *Likeness to God*

Ambrose. *On Duties. NPNF.*

Augustine. *On the Morals of the Catholic Church. NPNF* and *FOC.*

Clement of Alexandria. *The Instructor. ANF*; also as *Christ the Educator,* translated by Simon Wood. *FOC.*

Gregory of Nyssa. *Homilies on the Beatitudes.* In *Gregory of Nyssa on the Beatitudes.* Edited by Hubertus R. Drobner and Albert Viciano. Translated by Stuart George Hall. Leyden, 2000. Also translated in *ACW.*

Gregory Thaumaturgus. *Address of Thanksgiving to Origen.* In *St. Gregory Thaumaturgus: Life and Works.* Translated by Michael Slusser. *FOC.*

John Cassian: The Conferences. Translated and annotated by Boniface Ramsey, O.P. *ACW.*

Tertullian. *On Patience. ANF.*

The Lives of the Desert Fathers: The Historia Monachorum in Aegypto. Translated by Norman Russell. Introduction by Benedicta Ward, S.L.G. London, 1980.

Hadot, Pierre. *Philosophy as a Way of Life.* Oxford, 1995.

Kirk, Kenneth E. *The Vision of God: The Christian Doctrine of the Summum Bonum.* London, 1932.

O'Donovan, Oliver. *The Problem of Self-Love in St. Augustine.* New Haven, 1980.

Pinckaers, Servais, O.P. *The Sources of Christian Ethics*. Washington, D.C., 1995.

Rabbow, Paul. *Seelenfuehrung: Methodik der Exerzitien in der Antike*. Munich, 1954.

Rist, John. *Augustine: Ancient Thought Baptized*. Cambridge, 1994.

Wetzel, James. *Augustine and the Limits of Virtue*. Cambridge, 1992.

Wilken, Robert L. "Alexandria: A School for Training in Virtue." In *Schools of Thought in the Christian Tradition*, edited by Patrick Henry. Philadelphia, 1984.

Chapter 12. *The Knowledge of Sensuous Intelligence*

From Glory to Glory: Texts from Gregory of Nyssa's Mystical Writings. Edited and Translated by Jean Daniélou, S.J. and Herbert Musurillo, S.J. New York, 1961.

Maximus the Confessor: Selected Writings. Translated by George Berthold. *Classics of Western Spirituality*. Mahwah, N.J., 1985.

Maximus the Confessor. Translated by Andrew Louth. *ECF*.

St. Maximus the Confessor: The Ascetic Life and Four Centuries on Charity. Translated by Polycarp Sherwood. *ACW*.

Origen of Alexandria, *The Song of Songs: Commentary and Homilies*. Translated by R. P. Lawson. *ACW*.

Lactantius. *Divine Institutes*. *ANF*.

Gregory of Nyssa. *On the Soul and Resurrection*. Translated by Catherine P. Roth. Crestwood, N.Y., 1993.

Blowers, Paul M. *Exegesis and Spiritual Pedagogy in Maximus the Confessor: An Invesigation of the "Quaestiones ad Thalassium."* Volume 7 of *Christianity and Judaism in Antiquity*. South Bend, 1991.

——. "Gentiles of the Soul: Maximus the Confessor on the Substructure and Transformation of the Human Passions." *Journal of Early Christian Studies* 4 (1996): 57–85.

Brock, Sebastian. *The Luminous Eye: The Spiritual World Vision of Saint Ephrem the Syrian*. 2d ed. Kalamazoo, 1992.

McGinn, Bernard. *The Presence of God*. Volume 1: *The Foundations of Mysticism*. New York, 1991. Volume 2: *The Growth of Mysticism*. New York, 1994.

Nussbaum, Martha. *The Therapy of Desire*. Princeton, 1994.

Sorabji, Richard. *Emotions and Peace of Mind: From Stoic Agitation to Christian Temptation*. New York, 2000.

Thunberg, Lars. *Man and Cosmos: The Vision of St. Maximus the Confessor.* Crestwood, N.Y., 1985.

———. *Microcosm and Mediator: The Theological Anthropology of Maximus the Confessor.* 2d ed. Chicago, 1995.

General Index

Index of Biblical Citations

Old Testament

New Testament